The Triune God

D0049339

EDITED BY

RONALD L. KOHL

PUBLISHING
P.O. BOX 817 • PHILLIPSBURG • NEW JERSEY 08865-0817

ISBN: 978-1-59638-981-6 (pbk)
ISBN: 978-1-59638-982-3 (ePub)
ISBN: 978-1-59638-983-0 (Mobi)

Printed in the United States of America

Library of Congress Control Number: 2014930953

To the flock at Grace Bible Fellowship Church,
which has embraced its pastor, warts and all.

To Kendra,
who daily shows me in a practical way what God's grace looks like
by loving me far better than I deserve.

"To the King of ages,
immortal, invisible, the only God,
be honor and glory forever and ever. Amen."

Contents

Editor's Preface

ONE OF MY SEMINARY professors said it succinctly: "Deny the Trinity and you will lose your soul. Try to explain the Trinity and you can lose your mind."

This is not a book that attempts to define or explain the Trinity, but it is a book that enriches the Christian's love for our triune God.

To start with, it assumes what the Bible assumes: that our God is One, yet is three distinct persons. "The heart of Christian faith in God," writes J. I. Packer, "is the revealed mystery of the Trinity. *Trinitas* is a Latin word meaning threeness. Christianity rests on the doctrine of the *trinitas*, the threeness, the tripersonality, of God."[1]

While the term *trinity* does not appear in Scripture but is credited to Tertullian, it is impossible to read Scripture without seeing both the presence and the coequality of the Father, Son, and Holy Spirit. At Jesus' baptism, the Father's voice boomed from heaven while the Spirit descended upon the Son. As Jesus spoke in what we know as his Great Commission, he commanded his disciples to "go therefore and make disciples of all nations, baptizing them in the name of the Father and of the Son and of the Holy Spirit" (Matt. 28:19).

One God. Three persons. Our triune God.

1. J. I. Packer, *Knowing God* (Downers Grove, IL: InterVarsity Press, 1973), 65.

"If there be one God subsisting in three persons," the great Puritan Thomas Watson noted, "then let us give equal reverence to all the persons in the Trinity. There is not more or less in the Trinity; the Father is not more God than the Son and Holy Ghost."[2]

The essays that comprise this book—five for each member of the Trinity—were originally sermons delivered at conferences sponsored by the Alliance of Confessing Evangelicals. The chapters on God the Father come from the 2011 Quakertown Regional Conference on Reformed Theology (QrCRT), whose theme was simply "Our Great God." In 2010 QrCRT's theme of "Our Glorious Lord and Savior, Jesus Christ" produced this book's essays on God the Son. The chapters on the Holy Spirit draw from a deeper well, however: the Philadelphia Conference on Reformed Theology (PCRT), the "mother lode" of Reformed theology conferences, started in 1974 by the late Dr. James Montgomery Boice. In 2002 PCRT's theme of "The Promised Holy Spirit" provided rich material for this collection.

The process of editing, while at times demanding, allowed me the great privilege of walking through the fertile minds of great practical theologians as they interacted with inspired, infallible, inerrant texts. For that I am both thankful and grateful. As I read through their sermons, many of which I had heard before, my heart and mind were blessed and I was reminded of the depth and width and breadth of the Bible's teaching on "God in Three Persons, blessed Trinity."[3]

I am thankful to the men who have contributed their wisdom and labors to this endeavor by addressing such an inexhaustible subject. To Joel Beeke, D. A. Carson, Bryan Chapell, Kevin

2. Thomas Watson, *A Body of Divinity* (Grand Rapids: Christian Classics Ethereal Library, n.d.), 108, available online at http://www.ccel.org/ccel/watson/divinity.pdf.
3. Reginald Heber, "Holy, Holy, Holy" (1826).

DeYoung, Iain Duguid, and Richard Phillips, thank you for your willingness to come to Quakertown, taking time out of your busy schedules to provide your insights and edify the saints.

To those who spoke in 2002 at Tenth Presbyterian Church in Philadelphia—D. A. Carson, Michael Horton, Hywel Jones, Philip Ryken, and R. C. Sproul—the conference Dr. Boice started so many years ago remains the inspiration for the many that have followed it. This editor has benefitted greatly from a long line of godly men who have graced the pulpit at Tenth; to glorify God while equipping believers through the careful teaching of the Word of God remains the highest calling of the preacher.

This book begins with a look at the character of the Father; while there is no possibility of exhausting God's attributes, five are singled out for closer examination. Bryan Chapell capably draws our attention to the greatness and love of God. Kevin DeYoung, with characteristic humor and sharpness, hones in on the subject of truth in relation to God. Richard Phillips uses careful exegesis of 2 Samuel 6 and Hebrews 10 to deal with the holiness and the wrath of God respectively.

Turning to the second person of the Trinity, D. A. Carson brings us to John 5 so that we may see the glory of the Son. From there the section on Christ flows in chronological fashion. Joel Beeke takes us to John 1 for the purpose of showing us the importance of the Word who "became flesh and dwelt among us" (v. 14). Iain Duguid brings his rich knowledge of the Old Testament to his chapter on the life and ministry of Jesus. From there Joel Beeke brings us to the cross, patiently but urgently showing us what Jesus endured and what he accomplished in suffering and dying as a ransom for sinners. And finally D. A. Carson shows us the wonder of Christ's resurrection through Thomas's eyes.

The chapters on the Holy Spirit unfold in yet a different way, with an emphasis on the Spirit's work and ministry. D. A. Carson introduces the section with what Jesus said in John 7 about the Spirit's coming, which produces "streams of living water." Michael Horton uses imagery and analogy as anchoring points in his essay on the "Age of the Spirit." Hywel Jones draws from Paul's great text, Romans 8, to describe what life in the Spirit looks like, while Philip Ryken uses a rich description of Jesus' discourse with Nicodemus in John 3 to detail what it means to be "born of the Spirit." The ministry of the Holy Spirit as Counselor is left in the very capable hands of R. C. Sproul.

As is always the case in a project of this size, there are many people whose encouragement, advice, and insights have been invaluable.

To those who have played major roles in the inception and growth of QrCRT: what started as a dream has, I think, exceeded any of our expectations. Thanks to the many who volunteer each year and especially to those who serve on the planning committee: Paul Bevan-Xenelis, Adam Dieffenbach, Torry Hinkle, Jesse Light, Doreen McIlwraith, Michael Roberts, Eric and Diane Wolfinger. Your willingness, sacrifice, and joy in giving of your time are an encouragement as you serve unto the Lord and not unto men.

To the kind folks at the Alliance of Confessing Evangelicals: Bob Brady, Karen Ciavolella, Jeffrey Waddington. Thanks for your encouragement—and your patience too! I hope I haven't driven you crazy by setting a new Guinness record for email frequency.

To Ian Thompson, Amanda Martin, and Aaron Gottier at P&R Publishing, thank you for entrusting me with this project and for believing it would be accomplished, even when I wasn't quite so sure.

Thanks to those who have reached out in special ways over these past few years. To Linda Boice, whose kind notes and precious words make me feel that her husband would be pleased with what we're doing in Quakertown. To Carl Trueman, Rick Phillips, and Philip Ryken, who have offered advice and time when they've probably had far more important things to do, showing true grace to a brother in Christ. To Michael Roberts, whose zeal for research—a real bulldog for footnote citations—have helped to prevent impending deadlines from adding more gray hairs to the editor's scalp.

To the congregation, pastors, elders, deacons, and staff of Grace Bible Fellowship Church in Quakertown, thank you for your love, your friendship, your hunger for God and for his Word, and your support and care for your pastor, allowing him to take on a project like this one. I thank my God in every remembrance of you.

To the precious gift who is my wife Kendra, please know that I love you, that you are my much-needed helpmate, and that, as I always say—and rightly so, as much as you may deny it—I "married up."

Most importantly, I am forever grateful to God for rescuing this sinner from the depths of his depravity and transferring him from the domain of darkness into the kingdom of his beloved Son.

May this work bring glory to the triune God, who alone is worthy to receive glory and honor and power.

Ronald L. Kohl
November 2013

PART 1

God the Father

1

The Greatness of God

BRYAN CHAPELL

YOU MAY CONSIDER the character of God, the attributes of God, the provision of God—all the things that are great in his doing and being—but the greatness of God is such a broad topic that, if there's any demerit in writing on it, it would be the difficulty of knowing where to even enter the subject.

God is great in more ways than any human can count, but one way he is great is in contradistinction to what we are.

A passage that makes that very plain is Romans 4. It is an explication of an amazing statement the apostle Paul has already made in Romans 3:28: "We hold that one is justified by faith apart from the works of the law." What an amazing, shocking statement: one is made right before God, by faith, apart from what one does (the works of the law). Surely there would be a challenge to such an audacious statement, and so the apostle decides to give an example. Particularly for the sake of the Jews who had been gathering in the Roman church with Gentile believers, the example would have to be that of Abraham. In effect Paul says concerning Abraham, "You must remember that he was justified by faith apart from the works of the law, because the law wasn't even there yet." But what that begins to demonstrate is not only the greatness of the provision of God but the greatness of his mercy toward us, that he would provide righteousness for those who could not provide it for themselves.

So we read in Romans 4:18, "In hope, [Abraham] believed against hope, that he should become the father of many nations, as he had been told, 'So shall your offspring be.'" What does it mean to hope against hope? Some of you know of the Stockdale Paradox, which was introduced to us in Jim Collins's book *Good to Great*. It refers to Admiral Jim Stockdale, the high-ranking officer who was the prisoner held longest in the infamous Hanoi Hilton during the Vietnam War—after being shot down and wounded, he was held there for seven and a half long years.

You may know what pressures were placed upon him, but many wonderful things were written about his leadership in a difficult time—he was even willing to continue to wound himself to prove to his captors that torture could not persuade him to betray his country. When Jim Collins asked Stockdale what had sustained him and given him hope when there was no hope, Stockdale answered, "I never lost faith in the end of the story. I never doubted not only that I would get out, but that I would prevail in the end and turn the experience into the defining moment of my life."

When Collins asked, "Who did not make it out of the Hanoi Hilton?" Stockdale replied, "That's easy. The optimists did not make it out. They are the ones who said, 'We're going to be out by Christmas,' and Christmas would come and Christmas would go. And then they'd say, 'We're going to be out by Easter.' And Easter would come and Easter would go. And then

Thanksgiving, and then it was Christmas again. And they died of a broken heart."

To such men, Stockdale said he would say, "We are not getting home by Christmas, so deal with it." He told Collins how he taught others and himself to deal with such deprivations and disappointments. He said, "This is the most important lesson. You must never confuse faith that you will prevail in the end, which you can never afford to lose, with the discipline to confront the most brutal facts of your current reality, whatever they may be."[1]

In a nutshell the Stockdale Paradox is this: believing profoundly that your life's story will turn out well, while at the same moment confronting the most brutal facts of your present reality.

Those are inspiring words, but for us as believers, there's a certain hollowness to them, because while Stockdale says with great firmness and stridency, "You must believe that the end will turn out well," you and I know there was no guarantee he would get out of prison alive. In essence, he was pitting one hope against another hope. His hope was optimism in a long-term good end, and he pitted that against others' optimism in a short-term good end. The reality is that both these types of optimism are human optimism with the limitation of human ability.

More Than Human Hope

When he speaks of hope against hope in Romans 4, the apostle is not saying, "There is one form of human optimism

---

1. Jim Collins, *Good to Great: Why Some Companies Make the Leap . . . and Others Don't* (New York: HarperBusiness, 2001), 83–85.

that's better than another form of human optimism." He is saying there has to be a totally different hope from human hope. It cannot be based on humanity's abilities, goodness, will, and resolve. There is a scriptural hope that is of a different nature and quality from human hope; it is a divine hope, a hope in the greatness of God, not in the greatness of human ability, resolve, or righteousness.

If you work through Paul's account of Abraham in Romans 4, you quite clearly recognize what he is saying. What we're forced to do initially is to face the brutal facts. We do that first because we're exposed to Abraham's "hoped for" end. What does Abraham hope for? "In hope he believed against hope, that he should become the father of many nations, as he had been told, 'So shall your offspring be'" (v. 18).

What was Abraham's initial hope? *Abraham* means "father of nations, father of a multitude." Keeping that in mind, the good outcome for which he hoped was simply that his name would come true. But the brutal reality he had to face is in verse 19. "He did not weaken in faith when he considered his own body, which was as good as dead (since he was about a hundred years old), or when he considered the barrenness of Sarah's womb." These are not pleasant or politically correct words: he's as good as dead, and she's barren.

Although we can read the words quickly, we understand the pain behind them. Abraham can't produce children anymore. He received the promise of God at age seventy-five, but now he's ninety-nine and has no children. His wife is barren, not just in that period of time, but since her youth. There was, particularly in that culture, a shame, a sense of unfulfillment that came to a couple—and particularly to a woman—who were unable to have children. But the brutal facts are these: he's as good as dead, and she's barren.

6

They lived in a different era. Abraham had longevity in a number of ways. He apparently was still strong enough to make a journey of several hundred miles by foot with a caravan, with all the travails that went into that. And even though his wife was older, Sarah was apparently beautiful, because she could still tempt kings. But neither of them is able to bear children. He's initially seventy-five and will be ninety-nine before he sees any fulfillment of promise; she has never been able to bear children. Neither is worthy. When God declares that the promise will be fulfilled, Abraham laughs and falls on his face. Sarah laughs and lies about laughing. They're not able. They're not worthy. The brutal fact is that this had to be a horrible waiting period as they faced the reality of their own inability.

What must it have been like for Abraham to have been told at age seventy-five that he was going to have a son—and then to have to wait for almost twenty-five years? Ray Pritchard described it this way:

> At age 76 Abraham buys a crib. Imagine going to the store. "Well, Grandpa, for the grandkid?" "No this is for me and my wife." Age 77, pick out colors for the baby's room and paint the room. Age 78, the list of baby names is getting really long. Age 80, sign up for a diaper service. Age 82, subscribe to *New Parents* magazine. Age 85, re-subscribe to *New Parents* magazine. Age 95, repaint the baby's room. Age 99, attend Lamaze classes with your wife, and between blows (puff, puff, puff), scratch your head and say, "Was God just kidding?"[2]

In Genesis 18, when he is given the announcement of the coming of Isaac, Abraham laughs and falls on his face. You have

---

2. Paraphrased from Ray Pritchard, "The Oldest Dad in the Nursery—Romans 4:18–25," *Keep Believing Ministries*, accessed November 26, 2013, http://www.keepbelieving.com/sermon/1992-05-24-The-Oldest-Dad-in-the-Nursery/.

to understand his response is not humor but the release of deep emotional pain. He collapses. He is not able to take the news. Yet Paul declares, "No distrust made him waiver concerning the promise of God, but he grew strong in his faith as he gave glory to God" (Rom. 4:20).

How astounding to say that Abraham is not trusting in the character of his circumstances, for they are terrible. No, he is trusting in the character of his God. "Why should I keep trusting? Why should I not waiver in faith? It's not because my circumstances indicate that I shouldn't waiver in faith; it's because I have trust in my God." What Abraham has from his God is the promise of a son, and because he has that promise he does not waiver. The reason we are not to waiver in the awful circumstances we face is not because of the promise of a son but because of the *provision* of a Son. That is what God has shown to us, and it's one of the most difficult but important aspects of pastoral ministry and Christian faith: to say, "When my circumstances give me no reason to trust God, I trust him because of his character."

A few years ago I was picked up prior to a theology conference. The man who drove me from the airport to the conference was a man I'd known for some time, a ruling elder in a Presbyterian church. As he was driving me from the airport, he began to unfold the details of his life in recent years. He had a son in prison, a daughter living with a man who was not her husband, a church in turmoil, and no sense that anybody was coming around him to support him and his family despite his suffering. Finally he asked me, "Bryan, how do I trust God in the midst of all this?" I don't know if you are like me, but in those moments I feel absolutely tongue-tied. I'm supposed to know the ready answers, but all I could say was, "I trust him because he sent Jesus." God's Word tells

me that this is a fallen world, that we will go through a veil
of tears because it is a corrupted world, and that if you are
looking to trust God on the basis of circumstances, you will
be sorely and awfully disappointed. We do not look to circumstances; we look to God.

My early pastoral experience was spent ministering in a
mining and farming community. I learned so much about
faith from people of faith, though not quite in the terms I had
learned in seminary. I learned what it meant to trust God in
the hardest of times by hearing the account of an older miner
who had been injured early in life in the mines. Because of
what had happened, he spent the rest of his life as an invalid,
watching family and friends prosper while he himself lived in
great deprivation.

In old age he was approached one day by a younger man,
who said to him, "I hear that you are a man of faith. How can
you be one who trusts in God, with all the hardships that have
happened in your life?"

Lying on his bed as an invalid, the older man said with
great candor and honesty, "You are right. There are times
when Satan sits in the chair that you are sitting in and asks
me those very questions. He points out the window to men
who are my age who have worked in the mine and have pros-
pered, and he points to their fine homes and their expanded
families when I have none. Satan says to me, 'Does Jesus
really love you?' Satan points to younger men and older men
whose bodies are still strong, without the broken legs that I
have, and Satan points to their healthy bodies and says, 'Does
Jesus really love you?' "

The younger man was left aghast at the honesty of the
older. "What do you say? What do you say when Satan speaks
to you that way?"

The older man said, "I take Satan by the hand, and I take him to a hill called Calvary. And I point to the thorns on the brow and the nails in the hands and I say to him, 'Doesn't Jesus love me?'"

Abraham looks at his circumstances, with perhaps no reason to believe in the goodness or the greatness of God, but he looks to the character of God and says, "He has promised me a son. His righteousness is yet on display in the character that he is showing me. I have no basis of faith in my circumstances, but my faith is based on the character of my God. And for that reason, I endure." What is the nature of that faith that will sustain such hope? It is that God is great and good and is accomplishing his purposes despite the denial of apparent circumstances. What is the faith that really sustains hope? Paul notes, "No distrust made him waiver concerning the promise of God," because he believed in the God who had promised him a son (Rom. 4:20).

Not the Faith of a Perfect Man

If you think of the kind of faith that sustains hope in a great God, you must know first that it is not the faith of a perfect man. After all, what do we know about the life of Abraham? Yes, God gives him a promise: "I am going to give you a son." And Abraham believes, but he's not exactly sure how God is going to bring that about, so he decides to contribute a little bit by taking his wife's handmaiden to bed. And then, after she conceives, there is dissension in the house—surprise, surprise—and he casts out of his home the very woman he has taken advantage of, knowing that this will probably be a death sentence for her. "You take care of yourself. My wife is upset with you because of what I have done with you."

Although he does take her back into his home, Abraham's unfaithfulness is not just to his mistress. He is also unfaithful, and repeatedly so, to his wife. The jeopardy of being in a foreign land with an attractive wife causes him twice to give her away to other men in order to protect himself.

Beyond that, remember the haggling over Sodom? "Lord, I know it's filthy sin, but if there are just fifty righteous people there, or forty-five, or forty, or thirty, or twenty, or ten . . ." He haggles to protect the sinful.

Not only does he laugh when Isaac is promised, but he also decides he has to take care of the problem he has created through his wife's handmaiden. Because she has borne his own biological son, he takes the two of them and sends them out into the desert to die of exposure. This is not the faith of a perfect man. If God is going to save him, there is going to be some great mercy on display. That great goodness of God is what we see in verse 21: "[Abraham was] fully convinced that God was able to do what he had promised."

What is Abraham convinced of? Not of his goodness, but of God's greatness. He can do as he promised. Abraham can say, "I'm ninety-nine years old, my wife has been barren for our whole marriage, but God is able to do as he has promised. He can bring dead things to life. That is the nature of my God, and I will believe that."

If it seems hypocritical of Abraham to say that, you have to understand that in Scripture it is the nature of faith to be often expressed by very imperfect people. The greatness of God's provision on display is not the greatness of the people who express faith; it's the greatness of a God who would receive such defective faith. Note the instance of the man who comes to Jesus saying,

"Save my child." Jesus says, "All things are possible for one who believes," but then the man says, "I believe; help my unbelief!" (see Mark 9:24).

Here is Abraham. You recognize the Scriptures are extolling his faith over and over, but you know enough about his life to know his is a very defective faith. It just barely holds on to the notion, "I guess God is able. Maybe I've got to help him, but he's going to do it some way." And I myself need to be reminded from time to time that God is blessing me, holding me, maintaining his faithfulness not because of *my* faithfulness but because of *his*. My faithfulness is too weak; it's too stretched despite all that I know in my head.

I recently spoke with a church elder who said, "When God took my son, my faith became stretched like taffy, so thin and so transparent I was sure it would break. It was that thin. I wasn't sure I had faith anymore. And still God honored it. I still believe his promises are eternal; I still believe that he has my son even if I don't and that in the great day I will see him again."

What does it mean to believe that you're trusting in the greatness of God and not in the greatness of you? It means that you understand that the circumstances are meant to strip you away from confidence in you so that there's nothing left but faith in God. That's what's happening to Abraham. He has left home, familiarity, wealth, and security to give himself to this God who has called him to a foreign land, and now this God seems to be supplying nothing, and it's almost as though the circumstances of his life are stripping away every confidence that Abraham might have in his own ability and supply so that there may be nothing left but God. What else would he have? God is all he has left.

In *The Voyage of the Dawn Treader*, the spoiled kid Eustace sails away and ends up on an island, where he discovers what he thinks he wants: a great treasure in a cave. Having found the treasure and rejoiced over it, he lies down on it and falls asleep, not knowing that in this magical cave what he dreams will now shape and form him. As he lies on this treasure, he dreams of the vengeance that he will wreak on all those who he perceives have wronged him in life, and when he wakes up, he has been transformed into a dragon: ugly, awful, mean, bitter, and dangerous to all around him. He doesn't want to be a dragon, but that is what he is.

But the great lion Aslan shows up and tells the boy, now covered in dragon skin, that he must undress. After balking initially, thinking that he can't undress because he isn't wearing any clothes, the boy-turned-dragon realizes that he can cast his skin.

Telling the story afterward, Eustace explains, "I started scratching myself and my scales began coming off all over the place. And then I scratched a little deeper and, instead of just scales coming off here and there, my whole skin started peeling off beautifully, like it does after an illness, or as if I was a banana."

But although he is able to step out of his skin entirely, he finds that he has another ugly dragon's skin underneath the first one. Although his scratching tears it away, he finds another ugly skin under that one too. "And I thought to myself," Eustace relates in retrospect, " 'Oh dear, how ever many skins have I got to take off?' "

Finally Aslan takes over. "You will have to let me undress you." Eustace is afraid of the lion's claws, but he is desperate. "The very first tear he made," Eustace remembers, "was so deep that I thought it had gone right into my heart. And when he began pulling the skin off, it hurt worse than anything I've ever felt. The only thing that made me able to bear it was just the pleasure of feeling the stuff peel off."[3]

3. C. S. Lewis, *The Voyage of the Dawn Treader* (New York: MacMillan, 1970), 89–90.

Do you know what I'm talking about? You thought you had it, you thought you understood it, you thought your faith was worked out, you thought it was kind of sweet the way this God was taking care of you, and you and God were walking along together and you were doing just fine. And because you were doing just fine, he was loving you so well and life was pleasant—but then suddenly you find out he is saying, "Are you depending on you or on me? Where is your faith? Is it in the adequacy of your faith, your performance, your doing? If that's the case, you're going to have to let me go deeper, to let me undress you."

You may know exactly what I mean, through a loss or a pain or a failure or a disquieting uncertainty about your adequacy such as you've never known before. You must recognize that God is saying, "When you strip away every aspect of your life in which you have confidence, there's nothing left for you but to put faith in me. There's nothing else left." The reason you can put faith in the adequacy of your God is because, even though you are quite imperfect, he is great. The degrees and nature of his greatness are now being unfolded to us because he is able. That was what Abraham believed: not that Abraham was able, but that his God was able.

Paul writes of Abraham, "His faith was counted to him as righteousness" (Rom. 4:22). We're learning something not just about the nature of faith that sustains hope but about the nature of faith that is attached to grace. What is the grace that provides the hope that is so exemplified in the faith of Abraham? It's plainly stated: "His faith was counted to him as righteousness." But how could that be?

Faith . . . Counted to Him as Righteousness

You have to back up to verse 20 again to understand the point the apostle is making. "No distrust made [Abraham] waiver concerning the promise of God, but he grew strong in his faith as he gave glory to God." You have to clearly understand one thing: if Abraham grew strong in his faith, that means that at some point his faith was not as strong as it later became. There was a defect, a weakness in his faith so that it wasn't what it ultimately became. What it ultimately became was a consequence of his giving glory to God.

The faith that was counted to him for righteousness was that faith that had every aspect of self-confidence stripped away so that all Abraham could do was give glory to God. That's all that was left, to the point where Abraham could say, "God is all I have. God's the only thing left. He can be faithful to his promise. I don't know how, I don't know when, but I believe that God can do what God says he's going to do." Abraham had buried himself, his hope, his ability—he had buried everything in his hope of what God is and what God can do. There was no hope in himself anymore. It's the Old Testament image of being clothed in God. All he had left was the glory of God, and we are told that this is where his faith ended up, not where it began.

There had to be the stripping away of trust in self to the point where Abraham ultimately said, "It's just God; there is nothing else. Not my faith, not my doing, not my performing. All I've got is God. I can't even trust my own faithfulness; all I've got is him." When that's what we have, we understand that God is saying, "If you have buried yourself in me, what's true of me is true of you. I am the righteous God who will keep my promises and who is able to do so. Great in righteousness, great in power—when you bury yourself in me, what's true of me is now true of you."

That's the great promise of the gospel, isn't it? Faith is counted as righteousness. That's as true for us as it was for Abraham.

The great promise of Scripture is not just that Abraham's faith was counted for righteousness; it's the promise available to all believers that faith still is counted for righteousness, as Paul proclaims in Romans 4:23–24:

> But the words "it was counted to him" were not written for his sake alone, but for ours also. It will be counted to us who believe in him who raised from the dead Jesus our Lord.

Faith in God's Power and Provision

What is your faith? It must be faith in the greatness of the power of God. He can make dead things alive. He could make Abraham, who was as good as dead in his ability to produce children, alive. He can make a dead man alive. He can make a dead womb alive. He could make a dead Jesus alive. And he can make a dead *you* alive. That's what we're ultimately trusting in. Here is a God so great that he makes dead things live. Ultimately I need to know this because, when I have been stripped of every confidence in myself, stripped of every confidence in my performance, I have to believe there's nothing I bring to this equation. There's no reason that God should love me or provide for me or equip me with his righteousness. I just trust him—faith alone in a God who makes dead things live—because that is faith in the greatness of the power of God alone and distinct from any power I possess.

But it's not just faith in God's power. Ultimately it's faith in God's provision. God raised from the dead Jesus our Lord, who Paul tells us in verse 25 "was delivered up for our trespasses and raised for our justification." What is this greatness of God? Paul has expressed it already in Romans 3:25. "[This Jesus] God put forward as a propitiation by his blood, to be received by faith." Recognizing the inadequacy of his people, our great God provided his own Son as the sacrifice, taking upon himself your sin, my sin, and the sin of the world. What we don't quite understand is the greatness of God's provision. Sufficient for the sin of the world is this sacrifice of Jesus Christ. He took all that we deserve. That penalty, taken upon him, is taken off those who put their faith upon him. It is a great provision.

The hard part for many theologians is not the first part of Romans 4:25, that Jesus "was delivered up for our trespasses." We know what that's about: the penalty our sins deserve. The harder part is "and raised for our justification." I thought he was crucified for our justification, but here Paul tells us that Christ was "raised for our justification." It's the apostle's reminder of the greatness of the power of God that makes us right before God.

I think of the similarities between these words and those in the incident of Jesus and the paralytic. The paralytic can't move, and his friends can't move him through the crowd, so what do they do? They let him down through a hole they make in the roof, and Jesus, instead of verbally declaring to him the ability to walk, says, "Son, your sins are forgiven" (Mark 2:5). Of course, everybody's really happy about this, right? "Why does this man speak like that? He is blaspheming! Who can forgive sins but God alone?" (v. 7). In response Jesus says, "But that you may know that the Son of Man has authority on earth to forgive sins . . . I say to you, rise, pick up your bed, and go home" (vv. 10–11).

When he gives life to dead things, as Jesus did with this man's paralyzed legs, we know that God has such power; the

One who says, "I will take away your sins" can do it. It is the life of Jesus, raised from the tomb, that gives the proof that we are justified before God. Our sin has been put away, and the fact that he is raised again proves that God says, "Your sins are forgiven."

Christ has accomplished this. It is God's ability to give life to dead things that ultimately proves not only his greatness but also the greatness of his mercy toward us. As we are fond of saying, where there is life, there is hope. It is the life of Christ, which you and I share by virtue of faith in him, not in anything in us, that ultimately gives us hope in the greatness of a God whose greatness extends not only to his power but to his mercy toward us.

Do you remember the great earthquake in Haiti in 2010? One of the amazing stories that came out of that disaster was of Frank and Jill Thorpe. Frank was almost a hundred miles away in the mountains when he received a call from his wife on her cell phone. She was trapped underground in the rubble of a building. He immediately drove for six hours through the devastated country to get to his wife, and upon arriving where she was, he dug for hours to get to her. Why would he go through all this effort? Because where there is life, there is hope. He knew that it was worth the striving, worth the faith to go after his wife, worth the willingness to live, to dig, to serve, to honor.

Because Jesus is alive, I believe that my God is able to fulfill his promises, just as he provided a son for Abraham when there was no hope in all that was human. But there was a divine hope that sustained faith. The fact that Jesus was raised from the dead gives me reason to believe and have faith when my faith is defective. When my hope seems almost gone, I hope against human hope in the divine work of God, because he has shown me the greatness of his power and mercy in the provision of Jesus Christ. When I believe in him, then when all else has abandoned me and I have no hope in anything else, I bring to the table faith alone in God alone. That is my hope: because he is so great, when all my efforts fail, all his greatness is in my path.

2

The Holiness of God

RICHARD D. PHILLIPS

HOLINESS IS THE MOST difficult of God's attributes to define because, in its essence, it refers to the way that God is "other"—the way that he is wholly above his people. We can't quite point to it; it is much more simple to point to what holiness is *not* than to pinpoint what it is. We tend to think of holiness in terms of moral purity, and that's certainly part of God's holiness. Yet it's not the essence of what it means for God to be holy. Most basically, holiness carries the meaning of being set apart. When we speak of holy places, holy vessels, and holy men, we're referring to places, things, and people that have been set apart from their normal use to be used for God. When we speak of God's holiness, we refer to his absolute transcendence above and apart from all that he has made. The word *holy* comes from a root word that means "to cut" or "to separate." It means that God is a cut above all that he has made.

R. C. Sproul has written that holiness refers to

that sense in which God is above and beyond us. It tries to get at his supreme absolute greatness. . . . He is higher than

21

the world. He has absolute power over the world. The world has no power over Him. Transcendence describes God in His consuming majesty, His exalted loftiness. It points to the infinite distance that separates Him from every creature. He is an infinite cut above everything else.[1]

We realize how important God's holiness is to the Christian when we remember that the first petition that Jesus taught us to offer after saying "Our Father in heaven" was "May you be holy," or "Hallowed be your name." Christians need to learn the holiness of God. We need to learn God's holiness for our worship and for our service unto him. David needed to comprehend God's holiness, and 2 Samuel 6 records the event in which the lesson of holiness was sharply taught to David by God.

The events of 2 Samuel 6 take place after David finally enters into the kingship over a united Israel. In chapter 5 David has shown us he has great understanding when it comes to leading men on behalf of God. In that chapter he captures Jerusalem, unifies the country, and leads it on a great mission. Chapter 6 reminds and shows us, however, that David, while he knows how to stand before men on God's behalf, still has much to learn when it comes to standing before God as a man.

The event described in this chapter is the bringing of the ark of the covenant to Jerusalem. The chapter's message about God's holiness comes not only through what David does and how God reacts to it, but first of all through the very careful description that is given to the ark of the covenant itself at the beginning of the chapter. Verse 2 provides a very interesting description of the ark. It tells us that David went to where the ark had been housed, and it refers to the ark as "the ark of God, which is

---

1. R. C. Sproul, *The Holiness of God* (Wheaton, IL: Tyndale House, 1985), 55.

called by the name of the LORD of hosts who sits enthroned on the cherubim." That's not an incidental description of the ark; it's a vital theological statement that tells us much about how the holy, transcendent God reveals himself and also dwells in the midst of his people. What does the text mean when it says that the ark was called by the name of "the LORD of hosts"? In saying this, verse 2 establishes a sacramental relationship between the ark of the covenant and God.

So close is this association that, during the exodus, when the ark would set out, Moses would cry out, "Arise, O Lord." At the end of the day, when the ark ceased moving, he would cry out, "Return, O Lord." In Psalm 24, when David announces the arrival of the ark within the city, he says, "Be lifted up, O ancient doors, that the King of glory may come in." There is a relationship between the ark and God himself.

How a Holy God Reveals Himself

David knows, and Moses knew before him, that the ark is not God—God is not in the box—but rather that God has established so close a relationship that where the ark is present, there God is present in his holy glory. It is necessary for God in his holiness to provide revelation of himself.

God is so holy, so separate, so above and beyond us that his spiritual essence cannot be seen. His infinite majesty and glory are, frankly, beyond the comprehension of our finite minds, so God for our benefit has placed emblems before us. I've heard it said before, I think very helpfully, that because you and I are not holy or infinite beings, we reveal ourselves by taking things off. We reveal more of ourselves by removing clothing, although that has obvious limitations. But God, who cannot be seen because he's so other than his creation, reveals himself by putting things on. The ark of the covenant is one of those things. It's an emblem that he places before his people to represent his being and character.

John Calvin wrote, "When we want to approach God, it is certain that we will not be able to and that he is totally inaccessible to us. Therefore, he must come down to us when we cannot reach up to him. And how does he come down? It is not that he changes his place as far as his essence is concerned, but he must make himself known in a familiar manner."[2]

This information is useful to us because the ark of the covenant was a sacrament in a manner similar to the New Testament sacraments. Sacraments serve as divinely ordained signs that point to something about God and that officially seal his validation upon his people. Baptism signifies our cleansing from sin by Christ's blood and our renewal by the washing of the Holy Spirit, and it seals us as belonging to God's people. The Lord's Supper emblemizes Christ's atoning death and its saving benefits. In these ways, the holy God reveals his grace to forgive and receive those who belong to his Son, Jesus.

What the Ark Signified about God

What then did the ark of the covenant show about God? First, it conveyed God's *rulership*, his sovereign kingship. It represented God as the sovereign ruler of his people. Verse 2 refers to God as "the LORD of hosts who sits enthroned on the cherubim." The ancient Israelites did not believe that God was

---

2. John Calvin, *Sermons on 2 Samuel, 1–13*, trans. Douglas Kelly (Edinburgh: Banner of Truth, 1992), 233.

locally present between the two angels that adorned the cover of the ark. Instead, Calvin noted, "The ark was a standing witness that God wanted to dwell in the midst of his people."[3] Since the ark was conceived as the footstool of a divine throne, God dwelled as King and Sovereign and Lord in the midst of his people. The ark of the covenant was an emblem of his kingship and lordship.

The ark also conveyed the Lord's *reconciliation*. On the annual Day of Atonement, the high priest would come before the ark and sprinkle the sacrificial, atoning blood as a sin offering on the lid on top of the ark. By this action, the people realized they had been restored to God; though they were sinners, an atonement had been made and their sin was covered. God did not see the broken law (for in the box was the law of God). Instead God saw that atonement had been made by a fitting sacrifice.

Third, "the ark emphasizes God's *revelation*, for the stone tables containing the covenant commandments were placed inside the ark (Ex. 25:16, 21; Dt. 10:1–5)."[4] These were things Israel needed to know to trust and worship the God represented by the ark: the Lord is ruler, reconciler, and revealer for his trusting people.

Beyond that, it's worth noticing that the ark of the covenant did not involve any attempt to visually represent God. I find it very interesting that here the ark is, in the midst of God's people—the focus of their life and their worship—yet it is not a picture of God. Why? Because he is holy. Because he cannot be grasped in that way. The second commandment forbids the making of images to aid in worship.

3. Ibid.

4. Dale Ralph Davis, *2 Samuel: Out of Every Adversity* (Ross-shire, UK: Christian Focus, 1999), 62.

What's interesting is that the temple later in Israel's history is itself adorned with images. You have creation imagery: palm trees and fruits and pomegranates. God even commands angels to be woven into the fabric to be placed atop the ark of the covenant. The point is not that no images can be made, but that they cannot be made to represent God and to mediate the worship of his people. We are barred from the garden, and that imagery is found there, with the angels barring the way to the tree of life. Note the cherubim atop the ark. There is a theological depiction of a God who cannot be seen.

The problem with worshiping God through pictures and other images is that they always involve an imaginary but inevitably false representation of God. Why? Because he is holy. We tend to see pictures of Jesus, and they're usually nice pictures. But you know what? When you read in the New Testament of people actually confronting Jesus, theirs is a holy encounter. You have Peter saying, "Depart from me, for I am a sinful man, O Lord" (Luke 5:8). You have the temple guards who are sent to arrest him, and they fall back. Why? Because to encounter the Lord Jesus in the flesh is to encounter the holy, and no picture we make can ever do that. The ark is a theological description of God. Why? Because he is holy, and the ark makes accessible, in propositional truth, the God who is so holy that he cannot be seen.

The neglect or the pollution of worship is always a sign of spiritual decline among any people, and this is the problem that David is dealing with in 2 Samuel 6. David recognizes the problem—the worship of God reveals spiritual decline—and so now that he has established his kingdom, he wants to do something about it.

It is important to note that a generation earlier God had judged Israel by allowing the ark of the covenant to fall into

Philistine hands at the first battle of Ebenezer. This was during the time of Hophni and Phinehas, those corrupted priests who were sinning so terribly at the tabernacle at Shiloh. The Philistines were coming in power, and in response to that threat, the Israelites said, "Hey, somebody get that God-box. We need some power. Get God up here, and we'll employ God for our purposes."

But God is holy and doesn't allow himself to be used that way. Not only was Israel defeated in 1 Samuel 4, but the ark of the covenant actually fell into the hands of the Philistines. You may know the great story of how the Philistines placed the ark of the covenant on the shelf next to Dagon (1 Sam. 5). It didn't work out so well; God destroyed Dagon by cutting off his head and his hands, showing that the reason Israel was defeated was not because the Philistines were so great—God could handle them—but because the Israelites were not trusting him or walking close to him.

I hear all the time today: "Oh, the culture's too strong. You can't just preach the Bible. People won't buy that. You can't just do biblical worship. People aren't interested in that. We have to do it the way of the Philistine culture, or we'll lose."

God reminds us that he can handle the Philistines. The ark is in no danger at all. In fact, pretty soon the Philistines want to get rid of it. They start saying, "What are we going to do with this holy God, because he is killing people around here." He not only kills the idol; he kills the idol worshipers. Tumors are growing on people. He's in Gath, and there's a plague in Gath, so they move the ark to the next city, into Ashdod. The same thing happens there. They try to move the ark to Ekron, but the people rise up. "Don't bring this holy God into our precinct," they say. Finally they put the ark on a cart with some milk cows and send it back to Israel. It spends a generation in the home of a man named Abinadab, in the town of Kiriath-jearim. First Chronicles 13:3 says Israel did not see the ark of the covenant in all the days of Saul.

This is a picture of a generation in spiritual decline, and that decline coincides with the reign of Saul. The people did not even seek the particular revelation of God given to them to signify his saving presence and lordship among his people. Now David, having come to the unified kingdom and taken up his throne, seeks to have a revival of true faith. He wants the people to be restored to the divinely appointed institutions of worship and covenant life. The ungodly prior generation had forsaken true worship, so David wants holy reverence and worship to be prioritized.

The parallel account in 1 Chronicles 13 tells us that David called an assembly of all the nation's elders and other leaders and proposed this: "If it seems good to you and from the LORD our God, let us send abroad to our brothers who remain in all the lands of Israel, as well as to the priests and Levites in the cities that have pasturelands, that they may be gathered to us. Then let us bring again the ark of our God to us" (vv. 2–3). This is a wonderful moment: David wants to assemble representative leaders from the entire tribe. They don't need that many people to bring the ark up, but they want to say that God is holy and that all the leading people are going to help to reprioritize the worship of the people. They want everyone to be represented, because they are going to reestablish biblical worship because God is holy.

William Blaikie commends the godliness of David and his followers: "The people, numerous as they were, grudged neither the time, the trouble, nor the expense. A handful might have sufficed for the actual labor that was required; but thousands of the chief people were summoned to be present . . . rendering due honor to God."[5] David's emphasis on restoring worship to the Lord bears testimony to his conviction that God is holy.

Sometimes people say to me, "Pastor, why should I go to church?" There are many good reasons to go to church. We might say, "You'll benefit from the fellowship; we've got nice people here. You might meet a nice girl here, or a nice boy here. There are big business contacts here. You'll enjoy the music. Maybe the preaching will be interesting." Some of this is true to one extent or another, but the reason for us to gather with excitement and to prepare for worship, to set aside time, to come together as the people of God is because God is holy. He is the holy, exalted, transcendent God, and he demands and deserves our worship. He is holy, and when we emphasize and prioritize true worship, we bear testimony to that before the world.

The Israelites under David do not deem worship to be an optional or insignificant activity; they understand it is essential to the well-being of the nation. Whenever Christians realize the holiness of God, they also will prioritize their participation in worship. God is not to be taken for granted. He is not to be treated lightly. He is holy; he is exalted and transcended above us, and so we should be diligent to attend the preaching of his Word. Why? Because it's the Word of the holy God that's being proclaimed.

Sometimes I don't think I'm preaching well or I don't think people are responding, and I'm overwhelmed with this reminder: "Rick, you are preaching the Word of the holy God to people." What a thing that is, and how we ought to devote ourselves to it, along with prayer and the sacraments. The Israelites were to reverence God in the presence of the

5. William G. Blaikie, *Expository Lectures on the Book of Second Samuel* (1887; repr., Birmingham, AL: Solid Ground Christian Books, 2005), 85–86.

ark, and likewise believers today should account him as holy as we attend the ordinances that Christ has commanded for his church.

As we turn to verse 5, we see the attitude of David and his followers toward worship. In the expression of their joy, David and all the house of Israel are making merry before the Lord with songs and lyres and harps and tambourines and castanets and cymbals. How interesting that they don't consider biblical worship to be boring or irrelevant.

Whenever you find people having a true encounter with God as he is revealing himself, the one description you'll never use is that they're bored. Terrified, yes. Bored, no. Meeting with our God will never be a disappointment. Blaikie writes, "The happiness with which this service was entered on by David and his people is surely a type of the spirit in which all service to God should be rendered by those whose sins He has blotted out, and on whom he has bestowed the privileges of his children."[6]

This passage is not calling for triviality, for worldly revelry in worship. Some of us worship in different ways. I'm the kind of person who, when I'm really drawing close to God, becomes more quiet. Others express it in other ways. The point is that our hearts should be lifted up however we express it. Why? Because of the great privilege that we can know and worship God and be received by him.

There is therefore much to commend in David as he takes action to restore worship in Israel. David understands that the holy God cannot be worshiped by human contrivance, so he desires to return to the rightful worship of God among the people. Yet we find that he nonetheless underappreciates just how

6. Ibid., 87.

30

holy God is. By doing so, he learns a lesson about the holiness of God that makes him angry and dismays him and repels him and frightens him.

To grasp this fully, we need to understand what happened during David's procession of the ark, because David errs greatly in the manner of his transportation of this holy object. That's what we note in verses 3–4, starting with "And they carried the ark of God on a new cart." Apparently the idea behind using a new cart was that such a valuable object showed respect to God. Thus arranged on this new cart, the ark is brought out of Abinadab's house. One of Abinadab's sons, Uzzah, is driving it, and the other, Ahio, is walking before it.

The Perils of Casual Ignorance in Worshiping a Holy God

We practice what is called the Regulative Principle of Worship, which answers the question, "What is worship that is acceptable to God?"

I just finished teaching a new members class at the church I pastor. My last lesson was on Reformed worship. Because it alarms people and that's fun for me, I always like to begin by saying, "You need to know that Second Presbyterian Church is committed to consumer-driven worship." *Gasp!* I say, "It's true. We have a target audience; we're seeking to please our target audience. We study the preferences of our target audience, the likes and dislikes, because we want our target audience to be pleased. We would like the worship to be pleasant and for our target audience to come back."

By this point in the class, the more conservative Reformed people are moving toward the door. Before they leave, I have to slip in, "And our target audience is a thrice-holy triune God." We want worship to be acceptable to him. When we ask the question, "What is acceptable worship?" people immediately say, "Well, according to whom?" According to God, and God in his Word has revealed how he is to be worshiped.

If you are a careful Bible student, you are going to be distressed by how Uzzah and Ahio are treating the ark of the covenant, because in those days, God's revelation of how he is to be worshiped included rather specific instructions for the transportation of the ark of the covenant. It could not be casually moved about. God is holy, and he wants to reinforce his holiness in the way things are treated. According to Numbers 4:5–15, the ark could be handled only by a certain sub-clan of the Levites known as the Kohathites, men who were made holy so as to belong to the ark for service. They were set apart simply for this function of caring for the movement of the ark of the covenant.

In order to move the ark, you had to cover it with goatskin. Why? Because if you even looked upon the ark without the right to do so, you would be punished with death. In 1 Samuel 6, when the ark comes back to the Israelites from the Philistines, the men of Beth-shemesh learn that lesson. They make the ark a tourist attraction, and seventy people are slain. Once the ark is covered, it is to be carried only by Kohathites on the wooden poles provided for the ark's transportation. Numbers 4:15 warns that those carrying the ark must not touch the holy things lest they die.

Given these clear biblical instructions and warnings, David's casual, biblically ignorant manner of bringing up the ark is dismaying for its folly and danger. We may rightly ask, "What was David thinking?" John Calvin suggests this was simply the result of ignorance of the previous generation, and how true that is when there is a decline in spiritual things. "This shows us what happens when people are not used to participating in the worship of God . . . and are total novices in it. . . . What was the cause of this failure except that the people had increasingly adulterated themselves, were not accustomed to the worship of God, and were ignorant of the simple elements of it?"[7]

You can't deny that that must be the case, but I think something else is going on with David. We remember that when the Philistines were ridding themselves of the ark, they put it on a cart drawn by oxen. We can imagine David going to Abinadab's house, where the ark was being kept, and asking him and his son, Eleazar, "What do you know about the transportation of the ark?" It wouldn't be surprising for them to say, "It came to us on an ox-drawn new cart, and that seemed to work fine." David seems to have taken them up on that, and his example warns us of the peril of drawing ideas about worship from the practice of the world, even if those practices appear to be blessed. That's essentially what's going on here. "What are your thoughts, Abinadab, about worship?" "Well, here are my thoughts. Here's what seems to have worked before." People today say, "I have an idea about worship."

I know just enough about my own sinfulness to worry whether something that makes sense to me is a good idea in worship. The fact that it makes sense to me does not mean that it commends itself to God. Many people today may sincerely be trying to worship God in a certain way, but the question they should be asking is, "How does God want to be worshiped?" That's the lesson being taught here in 2 Samuel 6.

7. Calvin, *Sermons on 2 Samuel*, 237–38.

33

Blaikie comments, "The great lesson for all time is to beware of following our own devices in the worship of God when we have clear instructions in His word how we are to worship Him."[8] I don't think it's a stretch to say that we're living in a generation when many well-meaning Christians are growing weak in the faith because they are employing worldly methods instead of those given by the Word. Instead of what some would consider a long, boring sermon, churches are using video clips and drama clips. It makes sense to them, but it's not what God has ordained, and so we engage in artifices that make sense to us, that seem to have blessing. The people of God are weakened when we worship in any other way than according to the Bible.

Uzzah's Death: No Minor Indiscretion

Let's be honest: in our judgment this is nonetheless a pretty minor indiscretion. Surely it can be set aside against David's more fundamental desire: his fine devotion to the worship of God. The reason that you and I think this is not a big deal is that we forget just how holy God is. But God has not forgotten. David is in fact courting deadly danger, as is proved by what happens along the way from Kiriath-jearim to Jerusalem. As the procession advances, suddenly the cart stops and the dancing is interrupted. As they look back, they see that one of the ark's attendants, Uzzah, is lying on the ground, so they go back to him. Upon inspection they find that he is dead. Here's what the text says:

> And when they came to the threshing floor of Nacon, Uzzah put out his hand to the ark of God and took hold

8. Blaikie, *Expository Lectures on the Book of Second Samuel*, 88.

of it, for the oxen stumbled. And the anger of the LORD was kindled against Uzzah, and God struck him down there because of his error, and he died there beside the ark of God. (vv. 6–7)

These words rule out any idea that an accident happened. Uzzah dies because he is slain by God for touching his holy ark. This, if anything else, should bring us up short in our casual thinking about dealing with God, especially when it comes to worship. God is holy, and this passage, among others, reveals that he cares about his worship with a holy and fierce passion. That's the lesson that God taught the Philistines when the ark was among them, and now he's teaching it to Israel. Verse 7 says, "The anger of the LORD was kindled against Uzzah." Another way to translate this is that God's wrath "broke out" against him. That connects us with the previous chapter, where the same Hebrew verb is used in saying that God's power "broke out" against the Philistines when David defeated them in battle. On that occasion, David named the place Baal-perazim, meaning that God had broken out against the followers of Baal (2 Sam. 5:20). The place where Uzzah died was named Perez-uzzah (2 Sam. 6:8). God's wrath was equally deadly in breaking out against his irreverent people.

The Bible is honest in telling us of David's reaction to Uzzah's death. David is angry because the Lord has burst forth against Uzzah (v. 8). David is not the only one who has been appalled by God's slaying of this man, since this explosion of wrath seems an overreaction against the actual importance of what Uzzah had done. Wasn't he just trying to honor God's holy ark by keeping it out of the mud? Was this transgression so serious that he actually deserved to die?

Dale Ralph Davis writes that this and similar stories in the Bible show us the supernatural origin of the Bible. No man wrote this passage. It would never occur to any human author to reveal this about God. "This Uzzah story goes so against the grain of human preferences. We would never have 'invented' a God like this—not if we want to win converts and influence people. This God is not very marketable."[9] That's precisely the statement God wanted to make. He is a holy God against whom the slightest transgression is a capital offense.

David's anger partly reflects his own embarrassment as the ark's procession grinds to a halt. He's got this big endeavor; he's called all these people from all the nations. He's got an important thing going on, and here is God getting in the way. Yet from the Bible's point of view, the Lord's response is entirely appropriate. God, after all, had given ample warning of what would happen if anyone touched his holy ark. Numbers 4 made that very clear. We need to be careful not to think of God being petulant or unjust in striking out in his anger.

The wrath of God is not a capricious anger. It's never an unworthy outbreak of anger the way anger often is among you and me. God's anger is always the appropriate and righteous response of God in his holiness to sin in the creature. If we have any problem with Uzzah's death, it only shows that we, like David, still have much to learn about the holiness of God.

It is true that Uzzah's was not a premeditated act of disobedience to God. Moreover, what the man did seemed right to him at the time. He was in the presence of God. R. C. Sproul puts it this way, "We think that Uzzah should have heard the voice of God shouting down from heaven, 'Thank you, Uzzah.' God didn't do that. Instead He killed him. He slaughtered him on the spot."[10] Why would God react this way?

9. Dale Ralph Davis, *2 Samuel*, 64.
10. Sproul, *The Holiness of God*, 138–39.

The answer is that Uzzah's action in touching the holy ark of God was not a heroic act of devotion but a horrific sin of arrogant presumption. Sproul explains: "Uzzah assumed that his hand was less polluted than the earth. But it wasn't the ground or the mud that would desecrate the ark; it was the touch of man. The earth is an obedient creature. It does what God tells it to do. . . . The ground doesn't commit cosmic treason. There is nothing polluted about the ground."[11] But man's touch is polluted, since man has committed cosmic treason by revolting against God's law in sin.

I noted earlier that holiness is not exactly moral purity; it's this transcendent "otherness." But it certainly involves God's moral purity. Moral purity is inseparable from God's holiness. God is set apart in his moral perfection that is infinitely higher than we can ever conceive, with the practical result that the holy God cannot abide any sin. This is why Uzzah's death is not the result of capricious wrath; it is not an arbitrary judgment. If the shock of Uzzah's death offends us, as it did David, then we simply have not comprehended the heinous, horrific results and reality of our sin.

Think of the famous words Anselm of Canterbury wrote in *Cur Deus homo?* when he responded to Boso his inquirer, "You have not yet considered what a heavy weight sin is."[12] That's what we do not get. We are sinful. God is holy. And so the man who touches God's ark must be slain.

The ark is coming up to Jerusalem for the first time. It's going to be enthroned on Mt. Zion, and God wants to make sure that his people understand what his holiness means. God normally does not do this kind of thing.

Sproul uses an illustration from his days as a college professor to draw an appropriate parallel. He had assigned his students a

11. Ibid., 141.
12. St. Anselm of Canterbury, *Cur deus homo?*, book 1, chap. 21.

paper that was due on a certain date, but the papers were not turned in on time. His students offered various excuses: lots of midterms, trouble adjusting to college, problems at home. So Sproul said, "Okay, it's the first time. I'm going to show you mercy." Of course they praised him as a great teacher.

He assigned a second paper. When it came due, half the students did not turn it in on time. Sproul warned them this was the last time late papers would be accepted. The third time, he made good on his threats. When three-quarters of the class showed up without the papers he had assigned, to their amazement, each received an F in the grade book.

What do you think was their reaction? "That's not fair," they said. But of course it *was* fair. It would have been fair if he had done it the first time they had been late in turning in a paper. He had shown mercy, and they took his mercy for granted.

So it is in our reading of the Bible. The Old Testament is a long record of God's patient loving-kindness, his mercy after mercy upon his sinful people. But the time comes when God's wrath breaks forth against sin and God punishes a sinner. When that happens, he is not being unjust. Sproul elaborates: "It is the confusion between justice and mercy that makes us shrink in horror when we read the [story] . . . of Uzzah. When God's justice falls, we are offended because we think God owes us perpetual mercy."[13]

It's not something that occurs to us in our lives. I love myself and have a wonderful plan for my life. It's called happiness, smooth sailing, God being faithful as I define faithfulness. But God loves me more than I love myself, and he has another plan for my life. It's called holiness. He wants me to grow in faith. In fact, he designed me to partake of his glory, and he's fitting me

13. Ibid., 161–67.

down here so I'll fit in up there. He sees fit to put in the trials that I never would have, and he disciplines me and chastises me, and it is not an abandonment of his grace when he does so. We need to learn the lesson of God's holiness. His ways are holy. They are working toward holy objectives. We therefore need to serve the Lord, not in servile terror, but in the awe that looks upon him as a holy God.

What Shall We Do with This Holy God?

David's first mistaken response was to be angry. His second response to Uzzah's death was equally mistaken.

> And David was afraid of the LORD that day, and he said, "How can the ark of the LORD come to me?" So David was not willing to take the ark of the LORD into the city of David. But David took it aside to the house of Obed-edom, the Gittite. (2 Sam. 6:9–10)

David concludes from Uzzah's death that God is simply too dangerous to be dealt with. If he really is that holy, who can handle him? As the Philistines said a generation before him, "What shall we do with this holy God?" The one thing we want to do is get away from him. "Put it aside," David says in effect. "It would be better to set aside the true revelation of God than to have to deal with the God of holiness and wrath against sin."

Isn't that the way we often feel? God is holy. He does not do the things we think he should do. He does not run our lives the way we think he should. His purposes are other than ours. His goals are higher than ours. He's a holy God. He wants to bring us to real faith. He wants to go deeper in our lives. In response we say, "Who can handle a God like this?

What's David's error? We see it here: "And the ark of the LORD remained in the house of Obed-edom the Gittite three months, and the LORD blessed Obed-edom and all his household" (v. 11).

Here we have an epilogue to David's failure at Uzzah's expense, and it tells us that God comes among us to be our God. He is enthroned in the midst of his people. He is a holy God, so his coming among us will be on his terms, according to his Word, with the aim that he will bless us in a holy way—far more than we could ask or imagine.

Sinners naturally shy away from the holy. That's why preachers tend not to be popular in the world. That's why churches often draw less interest than professional football on Sundays. But if David had reflected on the revelation of God provided by the ark that he had cast aside, he might have realized that it offered a treasure that is worth any expense to obtain.

I noted earlier that the ark of the covenant provides a theological revelation of God. The God represented by the ark is a God of rulership, reconciliation, and revelation, and insightful readers will realize that in all these things, the ark of the covenant is fulfilled in the coming of God's holy Son, the Lord Jesus Christ.

The response that people had to the ark is very much the response people have to the biblical presentation of Jesus. The Westminster Shorter Catechism explains Jesus' saving works in terms of three offices: he is Prophet, Priest, and King, the very things declared by the ark. As King, Jesus brings God's blessed rule to earth with righteousness and peace for those who believe. As Priest, Jesus died to reconcile his people from their sin, bearing in their place the outburst of God's wrath that their sins deserve. As Prophet, Jesus gives us the true revelation of God. Jesus said, "Whoever has seen me has seen the Father" (John 14:9), which tells us that if you ever wonder what God is like, the answer is that God is Christlike in all things. He is the perfect revelation of God.

By knowing the God revealed by the ark and ultimately by trusting his Son, Jesus Christ, we gain the blessings of life that were only prefigured in the house of Obed-edom the Gittite.

The Gospel: A Holy Revelation of Salvation

Just as God is holy, so also is the gospel of Jesus Christ a holy revelation of salvation. It is something we never would have imagined in a million years, that the holy God who breaks out in wrath against sin would nonetheless bless his people by entering into the world in his Son to bear that sin. Of course, again the ark of the covenant provides an illustration. If you'd gotten a priest and said, "Do you have a copy of the Bible? Can you tell us what the ark of the covenant meant?" he would have said it means that God, through the atonement, meets with his people. "What did God say to Moses?" "I will meet with you above the mercy seat. I will be your God in the place where the blood is sprinkled on the ark of the covenant, covering the breaking of the law. And I will bless you."

We come to the cross of Jesus Christ. Many in our day are saying, "The cross offends us." But it is a holy cross that comes from God, and we must receive it. We must humble ourselves. We must confess our sins and lay them on the cross of Christ if we are to meet with God. There is no

41

other. We must not treat it casually. We dare not neglect the offer purchased by the blood of God's Son. If Uzzah suffered a temporal death by violating God's law, I am going to presume that his soul was saved through faith. He died a temporal death. But we risk a far greater eternal death if we despise the holy gospel of Jesus Christ. John 3:36 warns us, "Whoever believes in the Son has eternal life; whoever does not obey the Son shall not see life, but the wrath of God remains on him."

C. S. Lewis's classic work *The Silver Chair* provides a fitting illustration to conclude this lesson about the holiness of God. Using the biblical image of the holy majesty of Christ, a great lion, Lewis represents his holy majesty in the character Aslan. In *The Silver Chair*, Jill encounters this majestic and terrifying lion when she is famished with thirst in a forest. She approaches because she hears the bubbling of a stream, but as she draws near, she is horrified to see the frightening lion, his menacing form resting before the stream.

Like David, Jill is arrested by holiness, and she starts to back away, but to her surprise, the lion beckons her to come forward. He says, "If you are thirsty, come and drink." Jill is very thirsty, but the lion is simply too frightening. Afraid of his holiness, she stammers, "I daren't come and drink." The lion answers, "Then you will die of thirst."

"Oh dear!" cries Jill. But she reasons, "I suppose I must go and look for another stream then." To her shock, the lion answers, "There is no other stream."[14]

So it is with this holy God who breaks out in anger against all sin and who reveals himself to us in his way, in a worship that will conform to his desires and in the gospel that reveals

14. C. S. Lewis, *The Silver Chair* (New York, Macmillan, 1970), 16–17.

his only way of salvation. Yes, it is very frightening. Yes, much that we will consider loss must take place if we will draw near to him. Yes, he will have his holy way with us according to his will and the display of his holy majesty. And we must come to him on his holy terms only.

But when we do, we find salvation, for he is the God of holy grace, and those among whom he dwells receive life and blessing, as Obed-edom and his family did. That's what Jesus says in John 5:24: "Truly, truly I say to you, whoever hears my word and believes him who sent me"—his holy Word, the holy God, through his holy gospel—"has eternal life. He does not come into judgment, but has passed from death to life."

3

The Truth of God

KEVIN DEYOUNG

WITH A HOUSE FULL OF KIDS, we read a number of children's books. You may be familiar with some of the classics. We have various favorites; sometimes my wife and I disagree on what are the best ones. She is a big fan of *Goodnight Moon.*

My wife and my two-year-old also like *Good Night, Gorilla.* There's not a lot of dialogue; it's pretty much a gorilla taking the zookeeper's keys, releasing all the animals, following the zookeeper to his house, and climbing in bed. You have to suspend your disbelief and make up things because each page just has a few pictures.

One of the books someone gave us is called *What Is God's Name?*[1] It says on the inside back cover, "Endorsed by Protestant, Catholic, Jewish and Buddhist religious leaders," so that makes you a little nervous—it's a multicultural, nondenominational, nonsectarian book. In the book, God creates

---

1. Sandy Eisenberg Sasso, *What Is God's Name?* (Woodstock, VT: Skylight Paths Publishing, 1999).

the world. All living things have a name, but no one knows the name for God, so people have to make up a name for God themselves: a shepherd calls God *Shepherd*, a nurse calls God *Healer*, and so on. They all think they have the best name for God until one day they come together to kneel by a lake, where they see their own faces and the faces of the people around them reflected in the water. They realize they have all come up with good names for God, so together they call God *One*, and God is pleased.

I had to order an extra copy of this book because I had thrown away the copy that was given to me. Then I thought, "I'm going to use this with some sermons."

Your first reaction may be, "That book could really use some theology." But upon closer inspection you realize, no, this little kids' book is chock-full of theology. Think of some of the theological "truths" that undergird that little story.

The book tells us, for instance, that religion is a process of discovery, not revelation—each person is trying to determine what he thinks God ought to be called, so religion is a journey of finding based upon our own discovery. We see that our knowledge of God cannot escape our own culture, our own needs, our own personality. Each person thinks of God in terms of his own experience and need—whether he needs a shepherd or a father or a mother.

We see too that God is whatever we call him, because he transcends all definition. So the last part says, "And they all called God 'One,'" which may mean there is only one God, though I doubt that's what the book is saying. It may mean God is a unifying God. It may mean that God is one with everything and everyone.

The point is, there is a lot of theology packed into this very bad book.

Truth . . . Indispensible to Christianity

Truth is indispensible to Christianity. Paul shows us just how important truth is to the gospel in 2 Timothy 1. In verse 11, Paul calls himself a preacher, an apostle, and a teacher, so his role is not just to be an active listener, one who comes and puts an arm around you and hugs you, but part of it is to communicate something: to preach, to teach. According to verse 12, he is willing to suffer for his message. He is not ashamed. Indeed, he is most likely about to face death; he knows that the time is coming soon and that he is facing his imminent departure because of his stand for the truth of the gospel.

Verse 13 notes that we are to follow a pattern of sound words. Verse 14 describes it as a "good deposit." So Christianity is fundamentally conservative. By that I simply mean that we believe there is something to be conserved, something to be preserved—there is a truth that is not meant to be reshaped and reimagined and reinvented in each generation, but there is a pattern that you must follow. There is a good deposit. There is an apostolic message that we must embrace and adhere to. Truth is indispensible to Christianity.

I think people actually still believe in truth. You say, "No, they don't. I meet people all the time who say, 'You have your truth, and I have my truth, and all truth is relative.'" But I think people actually believe in truth. Think again about *What Is God's Name?* Its author believes a number of things to be true: she believes that God is one, that God is pleased when the people of the world get along, that God likes to be called Father, Mother, Friend, Shepherd, or whatever else people want to call God. The author believes in truth.

People around you believe in truth; they just may be selective about it. The events concerning former Penn State football coach

Joe Paterno confirm that. I don't want to get into what should have happened or what you should think about JoePa; he is a great hero and still has a wonderful legacy in many ways. But when I listened to sports commentary as the story broke about the events concerning Jerry Sandusky and how the situation was handled, everyone had opinions. People may have disagreed about this, that, and the other thing, but every single person agreed that the allegations of abuse and molestation, if proved true, were a heinous and despicable thing. That was not up for debate with anyone.

Where did all the relativists suddenly go? Where was everyone who says, "Your truth is your truth, and whatever makes you feel good is fine for you"? Suddenly people had very strong opinions about truth and wanted with all their might to see truth upheld. It wasn't enough to merely go by the book; suddenly everyone determined that we have moral responsibilities.

People may say, "There's no such thing as truth" or "I don't believe in absolute truth," but I think we all do. The issue is not so much a matter of philosophy, as in "Is there truth or not?" For your average person in the world, I think the issue is epistemology, the study of how we know what we know. The question isn't whether there is a category of truth; philosophers might debate that, but not normal people. Normal people live their lives believing in right and wrong. You pick anybody's pocket, take the money out of his wallet, steal his iPhone, and suddenly he is a firm believer in truth. Something is wrong.

The question then is "How do we know truth?" Because the world believes there is a God. In the United States most people believe that there is a God, but that we should not speak too confidently about him, her, or it, because no one can fully ascertain the truth about this god or about his, her, or its ways. People think there is a God and that we can be very sure of some things, but that we cannot be very sure about God because no one can really ascertain his, her, or its ways or what he, she, or it is like.

I want to give you three misconceptions about truth that we must combat and one vital truth that we must remember.

Misconception: Sincerity Is the Measure of Truth

We must combat the misconception that sincerity is the measure of truth. I went to one of our denomination's colleges, a Christian college, but you could find anyone there: evangelicals, liberals, atheists, everyone. It was a time when I grew a lot in my faith, but also—as often happens to college students—there were seasons of doubt and exploration and wondering, "What do I really believe, and how do I know it's really true?"

I would see classmates who said they were Christians, but Christianity didn't seem to matter much to them. Instinctively, without realizing it, I began to believe that what I believed was true and had to be true because I really believed it. A lot of my classmates were surface level in their faith, kind of faking, going through the motions, but I *knew*. I really believed these things of the faith, and I was cutting my teeth on John Calvin and David Wells and Martyn Lloyd-Jones and the Puritans and Reformed people. I knew this was true.

Then I began having conversations with a friend of mine who was Catholic, and lo and behold, she was also very certain and very sincere in what she believed. One time she told me (how's this for an insult masquerading as a compliment?), "You're too smart, Kevin, not to become Catholic someday." We would have good conversations. It wasn't that any of her arguments for the Pope or indulgences or whatever were particularly challenging.

It wasn't that I thought, "Well, that's an argument I've never heard before." What rattled me a little bit was that she was so sincere. She was very sure. Her beliefs were as important to her as my beliefs were to me. So what did I do with that? I had to realize that sincerity itself cannot be the measure of truth.

What Paul writes in Philippians 1 turns some of our culture's notions of truth on their heads.

> Some indeed preach Christ from envy and rivalry, but others from good will. The latter do it out of love, knowing that I am put here for the defense of the gospel. The former proclaim Christ out of selfish ambition, not sincerely but thinking to afflict me in my imprisonment. What then? Only that in every way, whether in pretense or in truth, Christ is proclaimed, and in that I rejoice. (Phil. 1:15–18)

When I went to college and a number of professors were out-and-out hostile to Christianity, people would often say, "But he's a very nice man. He has students over to his home, and we have sloppy joes together. He's such a nice man. He's so earnest and sincere." But Paul moves in the opposite direction. He says, "I'm here in prison. I know there are some people who preach the gospel who are sincere and really mean it, and then there are some people who just want to get me in trouble, and they're doing it out of rivalry. They want to afflict me in my imprisonment, to draw more attention to me and my gospel." Paul says, "I'm just happy the gospel's getting out."

I know this is not the sort of blueprint for your pastoral search committee, but it does show us something. What matters to us and our culture is, "Well, at least he's really sincere." Paul says, "I know some of them aren't even sincere. I'm just happy objectively that the truth is being told, that the gospel is going out."

So sincerity cannot be the measure of truth. Conveniently in *What Is God's Name?* the author finds a soldier who is tired and calls God *Bringer of Peace.* What if the soldier wasn't tired and called God *Warrior?* That's actually biblical imagery, but it didn't make it into that book. What about the rich man who called God *Money?* What about the sex-crazed man who called God *Prostitute?* Or the racist man who called God *Aryan?* Or the bitter woman who called God *Revenge?* Is God still happy with all the names, or is there a limit? Is it really true that whatever you think God to be, he's happy with it? What is the basis for believing, feeling, and thinking as you do?

It is not enough to just say, "I think it ought to be so." You need more than your own sincere opinions of the truth, and if people would stop to think about it, no one really wants a world where sincerely held beliefs must be true beliefs. September 11, 2001, was a day when many people were acting on their incredibly sincere beliefs about their god. They were very mistaken beliefs too.

Misconception: Humility Entails Uncertainty

In our world, you can believe almost anything you want as long as you don't really believe it—as long as you don't think that what you believe is actually objectively true and that other people ought to recognize it. Religion in our world has become personalized, psychologized, and pragmatized so that religion is what makes you happy, what makes you feel good, what helps you cope in life. As long as you think of religion in those terms, you're okay.

People are always asking, "You Christians, why can't you just accept me for my beliefs? Why do you have to be so exclusive?"

What people are actually asking you to do, though they don't realize it and you may not realize it, is to embrace their worldview and abandon your own. Their worldview says God is not objectively real but helps us cope with life's problems and makes us feel good. They're asking, "Why can't your Jesus be like that?"

You must say in response, "He can't be like that, because my Jesus actually lived, died, and rose again, and he is even now Lord. He's not a territorial Lord; he is Lord over all. He's not just my Lord; he's also your Lord, whether you will acknowledge him or not."

It is said in our day that humility is inconsistent with certainty. This is perhaps one of the reasons why so many of us, especially young people, have forgotten how to speak like, you know, whatever. We have these little verbal hiccups because we're afraid to say, like, something with, like, authority.

A few years ago, I took my kids to see the *Curious George* movie and I thought, "The music here is really fun." It's by an artist named Jack Johnson, who's a Hawaiian with a really chill sort of acoustic sound. I've gotten some of his CDs, and he's fun to listen to. He has a song called "Never Know."[2] It's a really fun song, and it makes you feel like surfing—until you pay attention to the words. In an interview, Johnson said he was trying to combat this idea that there's one right way to God—people are killing each other over their own metaphors of what God is like, but all any of us have are different expressions for the same thing.

He was very influenced, he said, by the Joseph Campbell book called *The Hero with a Thousand Faces*,[3] which was also

---

2. Jack Johnson, "Never Know," *In Between Dreams*, released March 1, 2005, Brushfire B0004149-02, compact disc.

3. Joseph Campbell, *The Hero with a Thousand Faces* (Princeton, NJ: Bollingen Foundation, 1949).

very influential with George Lucas as he made the *Star Wars* movies. Campbell's book suggested that there's a hero with a thousand faces and that every culture and religion is just retelling the same primeval story with its own metaphors, so you can't really be sure that your version is the correct version. In fact, if you're sure, that sureness probably leads you to fanaticism and killing. Any assurance of religious belief is seen as arrogance; confidence is seen as cockiness.

A century ago, G. K. Chesterton said, "What we suffer from today is humility in the wrong place. Modesty has moved from the organ of ambition. Modesty has settled upon the organ of conviction; where it was never meant to be. A man was meant to be doubtful about himself, but undoubting about the truth; this has been exactly reversed."[4] He said we are making a race of men too meager to believe in the multiplication tables: "Five times five is twenty-five if that works for you, but you may be different."

I had a philosophy class in college, and we had to do deductive logic and work with symbols. It's very much like math. We would go through our homework in class, and there were right or wrong answers. The professor would say, "No, that's not right," and the philosophy majors would go crazy, saying, "No, no, no. I think this is true." The professor would say, "I know you think it is, and you ain't thinking right about it." It was just mind-boggling that there might be a wrong answer. You can be certain about something and still be humble.

John the Baptist did not call people to a conversation; he called people to repent. The apostles did not go into the Roman world inviting people on a journey of discovery; they told people who Jesus was, what he did, and what his life, atoning death,

4. G. K. Chesterton, *Orthodoxy* (Garden City, NY: Doubleday, 1957), 31–32.

and resurrection accomplished. J. Gresham Machen would say that the gospel is historical fact plus theological interpretation—something happened, and here's what it means. You need to help your neighbors and your churches see that Christianity is irreducibly historical. It isn't just a way of dealing with life's problems; we're declaring something that actually happened in history. Paul did not tell Timothy to dialogue the Word but to preach it.

Of course, every pastor knows there's a time in ministry when you're talking with a junior high school student who's really struggling. When that happens, you don't put on your best preacher voice and say, "Repent!" Instead you say, "Really? Tell me about it. What's hard for you?" You ask a lot of questions. We understand that. But there is a time in the ministry of the church, not simply for dialogue or journeying together, but for heralding. That's what Paul says in 2 Timothy 1:11: "I was appointed a preacher and apostle and teacher." *Didaskalos* is the word for teacher. The word for preacher is *kerus*, a herald—a man who will stand in the pulpit and say, "Hear ye, hear ye, I have a message from King Jesus." That's what needs to happen on Sunday morning.

When I was candidating at the church where I'm now serving, a literature major working on his PhD came up to me and asked, "If you become the pastor here, are you going to continue with these linear, modernistic, narrow, rigid, antiquated forms of communication? Are you open to more postmodern, dialogical, conversational modes of communication?" I said, "If you mean 'Are you going to stand up and talk for forty-five minutes and we'll listen,' yes, that's what I'm going to do." He left, which was probably good for him and good for me.

When we tell the truth to people, we don't have to say everything. Sometimes we get ourselves in trouble by doing that. Somebody comes up to you and says, "Isn't it a beautiful day?" You answer, "You know what? God created this day, and he also chooses and reprobates people." The person's stunned: "Where did that come from?" But you're just getting started. "Have you ever heard of Herman Bavinck? Well, you will now."

You don't have to say everything. Say something. Greg Koukl refers to it as putting a stone in someone's shoe.[5] That's what you're doing: just putting pebbles in people's shoes so that after they walk away from the conversation with you, while they haven't changed their minds, they go through the rest of the day saying, "Man, I've got something in my shoe"—just an idea, just a thought rattling around that they can't quite get out.

This certainly does not mean that you must be haughty when you share the truth. I think many people will listen to us even if we say hard things about heaven, hell, sexuality, and so on—they will listen if we show not anger or righteous indignation but brokenheartedness.

Paul went to Athens and was overcome with grief, agitated and distressed to see a city full of idols. But when he went to the statue of an unknown god, he did not say, "Hey, you worship an unknown god. This is going to be easy. I worship an unknown god. I don't know who he is either." No, Paul said, "What therefore you worship as unknown, this I proclaim to you" (Acts 17:23). He knew something. He was certain.

This doesn't mean we can't be winsome, respectful, wise, or brokenhearted. We can, but along with that we can also be certain. We can do better than to preach our doubts and our questions, though we will all go through seasons of doubts and questions. Luther reminded Erasmus, "The Holy Spirit is no skeptic, and the things He has written in our hearts are not

---

5. Greg Koukl, "A Stone in His Shoe," *Stand to Reason*, accessed November 26, 2013, www.str.org/articles/a-stone-in-his-shoe.

doubts or opinions, but assertions—surer and more certain than sense and life itself."[6] Humility does not entail uncertainty.

Misconception: All We Have Are Interpretations

We have to combat the notion that all we have are interpretations. We hear this all the time even from other Christians or from people who want to cast aspersions on Christianity. They say that Christians have a Bible and ten thousand different denominations and that no one agrees on anything. All we have are interpretations. Scripture is just a wax nose; you make of it what you want. How can we really know what the truth is?

This is a huge subject and space limitations won't allow me to unpack all of it. It gets to the issue of the perspicuity of Scripture. *Perspicuity* means clarity. People may not use that language, but that is the doctrine that is under attack in our day.

I did a lengthy review on my blog of a new book by Christian Smith.[7] Many of us have benefited from Smith's sociological work; his book *Soul Searching*, which talked about the religious lives of American teenagers, was very helpful to many. He has since become Catholic and has a new book called *The Bible Made Impossible* on what he calls "biblicism."[8] He gives a scholarly name to the problem he underlines in that book: "pervasive interpretive pluralism," which simply means there are many different interpretations. If the Bible is what we say it

6. Martin Luther, *The Bondage of the Will*, trans. J. I. Packer and O. R. Johnston (Westwood, NJ: Fleming H. Revell, 1957), 70.

7. Kevin DeYoung, "Christian Smith Makes the Bible Impossible," *DeYoung, Restless, and Reformed* (blog), *The Gospel Coalition*, August 2, 2011, http://thegospelcoalition.org /blogs/kevindeyoung/2011/08/02/christian-smith-makes-the-bible-impossible/.

8. Christian Smith, *The Bible Made Impossible: Why Biblicism Is Not a Truly Evangelical Reading of Scripture* (Ada, MI: Brazos Press, 2012).

is, how come there are all these books on Five Views of Church Government, and Three Views of Baptism, and Four Views of the End Times? Why can't we agree on what the Bible teaches? That's a huge question.

We might approach the subject of interpretive pluralism in a number of different ways. We might show how disagreement is often less than meets the eye—Christians often do agree on the essential matters. We might establish guidelines for interpreting Scripture. We might test our conclusions against tradition and confessions. We might distinguish between the meaning of Scripture and its significance; for example, someone might preach about the woman at the well in Samaria and make it a message about evangelism, while someone else preaches the same text and makes it a message about how Jesus knows our hearts. Does that mean they disagree on the passage? No, they're giving it a different significance. We need to be careful not to say more than Scripture says. Some of us get into problems because we get into issues God isn't addressing: "God tells you what diet you should be on. He's telling you how to lose weight. You can't eat carbs. No, no, no, eat the fat of the land. God says he wants us to eat Twinkies. That's what he wants for us."

This problem of interpretive pluralism is not a Protestant problem; it's a human problem. If you ever read Catholic writings, you realize they have the same issue, except they're disagreeing not about how to interpret Scripture but about how to interpret encyclicals or papal declarations. It's the same thing. At its heart, this is an issue about the fallibility of the human mind.

Another argument people use against the perspicuity of Scripture is the insistence that human language is too feeble to be an instrument of the divine. Sometimes people who are more sophisticated really stop you in your tracks by saying things like, "You think God can be put in a box? You think God can be confined to our little puny words that speak about him?" You say, "Wow, I don't want to put God in a box."

I once met an anthropology professor at Michigan State whose PhD was on evangelical Bible studies. His current research was on the emerging church, and he knew I had written a book on that subject, so he sought me out. We talked, and he invited me to a lecture he was giving on campus. Picture the scene: a lecture at Michigan State, an anthropology professor, thirty different people—grad students, professors, people from the department who have gathered for this lunchtime seminar at a Big Ten university. In explaining the traditional view of language versus the emergent view of language, he presented audio clips from John Piper and John MacArthur. It was fascinating—discouraging, but fascinating—to be a fly on the wall. Any time either John MacArthur or John Piper shared his view of language, there was audible laughing, scoffing, and disinterest from the audience. There weren't any believers as far as I could tell, but those present certainly gravitated more toward the emergent view that language is incapable of communicating truth.

The professor didn't come to any conclusions, but I thought he did describe a problem that has opened a fissure in some parts of Christianity. What is human language? John Piper and John MacArthur were saying that language is a gift of God by which he communicates to us. The others were saying, "No, language is so imperfect and frail that it can never really communicate to us the things of God."

I would argue, not surprisingly, for the former: God gives us language as a gift. Think about it. God's speaking is even prior to our human speaking. He said, "Let there be light," and there was light. He spoke, and light came into existence. God shows himself to be a speaking God, and he imparts to us this same ability. Part of being made in the image of God is that we can communicate with human language.

Do you remember how, in Exodus 4, Moses says, "I can't speak, and I can't go to the people"? God says, "I'm going to give you the words to say." Moses says, "No, I still can't do it. I'm no good. I stammer and lisp." Then God says, "I'll give you what to say, then you'll say it to Aaron, and then Aaron will speak my words to the people." At one point God says, "And you shall be as God to him" (v. 16). There's a transfer. God will speak his words to Moses, Moses will speak his words to Aaron, Aaron will speak Moses' words to the people, and those words will be from God, because God gives us the gift of human language and he can communicate his truth in it.

Think about how Jesus uses the Bible. It's always a good idea to have the same view of Scripture that Jesus had. He believed the Old Testament was understandable and accessible, so he claimed he was fulfilling Old Testament prophecy. He referred to the Old Testament as evidence for the truthfulness of his teaching. At other times, he chided the Jewish leaders for not understanding the Old Testament. Jesus could do that only if he worked with the assumption that there is an understandable meaning in the text that he recognized and that you should recognize. The apostles approached the Old Testament in the same way.

A few years ago I was participating in a panel discussion, back when the emerging church was really a big deal. Someone came up to me afterward and was very agitated, throwing out accusations like, "You're a Cartesian, and you worship at the throne of Descartes." I'm thinking, "Man, I don't even remember who you're talking about here." He was saying I was bound to reason, so I tried to explain. I quoted some Scripture. I said, "Paul reasoned in the hall of Tyrannus and in the synagogue. Reason is not a bad thing." Immediately he stopped me: "No!

You're just using the Bible as a trump card." I said, "Yes. That's what it's for." I was getting agitated and upset because he kept pushing back, and anytime I'd use Scripture, he'd say, "That's *your* interpretation of Scripture. You can't use the Bible. That's a trump card." I finally said, "Brother, then we've got nothing left. We can't even have a meaningful conversation."

You see Paul constantly making reference to the Old Testament, arguing that it has a meaning, that it has a shared set of values and interpretive borders. Even though we are centuries removed from the original text, there is still a meaning. When the book of the law was rediscovered in Josiah's day and the people read it, they understood it and knew what to do. Ezra read the book of the law to the exiles who returned to Jerusalem. It says in Nehemiah that the priests gave the meaning of the text so people could understand it (Neh. 8:8). The text was written years earlier, yet the leaders gave the meaning of it. The Bible doesn't say, "They gave an interpretation, all they had were interpretations, and there were many other interpretations." No, they gave the meaning of it, to which the people must respond, repent, and obey.

None of this is to suggest that the Bible is equally clear in all its parts. No Reformed confession, in talking about the clarity of Scripture, has ever said that. There are things that are hard to understand. Peter wrote that some things in Paul's writings are hard to understand. You get to that and say, "Thank you, Peter. There *are* some things in Paul that are hard to understand." But as you read on, Peter says, "There are some things in [Paul's letters] that are hard to understand, which the ignorant and unstable twist to their own destruction, as they do the other Scriptures" (2 Peter 3:16). Peter is recognizing that it's not a free-for-all. Paul's writings are hard to understand, but the understanding Peter is addressing is ignorant and unstable and twists God's intended meaning. There is a meaning even in hard texts.

Not everything is equally plain in Scripture, but the plain things are the main things and the main things are the plain things. The doctrines of Christ and salvation and what happened on the cross and how we are to be saved—these are the things that are given to us with clarity. God gives us the Spirit to illumine our minds and open the Scriptures, and God gets what he wants.

A Vital Truth to Remember

Let me conclude with one vital truth to remember: our God speaks.

Maybe you have run across the little poem about an elephant and six blind men.[9] If you haven't read it, you've probably heard allusions to it. The six blind men each touch a different part of the elephant. One feels its torso and says, "Bless me, it seems the elephant is very like a wall." Another pulls on the elephant's ear and says, "It's a fan." Another grabs his trunk and says, "It's a rope." The moral of the little poem is that we are all like that with God and religion. We're groping for things that we can't really see or understand. Each person has a little part of the truth, but we don't really know the truth. On a popular level, that's what many people think. We're blind men trying to touch an elephant.

The analogy breaks down, however, if the elephant can talk—if the elephant says, "I am an elephant." The blind men say, "No, you're a paradox." "No, I'm pretty sure I'm an elephant." At

9. Editor's note: The poem is known as "The Blind Men and the Elephant" and was written by John Godfrey Saxe.

that point, if the elephant speaks and you refuse to believe it, is it because you are so humble or is it because you refuse to listen?

What Is God's Name? gives a view of religion that is one of self-discovery, not revelation. The people in the world are saying, "Who is God? What's his name?" "I don't know. What's your experience? What do you think?" You never get the idea that God might say something to them.

That's why D. A. Carson wrote the book, *The Gagging of God*. That's what our world does, sounding very humble. "I'm just a human, and human language is so frail and imperfect. I could never know the truth about God. I could never really know." The super brainy people will use this kind of language: "You need to have a chastened epistemology; you need to have a hermeneutical humility." You come away convinced that, yes, you should. But so many of these terms effectively put a gag on God. God is speaking. He wants to be known, to say something to us.

Perspicuity is a crucial doctrine, not just because our understanding of the Bible is at stake but also because the doctrine is intimately connected to our understanding of God. Often when we talk about the doctrine of Scripture or truth, we don't connect the dots. We don't say, "What does this have to do with God?" Doctrines seem abstract and peripheral: "Well, I think the Bible is inspired." Yes, but how is it connected to your view of God?

One author says, "In short, a confession of the clarity of Scripture is an aspect of faith and a generous God who is willing and able to make himself and his purposes known."[10] The doctrine of Scripture starts with the doctrine of God, that there is a God who wants to be known and who speaks to us. He uses historical events, he uses inspired language and prophets, and he uses words written on a page. He finally shows himself

---

10. Mark D. Thompson, *A Clear and Present Word: The Clarity of Scripture* (Downers Grove, IL: InterVarsity Press, 2006), 170.

in the person of his Son. Before we think we have nothing but interpretations, we must remember that we also have a God who wants to be interpreted correctly. Look at Jesus and the apostles and see how they handled the Old Testament before you say, "We must have a chastened epistemology" or "I submit myself to the feet of your French philosophers." Let's not forget that God has something to say and he is very good at saying it.

Martin Luther said, "In a word: if Scripture is obscure or equivocal, why need it have been brought down to us by act of God? Surely we have enough obscurity and uncertainty within ourself, without our obscurity and uncertainty and darkness being augmented from heaven!"[11] God's Word is not beyond us, because God gave us his Word that we might know him. He wants to be known by the great ones and the small ones, by the brilliant and the unlearned, by the educated and the uneducated, by the kings and the princes, and by the plowboy, William Tyndale said.[12] God wants to be known, and so he is speaking.

R. C. Sproul says, "What kind of God would reveal his love and redemption in terms so technical, concepts so profound that only an elite core of professional scholars could understand them?"[13] We must remember that ultimately we are talking about the truth of God, and in doing so are talking about God himself. Is God wise enough to make himself known? Is he good enough to make himself accessible? Is he gracious enough to communicate in ways that even the simplest among us can understand?

11. Luther, *The Bondage of the Will*, 128

12. William Tyndale declared that "if God spared him life, ere many years he would cause a boy that driveth the plough to know more of the Scripture than [the pope] did." John Foxe, *Foxe's Book of Martyrs*, ed. William Byron Forbush (Grand Rapids: Zondervan, 1967), 178.

13. R. C. Sproul, *Knowing Scripture* (Downers Grove, IL, InterVarsity Press, 1977), 16.

Or does God give us commands and a self-revelation that reveals as many questions as answers?

Perhaps our problem is not so much with God speaking but with our hearing or our willingness to hear. I met a man who owned different clubs and had different cool, trendy folk bands come in. I would ask him, "What was the group like? What did you learn?" I'll never forget what he said: "I saw all these people come in, all these bands, all these artists. . . . I found that almost everyone was searching for truth and no one was willing to find it."

That is a description of our day. Everyone's searching. It's not that they aren't finding but that they don't want to find. God is an incessantly speaking God, but his creatures are not very good listeners. Think of all the language in Scripture. "Today, if you hear his voice, do not harden your hearts" (Heb. 3:15). The parable of the Sower and the seed asks what kind of ear you have to receive the Word of God. Jesus says, "My sheep hear my voice" (John 10:27). He is speaking; some are listening.

I started with a kids' book, and I'll end with a kids' book. You may have read the book or seen the movie *Horton Hears a Who!*[14] It's the story of an elephant called Horton who hears a voice. The voice belongs to the Mayor of Whoville, a microscopic, unseen world on a speck of dust. A mean kangaroo comes along and gets the speck of dust on a clover. The kangaroo mocks Horton and wants to get rid of the speck. Horton is chased by a bird, who takes the clover with Whoville on it and drops it in a whole patch of clover. Sinister monkeys lock Horton in a cage and are going to boil the speck in beezlenut oil. Everyone is mocking and scorning him because he claims to have heard

14. Dr. Seuss [Theodor Seuss Geisel], *Horton Hears a Who!* (New York: Random House, 1954).

an invisible voice—until the end, finally, when all the people of Whoville speak. Then everyone hears.

The great difference is this: we have a God who is not so microscopically small that we can't hear him, but we are such sinful, rebellious creatures that we refuse to hear him. There is still a parallel. In *Horton Hears a Who!* there is an invisible voice, belonging to someone you cannot see, speaking of a world you do not see—a reality that is just as real as everything in front of you, yet invisible to you. Will you listen to the voice?

God is speaking. There are unseen things that are as true and as real as we are, and a voice from that world is speaking to us, telling you about himself, telling you how to be saved, telling you how to live, telling you the truth. The problem isn't the voice; the problem isn't the reality or the clarity of the message. The problem is that we are not listening. So Jesus says, "He who has ears to hear, let him hear" (Matt. 11:15).

4

The Wrath of God

RICHARD D. PHILLIPS

HEBREWS 10 CONTAINS the fourth major warning in the book of Hebrews. The first appears in chapter 2, a warning against drifting away from Christ and an urging to instead hold fast to the gospel. Chapter 3 has the second exhortation, "Take care, brothers, lest there be in any of you an evil, unbelieving heart, leading you to fall away from the living God" (v. 12). In chapter 6 we read of the dire consequences of apostasy. In chapter 10 we are given a similar warning. Indeed, all these exhortations amount to the same thing. The writer's concern is that these Jewish Christians, living in a time when they're being persecuted for their faith in Christ, will not turn away in unbelief. Those who deliberately reject Christ, he says, have "a fearful expectation of judgment, and a fury of fire that will consume the adversaries" (v. 27). This passage makes clear a teaching that is widely denied today, even by many who call themselves evangelicals. This teaching has to do with the reality and the nature of hell.

RICHARD D. PHILLIPS

The Reality of Hell

Ours is a generation that doesn't like the idea of hell. In many cases, our generation simply will not accept it. I don't know how many times I've been told, "I am not willing to worship a God like that," referring to his wrath and hell. We live in a humanistic age, and we think of good mainly in humanistic terms: whatever is the greatest good for the greatest number of humans is the greatest good. Then we read someone such as Jonathan Edwards, who said, "The purpose of creation is that God might be glorified. That's the greatest good, that his perfections in glory might be displayed, including his wrath in the judgment of people in hell."[1] We, who have all been humanists and thought like humanists at some point, and to some extent still do, would—if we could—banish the lake of fire of which Scripture so plainly speaks.

In recent years the best discussion of the topic of hell and the reactions against it is D. A. Carson's *The Gagging of God*. It's a big book, but it's a great book, and it has an appendix on hell, annihilationism, and various attempts to either do away with hell or at least turn down the temperature on eternal punishment. Carson first talks about those who deny the idea of judgment and penal judgment in hell altogether, usually saying some version of, "It's unworthy of a loving God." Clark Pinnock expresses this idea very passionately.

> I consider the concept of hell as endless torment in body and mind an outrageous doctrine, a theological and moral enormity, a bad doctrine of the tradition which needs to be changed. . . . Everlasting torment is intolerable from a

1. Paraphrased from Edwards's argument in *A Dissertation Concerning the End for Which God Created the World*.

68

moral point of view because it makes God into a bloodthirsty monster who maintains an everlasting Auschwitz for victims whom he does not even allow to die.[2]

Others, who find themselves unable to brush aside the biblical data in the way Pinnock does, are attracted to the idea of total destruction as opposed to everlasting torment. These people are called *annihilationists*. They agree that God will punish the wicked—but not with eternal torment. Rather they are annihilated: they cease to exist altogether. A person in God's judgment will not suffer perpetually in hell; that person will simply cease to exist. Usually annihilationists will point to the imagery of fire that's associated with hell, observing that fire not only torments but consumes, with the effect that what has been burned is destroyed. They point out the strong theme of destruction in the Bible, using texts such as Philippians 3:19, 1 Thessalonians 5:3, and on and on.

John Stott, probably the most notable advocate of annihilationism, wrote, "If to kill is to deprive the body of life, hell would seem to be the deprivation of both physical and spiritual life, that is, an extinction of being. . . . It would seem strange . . . if people who are said to suffer destruction are not in fact destroyed."[3] Proponents have the idea that hell is annihilation, that it's not the endless torment of a wrathful God. However, I've been told that after expressing this—and this is to his credit—Stott changed his view. He abandoned this doctrine. Why? Because he was committed to the truths of the Bible. He said even back then,

2. Clark H. Pinnock, "The Conditional View," *Four Views on Hell*, ed. William Crockett (Grand Rapids: Zondervan, 1992), 149, quoted in D. A. Carson, *The Gagging of God* (Grand Rapids, MI: Zondervan, 1996), 519.

3. John Stott and David L. Edwards, *Evangelical Essentials: A Liberal-Evangelical Dialogue* (Downers Grove, IL: InterVarsity Press, 1989), quoted in Carson, *The Gagging of God*, 522.

when he held that view and was struggling with it, "As a committed Evangelical, my question must be—and is—not what does my heart tell me, but what does God's word say?"[4] That's always a good rule.

The Bible on Hell

What does the Bible say about hell? I do not intend an extended survey here of the whole Bible, but Hebrews 10 is very relevant in dealing with the subject of God's eternal judgment.

We find here inescapable affirmation of the judgment of God. We may not like the idea of a God who judges. We may prefer a God who only loves, at least as we would define love. Becoming a parent, and growing up, and going through life matures your view of love, but many people think that love rules out judgment. We may think that way, but the fact is that the Bible declares, "For we know him who said, 'Vengeance is mine; I will repay.' And again, 'The Lord will judge his people'" (Heb. 10:30). Verse 27 tells us that those who deliberately reject God have a fearful expectation of judgment and a fury of fire.

How do we reconcile the idea of divine wrath and judgment with a loving God? The answer is that God's goodness demands that he also be just; God's holiness entails a burning hatred of all evil. If we go straight to God's love, we see that his love demands his fervent opposition to things that are wicked, destructive, and offensive, and so God's wrath is not opposed to God's love; in fact, the two are inseparable. God has the same attitude toward sin and evil that a mother has for a fatal disease that threatens her home. J. I. Packer provides a helpful explanation:

4. Ibid., 520.

God's wrath in the Bible is never the capricious, self-indulgent, irritable, morally ignoble thing that human anger so often is. It is, instead, a right and necessary reaction to objective moral evil. God is only angry where anger is called for. . . . Would a God who did not react adversely to evil in his world really be morally perfect? Surely not. But it is precisely this adverse reaction to evil, which is a necessary part of moral perfection, that the Bible has in view when it speaks of God's wrath. . . . This is righteous anger. It is the right reaction of moral perfection in the Creator toward moral perversity in the creature. So far from the manifestation of God's wrath in punishing sin being morally doubtful, the thing that would be morally doubtful would be for him not to show wrath in this way.[5]

What people who reject the idea of judgment and wrath really oppose is the very idea of God. It's not how he exerts his sovereignty but that he *is* sovereign, that he rules—that's what humanistic mankind recoils against. If God is sovereign, then he is ultimately responsible for the disposition of all things, and he cannot be a God of love unless he is also a God of wrath. He cannot be good without also being just in his punishment of sin.

Again we see why many evangelicals are attracted to the idea of annihilation. They cannot hold a biblical view of God without accepting the idea of divine wrath, and yet they cannot stomach the idea of everlasting punishment. But they fail to reckon with many direct statements in Scripture. For instance, Jesus speaks of the danger of being cast into "eternal fire" (Matt. 18:8). Hell's fire does not burn out but is spoken of as being "eternal." In Mark 9:48, Jesus speaks of hell as a place "where their worm does not die and the fire is not quenched."

5. J. I. Packer, *Knowing God* (Downers Grove, IL: InterVarsity Press, 1973), 136, 166.

In Revelation 20, the scene of the great day of judgment, we receive clear instruction about what the final judgment will be like. We are told in verse 9 that fire will come down from heaven to "consume" the enemies of God's people. That word would seem to support annihilationism, but verse 10 goes on to explain what that consuming is. "And the devil who had deceived them was thrown into the lake of fire and sulfur where the beast and false prophet were, and they will be tormented day and night forever and ever." You may say, "That's talking about the Devil, not humans," but the Devil was a creature made by God, and if the Lord is able to send the Devil into perpetual suffering, he's capable of doing so to wicked, rebellious human beings.

The scene does not stop with the Devil, however. Verses 11–15 bring all humanity into the picture with these words:

> Then I saw a great white throne and him who was seated on it. From his presence earth and sky fled away, and no place was found for them. And I saw the dead, great and small, standing before the throne, and books were opened. Then another book was opened, which is the book of life. And the dead were judged by what was written in the books, according to what they had done. And the sea gave up the dead who were in it, Death and Hades gave up the dead who were in them, and they were judged, each one of them, according to what they had done. . . . And if anyone's name was not found written in the book of life, he was thrown into the lake of fire.

That is the same lake of burning sulfur where the Devil "will be tormented day and night forever and ever." The Bible's teaching on hell is that hell is God's holy, wrathful judgment on sin.

You may respond, "Why are you bringing all this up?" Because Hebrews 10 does so. But it's one thing to talk about God's wrath in the abstract; it's another to actually see the Bible's teaching of what the manifestation of wrath, which we are rightly to fear, involves: everlasting punishment and torment for the enemies of God. I don't have to like it. In fact, let me confess that I *don't* like it. I find it hard to deal with, but it is against this backdrop that we see the urgency of the writer of Hebrews as he's speaking to this Christian community. Clearly he speaks about the reality of God's wrath, and he says you need to know it. You need to know about hell. You need to know about God's wrath. Therefore he tells them, "It is a fearful thing to fall into the hands of the living God" (v. 31).

A Particular Warning to Believers

This passage does not give a general statement regarding sin and punishment but rather a particular warning to a community of Jewish people who had made professions of faith in Jesus Christ. The writer's concern is the same one that he voiced in the other exhortations, namely that they would not turn away from God in rejection of the gospel. There was pressure for them to do this. They were experiencing persecution and temptation, just as we are tempted to repudiate Christ by opposition from the flesh, the world, and the Devil. Therefore he warns them, "If we go on sinning deliberately after receiving the knowledge of the truth, there no longer remains a sacrifice for sins" (v. 26).

This is a verse we need to carefully exegete. We need to understand what he's talking about and what he's not talking about when the writer of Hebrews talks about going on sinning deliberately. This refers to a distinction that is carefully made in the Old Testament between intentional and unintentional sins. Moses spoke of this often, such as in Numbers 15:30: "But the person who does anything with a high hand, whether he is native or a sojourner, reviles the Lord, and that person shall be cut off from among his people."

In Hebrews 10:26, the key Greek word translated as "deliberately" is *hekousios*. It's a word that occurs only one other time in the New Testament—in 1 Peter 5:2, where it means "without compulsion." In other Greek writings, *hekousios* is used for those who serve as volunteers, who willfully, intentionally engage in something. This verse is not describing believers who are struggling with sin or even those who have besetting sins that plague their spiritual lives and surely displease the Lord. Rather, this refers to those who reject God's authority to tell them what to do and who flagrantly and deliberately flaunt their sin.

Solomon in Proverbs 2:13–15 also had this kind of person in mind, describing them as those

> who forsake the paths of uprightness
> to walk in the ways of darkness,
> who rejoice in doing evil
> and delight in the perverseness of evil,
> men whose paths are crooked,
> and who are devious in their ways.

Leon Morris comments,

> It is clear that the writer has apostasy in mind. He is referring to people who "have received the knowledge of the truth." . . . The people in question, then, know what God has done in Christ; their acquaintance with Christian teaching is more than superficial. If, knowing this, they revert to an attitude of rejection, of continual sin, then there remains no sacrifice

for sins. Such people have rejected the sacrifice of Christ, and the preceding argument has shown that there is no other.[6]

We should not fail to notice the apostolic writer's application of God's wrath and of hell in the motivation of his congregation. This is not a one-on-one encounter; he's dealing with a mixed congregation. Plainly there's a problem with people having made profession of Christ, having identified socially, culturally, and religiously with the church. They have probably been baptized, and then they fall away. He's talking to this mixed congregation, and I want you to note his freedom and his willingness to use the doctrine of wrath and hell in motivating a body of professing Christian people.

Wrath as a Motivation for Holiness

We're often told today that the only legitimate biblical motivation for godliness is gratitude for the amazing grace of God in justification. We'll frequently be told, "Don't use imperatives; that's legalism. Don't give the commands of God to people, because that's not what you do." The teaching is getting around in our churches that there is no other legitimate motivation for serving Christ than the joyful response to the gospel. I must note, of course, what a central motivation that is; it is a legitimate reflection on the gospel of Christ. In fact, the writer of Hebrews gives it to us in the verses before this: since Christ has died for me, I want to live for him. That is the principal motivation.

Last week, however, I was doing a question-and-answer session with a group of teenagers. They had a pizza gathering with

---

6. Leon Morris, "Hebrews," in *The Expositor's Bible Commentary*, ed. Frank E. Gaebelein (Grand Rapids: Zondervan, 1981), 12:106.

the youth group, and I took questions. A young woman at the Q&A said to me, "It is legalism for me to be told that I have to obey the Bible."

It hurts me to be called a legalist. I preach justification through grace alone by faith alone in Christ alone. I would never tell you that you're justified by your works. God give me the grace to be consumed by the fires before I deny justification by grace through faith alone in Christ alone. But it is not legalism to say that we are to obey the Bible. This young teenage woman, however, said to me, "I don't have to; it's legalism to tell me God's commands."

I said, "What about 'Thou shalt not murder'?"

She answered, "Oh, that's the state's law. I have to obey the state's law."

Here we are in our overreaction against fundamentalism. There is legitimate, deadly legalism, so we overreact. We're told, "Never warn a Christian about hell and wrath." The apostolic writer does not feel so bound. He argues against today's shallow perspective, and in verse 26 we have him warning this mixed community of believers that if, having made professions of faith in Christ, having been baptized, having become Christians, having raised their hands at the altar call and said the prayer, if after all that they then flout God's authority over their lives so as to sin in high-handed ways, they risk not just temporal chastisement, but God's eternal wrath on sin.

Why is that, theologically? The reason is because no one who is saved actually does that. The experience of salvation includes a progressive transforming work in your life. What does Paul say in Romans 6? "Are we to continue in sin that grace may abound?" (v. 1). His answer is *Me genoito*—"By no means!" (v. 2). How could that be? Nobody who's actually been born again reasons that way.

I've had a person come to me and actually say, "Pastor, my theology is impeccable." That got me worried right there. He said, "I believe everything, and I feel nothing. Is that okay?" No, it isn't. Then he went on to say, "My life has never been chaste." I said to him, "If your life has not been changed, if you don't even desire to be changed, you have just described yourself as a non-Christian. You can talk about your apprehension of theological truths, but the demons know the doctrine."

As a pastor, I've had a lot of people come to me and say, particularly after a sermon about the wrath of God, "I'm afraid I'm going to hell, because I sin and I'm just not doing that well." That person is always a Christian, categorically. The non-Christian never comes to the pastor and says, "Pastor, I'm burdened with my poor performance, and I'm going to hell." That conversation never takes place with anybody but a regenerate Christian.

We live in an evangelical culture in which the great want in many respects is a want of holiness, of lived experience. Why aren't we getting more traction in the United States? The results of the Southern Baptist study a few years ago of broad evangelicalism said that 88 percent of evangelical youth abandon the faith in college.[7] I think that's false. They have not abandoned the faith. They've never heard the faith. They've never seen the faith. If we are not persuading more than 12 percent of our children of the legitimacy and authenticity of Jesus Christ, then they are not experiencing actual Christianity.

I am not saying salvation is based on your performance. Works and transformation are necessary to your salvation, not as a condition but as a consequence. We will never be justified by our works. We *are* justified by works alone, but thank God they

7. Jon Walker, "Family Life Council says it's time to bring family back to life," *Southern Baptist Convention*, June 12, 2002, http://www.sbcannualmeeting.net /sbc02/newsroom/newspage.asp?ID=261.

are the works of Jesus received through faith alone, and before God I trust nothing that I have done. I trust what he has done for me. But the result of that necessarily will be an increasing sanctification in my life. I have been bought with a price. I no longer belong to myself. I'm a Christian, and I yield myself to God's sovereign lordship. If we reject that, Hebrews 10 tells us to fear lest we are not saved.

The author draws our attention to consider a positive direction in light of the blood of Christ.

> Let us draw near with a true heart in full assurance of faith, with our hearts sprinkled clean from an evil conscience and our bodies washed with pure water. Let us hold fast the confession of our hope without wavering, for he who promised is faithful. And let us consider how to stir up one another to love and good works. (vv. 22–24)

Given what he has written in these verses, the author doesn't hesitate to say in verse 26, "Look, if we live in a way that mocks what Jesus died for, if we sin high-handedly, there no longer remains a sacrifice for sins but a fearful expectation of judgment and a fury of fire."

Many years ago I had a pastoral situation that I have permission to share with you. It was very instructive to me. I came to faith at age thirty and was a college professor for a few years before I was called to the ministry. A young student at the college was very close to my wife and me. She was a fervent Christian, she had come to a strong Reformed conversion, her life was on fire—and then she went off after college and things didn't go so well.

We gave her all the normal admonitions: "Make sure in your new job that you identify yourself as a Christian. Find Christian friends." Well, she didn't do that. After about a year or so, we were very worried. Then she visited us and informed us that she had embraced a sinful lifestyle. In fact, she was involved in an adulterous relationship with a much older man in the workplace and was not willing to give it up. She lamented all this and said to me, "You know, I think I've lost my salvation."

What was interesting was my pastoral strategy.

On the first visit, I said, "Oh, you're a Christian. It's true that you never go to church; it's true that you're openly living in an adulterous relationship and aren't willing to give it up. But remember that night when we cried together while we were singing 'As the Deer'? Remember the time you cried after that sermon about God's grace? Remember the way you defended Calvinism against those who attacked our doctrine?" On I went, dredging up experiences from her past that argued against the reality of the flagrant sin that she expressed no interest in giving up.

After this meeting, our friend promised to start attending church again and to try to do better. However, she soon fell in with an unbelieving crowd. The next time I spoke with her, she informed me that she had come to realize the falsehood of Christianity. She had been unable to answer her atheist friends, had begun reading Nietzsche and other atheist philosophers, and had rejected the faith. I said to her, "Have some self-respect. Not Ayn Rand. Nietzsche is respectable atheism, but not Ayn Rand." She was still in the same relationship, and everything was just as bad as it had been before.

In the meantime, I had been pastorally instructed by reading Jonathan Edwards's great book *The Religious Affections*, which proves that emotional intensity in the past is not a proof of salvation. Only a living faith and its biblical fruits can attest to salvation—the very point being made by the writer of Hebrews.

Without the actual fruits of Christ living within us, we do not have the right to believe that we're Christians.

Our friend was leaving us again, saying, "I'm not a Christian; here are Nietzsche's answers; I'm still in this relationship, and I'm loving it." This time I said, with tears in my eyes, "Based on what you are saying about yourself, I have to agree that you are not saved. My final word to you is this: if you do not repent, you will perish everlastingly under the wrath of the God whom you have mocked." Those were the last words I said to this young woman, whom my wife and I dearly loved, for several years.

This makes an important point. Many Christians, especially young Christians, crave assurance of salvation while neglecting the biblical source of assurance—namely the fruit of a changed life. While justification does not come through good works and godly performance, assurance of salvation most definitely does! Peter writes, for instance, that we gain assurance of our election by supplementing our "faith with virtue," including "knowledge . . . self-control . . . steadfastness . . . godliness . . . brotherly affection, and . . . love" (2 Peter 1:5–7). First John grounds assurance of salvation in a true profession of faith, a morally changed life, and evidence of love for fellow believers (1 John 2:4, 9–11, 22; 3:4–6). Realizing the biblical grounds for assurance, and accepting their absence in the case of my dear friend, I realized that my pastoral duty was to warn my wayward friend of the wrath of God, just as the writer of Hebrews does.

Several years passed, and we were praying for our friend. I was asked to perform a wedding in her hometown of Memphis. The groom happened to be a former student from our same crowd, and I began praying that she would come to the wedding. Sure enough, at the reception after the wedding our friend was there, sticking out like a sore thumb in this Christian crowd by the way she dressed and acted. Reluctantly she approached me and, after a brief conversation, she agreed to drive me to the airport that evening.

Along the way, she recounted to me the various philosophies that had led her away from Christ, many of them similar to the ideas the writer of Hebrews wanted his own flock to avoid. I was tired after the wedding and reception and didn't think I could manage to keep straight the various Christian answers to each of these challenges. Instead I simply said to her, "Let me cut to the chase. Did you embrace a morally sinful and indulgent lifestyle because philosophy had proven that Christianity was wrong? Or isn't it really the truth that you did not live carefully and you gave yourself over to sexual temptation and later, in order to justify that, you turned to Nietzsche?"

We almost had a car wreck because she began weeping. Finally she said, "Yes, that's true." She insisted that she was no longer a Christian but an apostate. She had betrayed the Lord. Even if she wanted to come back, she said, citing passages such as this one in Hebrews, her sins had damned her forever.

As our conversation progressed, no longer in the car but at the airport, I confronted her with a question that is very much at the heart of what this passage is all about. "Do you renounce Jesus Christ? Can you say that he is not the Son of God, that he did not die upon the cross for sinners? Do you now repudiate Jesus Christ? If you can do that, I will admit that you are damned."

I don't know who was more nervous—she or I. But she could not repudiate Jesus. She did not, and that evening I had the privilege of evangelizing her all over again, starting with the cross where Jesus took the wrath of God in her place. She had been backslidden—badly so—but not apostate. To this day, she has repudiated her life of sin, is an active member in a Bible-believing church, and is growing steadily in the Lord.

In our conversations afterward, she told me that the most potent and helpful thing I had said to her during her time of rebellion was not the false assurance based on a past passion for Christ but the fearful warning of hell. She had been angry at the time and had denounced me, but she had not been able to rid herself of the knowledge that she must face God's wrath if she did not repent, and that was the doctrine that had stirred her in the midst of her rebellion.

The Horror of Apostasy

Sadly, not everyone repents. That's how you tell the difference between a backslider and an apostate. The backslider repents. There are real apostates. They are not real Christians, people who are actually saved but then fall away for a time. Apostates are professing Christians who have the outward appearance of Christians but never were saved. They show this by their subsequent repudiation of Jesus. John wrote of them, "They went out from us, but they were not of us; for if they had been of us, they would have continued with us" (1 John 2:19). They were never saved. Hebrews 10:29 makes it clear that there are apostates: people who mentally grasp the teaching of the gospel, who know and understand about Jesus, and yet have spurned the Son of God, profaned the blood of the covenant by which he was sanctified, and outraged the Spirit of grace. Such an apostate is deserving, the apostolic writer says, of an eternal punishment in hell and in fact is consigned to that by rejecting the only sacrifice that will atone for sins.

People who rejected Moses' law died without mercy, the writer says in verse 28. What will happen then to those who reject the grace of God in Jesus Christ? There is no other sacrifice for sin than the blood of Jesus Christ, and they have scorned it. There is nothing, therefore, but raging fire in the wrathful judgment of God.

This formulation makes clear that we are not talking about Christians struggling with sin. The statement of apostasy, according to Hebrews 10, involves the flagrant rejection of three things (v. 29): first, the person of Christ as Son of God ("one who has trampled underfoot the Son of God"); second, the atoning work of Christ on the cross ("has profaned the blood of the covenant by which he was sanctified"); and third, the Holy Spirit who has brought the gospel near ("has outraged the Spirit of grace").

That last reference helps us understand the teaching of the unforgivable sin in Matthew 12:32. How many people are plagued by thoughts of, "Maybe I've committed the unforgivable sin and I don't know it. Maybe it was kicking a dog and I kicked a dog. I don't know what the unforgivable sin is." All pastors have heard this. But it's clear in Matthew 12 and here in Hebrews 10:29 that the unforgivable sin is to have had the Holy Spirit make clear to you who Jesus is and what he has done, yet you reject him out of your rebellion against God and your love of the world and your hard-heartedness, such as the Pharisees exhibited.

Clark Pinnock calls any thought of eternal judgment an outrage against morality. But it is not an outrage for apostates to be damned. The outrage has to do with God sending his own precious Son into this world, and he came, as he said, not to judge us—he didn't need to come for that. We were already guilty. He came to save us. This is the God we're talking about when we talk about the wrath of God: the God who "so loved the world, that he gave his only Son, that whoever believes in him should not perish but have eternal life" (John 3:16). That is the great statement of God's abounding love and amazing grace.

That God should judge sinners is not the outrage. The outrage is that man, having received this gift from God, having heard it preached, having been enlightened at least to the extent that he knows what is being said, then despises it—that is the outrage. It is an outrage that we should trample underfoot the name of Jesus as God's Son, that we should treat the precious blood of Calvary as something unholy, that we should insult the Spirit of God who bears testimony to the gospel in this world.

That is the outrage, one the Bible asserts by the fact that John 3:16 leads to John 3:18: "Whoever does not believe is condemned already." Why? "Because he has not believed in the name of the only Son of God." Surely A. W. Tozer was right when he wrote, "There will only be one text in hell and it may be cut against the great walls of that terrible place. 'True and righteous are thy judgments, O Lord.'"[8]

The Gift of God's Love

That is what Hebrews 10 affirms.

> For we know him who said, "Vengeance is mine; I will repay." And again, "The Lord will judge his people." It is a fearful thing to fall into the hands of the living God. (vv. 30–31)

If one thing proves the reality of verse 31, it must be the experience of Jesus Christ as he contemplated this very truth. Jesus, on the night of his arrest, went into the garden of Gethsemane to pray. It was this dreadful wrath before him, which preyed upon his mind and soul. Luke tells us how he prayed, "Father, if you are

8. A. W. Tozer, *The Tozer Pulpit: Selections from His Pulpit Ministry* (Camp Hill, PA: Christian Publications, 1994), 1:89.

willing, remove this cup from me" (22:42). What a remarkable thing for God the Son to say. He was there in eternity past when the covenant of redemption was made. He says in other places that he came into the world to do this work. Jesus was not suddenly surprised by it, but now it is before him, and the dreadfulness is so great that he says, "If there's any way that I don't have to suffer this wrath, let it be, but nevertheless, thy will be done." That's what he says: "Not my will, but yours, be done" (22:42).

Luke records, "And being in an agony he prayed more earnestly; and his sweat became like great drops of blood falling to the ground" (22:44). James Montgomery Boice comments,

> This was not a man shrinking from mere physical death. It was the horror of the holy eternal Son of God as he faced the experience of being made sin for us and of bearing the wrath of the separation from the love of God in our place. He was delivered up so that we might be spared. He bore the wrath of God so that we, his people, might never have to bear it.[9]

God said that he would repay sin, visiting his vengeance on sinners. Verse 30 quotes two passages from Deuteronomy 32 that establish the judgment of God on sin. That truth, the proclamation that God will repay, that his judgment will be given, was proved—more than any other way, more than at any other time—by the death of God's Son as he bore the wrath that we deserved upon the cross. What Jesus experienced was incalculably dreadful. J. I. Packer describes it thusly:

> The physical pain, though great (for crucifixion remains the cruelest form of judicial execution the world has ever known),

9. James Montgomery Boice, *Romans: The Reign of Grace (Romans 5:1–5:39)* (Grand Rapids: Baker, 1992), 2:964.

was yet only a small part of the story; Jesus' chief sufferings were mental and spiritual, and what was packed into less than four hundred minutes was an eternity of agony—agony such that each minute was an eternity in itself.[10]

Is that dreadful? It is. But the point it makes is not that God is cruel, for it was God himself, in the second person of the Son, who bore that wrath. The point is not that God is terrible but that sin is terrible. That is what we find hard to accept. That is the point lost on those who complain about God's wrath. You and I don't realize what a personal offense it is, what a horror it is to the holy God when we sin. But the cross of Christ declares that it is so, even as it declares the holiness of God in letters of blood. For even when it was Jesus himself, the beloved Son of heaven, who bore our sins on the cross, the Father still poured out his wrath. J. C. Ryle therefore observes, "Terribly black must that guilt be for which nothing but the blood of the Son of God could make satisfaction. Heavy must that weight of human sin be which made Jesus groan and sweat drops of blood in agony at Gethsemane and cry at Golgotha, 'My God, my God, why hast thou forsaken me?' (Mt. 27:46)."[11]

The cross reveals the reality of sin as well as the reality of the truth of God's holy wrath against it. But the cross reveals something else: the answer to the question about how a God of wrath can be a God of love. According to the Bible, the cross reveals how high and wide and deep and broad is the love of God. This is what it took for God to satisfy his holy justice, to make full payment for the debt of sin. If this—God's own Son leaving heaven to come and bear that wrath upon the cross—is what was required for God to love the world and to offer the

10. J. I. Packer, *Knowing God* (Downers Grove, IL: InterVarsity, 1979), 176.
11. J. C. Ryle, *Holiness* (Darlington, UK: Evangelical Press, 1979), 6.

gospel legitimately, if this was what was required so that he might reconcile his own people to him with his love, so great is his love for you that he did it. The wrath of God on the cross is the measure of God's love for his people. God so loved the world, and the death of Jesus was the provision of God's love for you.

Therefore let us not trample Jesus Christ, God's Son, under our feet by unbelief and high-handed rebellion against his law. Let us never count as unholy that blood, so precious in its value and so saving in its virtue, that was shed for us. Let us not insult the Spirit of grace, who bears testimony of this love of God in our hearts.

When we sin—and we do sin—there is cleansing through the blood, applied by the Spirit to our souls. If anyone does sin, praise God we have an advocate with the Father, Jesus Christ the righteous. He is the propitiation for our sins. Thank God for that.

But should we repudiate Jesus as Lord, should we give allegiance to the world, should we spurn his gospel grace, then surely God will avenge and repay, and well he should. Even the very thought of falling into his holy hands for justice without the covering of Christ's atoning blood, received by faith alone, is dreadful. How terrible it will be for those who defy him now but who on that day will fall into those hands for condemnation.

5

The Love of God

BRYAN CHAPELL

THE LOVE OF GOD is expressed in incredible words by the apostle Paul in Romans 5:20: "Where sin increased, grace abounded all the more." That is wonderful love . . . and a great dilemma. W. H. Auden presented the dilemma this way: "I like committing crimes. God likes forgiving them. Really, the world is admirably arranged."[1] Challenged with such an attitude, Paul asks the question, "What shall we say then? Are we to continue in sin that grace may abound?" (Rom. 6:1).

That may seem to be just a theological question, but anyone who understands the doctrines of grace recognizes that it can create great trial and trauma in our lives. Do you recognize the phrase, "God will forgive me later"? I remember when the phrase was uttered to me as a pastor. A young couple had been attending our church, and we saw a wonderful fruit of grace in their lives. Their marriage had been struggling, but through

1. W. H. Auden, *For the Time Being: A Christmas Oratorio* (Princeton, NJ: Princeton University Press, 2013).

BRYAN CHAPELL

counseling they had reconciled, and we began to see growth in faith and faithfulness. She had come from a nominal Christian background, he from no church background, and seeing them grow was a special thing . . . until she had an illness and had to be hospitalized. While she was in the hospital, a man to whom her husband objected began to visit her. When she did not require the man to leave, the husband left her, and in an act of revenge and passion moved into a trailer with his old girlfriend.

Enter me as the pastor, knocking on the trailer door, telling him, "You need to get out of here and get back to your family." That's when he said those words: "God will forgive me later. I'm going to stay right here for now."

How do you respond to that? There was a sense in which what he said was entirely true. You can't deny the logic or the theology that God forgives sin, even the worst of it. But is it the intention of the gospel to say that because God will forgive you later, you indulge in sin for now? That's not what the gospel intends, and so Paul has to deal with this kind of thinking. How does the love of God claim us and motivate us at the very same moment? He asks the hard questions and makes this simple response: because you are united to Christ, you are not only freed from sin, but you are not to sin.

United to Christ

What does it mean to be united to Christ? This is the archetypal text in all Scripture of the central doctrine of what it means to have a provision from God, so much so that we are united to his Son in identity, and by that identification with his Son we are empowered for living the Christian life. It means that we have a new identity, and in that new identity we do not have a license to sin. Just because grace increases where sin was, that does not mean we have license to sin.

Paul's declaration is abundantly clear: "What shall we say then? Are we to continue in sin that grace may abound? By no means!" (Rom. 6:1–2). It's hard to have a stronger Greek declarative than the one the apostle uses right here. Just to make sure, he repeats it in verse 15. "What then? Are we to sin because we are not under law but under grace? By no means!"

The fact that you are a card-carrying Christian does not mean you have a license to sin. Instead Paul is saying that something else entirely has happened as a consequence of what Christ has done on your behalf.

Can we be honest? When many people come to an understanding of grace, they begin to see that God loves you not on the basis of your performance, nor does he reject you on the basis of your performance. God loves you not because of what you do; he loves you because of what Christ has done. If God's love is due to our faith in what he has accomplished and not due to what we do, for many of us, the pendulum swings. We have been in circles in which people have said, "You're loved when you do well enough." But now we hear people saying, "You're loved even when you fall. God's grace to you is based not upon how well you do, but on your faith in the finished act of Jesus Christ on your behalf."

How much of the guilt of your past sin was put on Christ? All of it. How much of the guilt of your present sin was put on Christ? All of it. How much of the guilt of your future sin was put on Christ? All of it. You are made right before God, not by what you do, but by what Christ has done. Many respond, "I like hearing that. If I've got my ticket to heaven stamped, then Sin City, here I come. This is going to be fun."

In response, Paul declares that you are united to Christ and that in him not only do you have his identity, but you also have

91

a purpose that the apostle now begins to explain, which is to make the glory of God resonate through your life, your body, and your doing for the world's sake and for the testimony of Christ himself. You do not have a license to sin. In fact, what you have, by virtue of your union with Christ, is a death certificate.

In Christ, Your Death Certificate

"How can we who died to sin still live in it?" (6:2). Paul declares that, by virtue of the work of grace in your life and your union with Christ, you are dead to sin. What is the death certificate? Your baptism. Your baptism is the coroner's notice; it's the notary seal that says, "This is God's statement: You're dead." That's verse 3: "Do you not know that all of us who have been baptized into Christ Jesus were baptized into his death?" Jesus was dead. He was crucified. If you are baptized into him, if you are united to him, then you are dead too.

It is hard for us to think this way because we're in a Christian culture in which baptism is an ordinary and regular occurrence; we don't recognize what it would have meant in the time of the apostle Paul, and what it still means in many nations of the world, to declare with whom you stand by virtue of your baptism. If you were in the church in Rome, where former pagans and Jews were worshiping together, and you declared to all those in your past, "By my baptism I am now aligning my life with the body of Christ," they would understand as clearly as you do that you had just said, "The past is dead to me. I now come under something new: a new life, a new way, a new identity."

You can see almost the same declaration today, in reverse, when people declare themselves to be Christians in a predominantly Hindu or Muslim country. What happens when a daughter or a son declares to her or his own Muslim or Hindu family, "I'm a Christian"? The family says, "You are now dead to us."

In October 2011, a young man in Morocco declared himself a Christian to his family. Walking out of his new church, he was attacked by a mob, stabbed repeatedly, and left for dead. Later it was discovered that his family had arranged the stabbing. He sought asylum in the United States and was allowed to emigrate, but his family basically said, "Not only are you dead to us, but we will arrange for you to be dead to us, because everything that you now say you live for means that the past is dead to you now."

As awful as it sounds to say that we, as those who have been baptized, have a death certificate, that we are now dead by virtue of our union with Christ, it is actually a good thing. For what does it mean to be dead? We are not just dead to our past, but we are dead with Christ.

See how specific Paul's wording is: "We were buried therefore with him by baptism into death" (6:4); "We have been united with him in a death like his" (6:5), "We know that our old self was crucified with him" (6:6). It is particularly important to understand who the old self is that is now dead. In the Greek, the word for "self" is *anthropos*—"man." Who is that "old man"? You must go back to the preceding chapter, to a reference to Adam and our union with him. "Just as sin came into the world through one man, and death through sin, and so death spread to all men . . ." (Rom. 5:12).

The "old man" is the one who is dead by his affiliation with Adam. That's what we also see in Romans 5:15: "Many died through one man's trespass." Adam did something that affected us all, his sin becoming ours. We came into union with him in that way, as Paul indicates in Romans 5:17: "If, because of one man's trespass, death reigned through that one man . . ." There is not just the identification with the sin of that man, but now there is the reign of death. There is a certain contamination, but beyond that there is also a control of the Adamic nature that is true of all those who are in Adam. "As one trespass led to condemnation for all men, so one act of righteousness leads to justification and life for all men" (v. 18).

But that old self is dead. This is the wonder of the gospel: all we recognize that is true about ourselves—our sin, our shame, the things that are wrong about our lives, our enslavement to sin, our inability not to sin—that aspect of us is dead. Yes, there can sometimes be confusion, even in Christian circles, in that we don't understand that we are fundamentally new creatures in Christ Jesus. We don't always understand that it means the old nature that was subject to the condemnation of God and subject only to the control of sin is now dead because we were baptized into the death of Christ. In that baptism, we were declaring before the world that our identification now is with him, and because we are with him, all that was past is dead to us.

What is the importance of that? We are free from the guilt of sin because we are dead with Christ. The old self, the one that was guilty of sin, the one that had the wrong in its life, that man is dead. That is an important concept, for reasons that Paul explains in Romans 7:1. "Do you not know, brothers—for I am speaking to those who know the law—that the law is binding on a person only as long as he lives?" That makes sense, of course. The law is binding on you only as long as you live.

Go back to Romans 5:13 and you'll see why this is so important. "Sin indeed was in the world before the law was given, but sin is not counted where there is no law." Put those two thoughts together. If you're dead, does the law apply to you? No. But if the law doesn't apply to you, is there guilt before the law? No. Sin is not counted where there is no law, and dead people have no law that applies to them.

A major highway runs in front of our house, and two years ago a truck driver, distracted while looking at his cell phone, topped a hill, ran into a line of traffic in front of him, and killed four people in a tragic accident. Yet not even a traffic ticket was issued to him. Why? Because he died in the accident. You don't give traffic tickets to dead people. A dead person cannot be sentenced. That's what the apostle wants us to understand here: if you identify with the One who died, then what is true of you is that you are dead and the law, with its sentence and guilt, does not apply to you. You are free from the guilt of your past sin because you are united to the death of Christ.

No Longer Enslaved to Sin

We are not simply free from the condemnation and the guilt of sin; Paul has more good news to declare in Romans 6:6. "We know that our old self was crucified with him in order that the body of sin might be brought to nothing, so that we would no longer be enslaved to sin." We must remember that that old nature was Adamic, and in our Adamic nature we could only sin. We were not able not to sin. In that nature, we were subject to our own passions as sinful creatures. Now we are fundamentally different because we're dead. Dead people are not under the control of temptation and sin. The apostle is building an argument for hope: you are not condemned by your past, and you're also not controlled by the old nature.

The first two churches I pastored were in farming communities, and I can remember a time when a father, being a father, allowed his young daughter to ride on the fender of the family tractor, which was a common experience. But they hit a ditch, and she fell off and was killed. After the funeral, we went to the family home for a meal and a time of fellowship and sharing. The television was on at one side of the room, and an anti-drug-use commercial came on showing a young woman going through the streets of a city, being tempted by the drug culture. In an amazing coherence of circumstances, the girl in the commercial looked almost exactly like the young girl we had just buried.

I expected the family to respond with shock and devastation, but instead the mother who had just put her daughter in the grave shook her finger at the television and said of the drug culture, which had no relationship to her own daughter, "You can't touch my baby. My baby cannot be controlled by you. Now she is with Jesus."

It was the most horrid of situations, but at the same time there was a great sense of hope. The woman's daughter is not under the control of sin. It can't touch her. Why? Because she is dead. She is united to Christ now—although not just by death, but by something else as well. That's what Paul is declaring: that we are not just united to Christ in his death, by which we are freed from the condemnation and the control of sin, but we are also united to Christ in his resurrection and his life.

That is Paul's repeated message here: we were with Christ by baptism united into death in order that "just as Christ was raised from the dead by the glory of the Father, we too might walk in newness of life" (v. 4). "We shall certainly be united with him in a resurrection like his" (v. 5). This is done "so that we would no longer be enslaved to sin" (v. 6). We have new life in us. There is newness of life that makes such things possible. The old self that was united to Christ is dead, but Christ is alive, and we're united to him in that too.

Crucified, Dead, and Buried

To begin to fully grasp the greatness of the love of God, you almost have to back away from what Paul is saying and engage your full understanding of what you know about the nature of Christ and then recognize that Paul is saying that it applies directly to you! Paul has just told us that our old self was crucified with Christ. He has declared that we have been united with Christ in a death like his so that we would be united with him in resurrection. We were buried therefore with him by baptism. Stop and think about what Paul has written: crucified, dead, and buried. Where do you usually hear that trio placed together? In the Apostles' Creed. The amazing thing is that in Romans 6 it's being applied not to Christ but to believers. We were crucified, dead, and buried with him.

Crucified. All the pain, shame, and suffering that we know was true of a life before and apart from Christ is dead. The heart stops and breath stops and our wrestling for approval and significance and affection is dead and buried with him. In the grave, my foot against his foot. Cold hand against cold hand, and darkness all around. All that was true of me is sealed in the grave. Dead—but that is not the end of the story. Crucified, dead, and buried, but on the third day Christ rose again from the dead, and we are united to him in his resurrection too.

Feel the weight of what the apostle is saying. In 2011 in Iowa, Gordon and Norma Yeager—she ninety years old, he ninety-four, married to each other for seventy-two years—were in an automobile accident. They were taken to the hospital and because of their long years together were allowed to lie in gurneys together while Gordon died. As his breathing stopped and the blood drained from his system, he became cold and lifeless; nonetheless, the heart monitor continued to show a heartbeat, because he was holding her hand. The monitors showed her life through him. In the same way, you are dead. All that shames you, all your lack of control, all that you wish no one knew about you but that you know that God knows—all that is dead. In its place is the life of Jesus Christ coursing through you.

If you're dead and Jesus is alive in you, whose identity do you have? You have the identity of Jesus Christ, which means that God loves you as much as he loves Jesus. As a new creature in Christ Jesus, you have gone from an old self—an Adamic nature that was contaminated, controlled, and condemned because of sin—to one that is in union with Christ, and in union with him you now have the identity of a child of God as precious to God as Jesus himself.

In John Bunyan's use of the mirror in *The Pilgrim's Progress*, we get a picture of how God views us. One side is just a regular mirror that reveals us as we are now, with wrinkles, blemishes, and flaws. But on the other side of the mirror is the image of Jesus Christ. That's the side from which God views us—from the "Christ" side—because you are dead, but Jesus is alive in you and the life of Christ now characterizes you. The love of God embraces you, based not upon your performance but upon the reality of the mercy of God in Christ given in your behalf. You are united to Christ, and his life is yours, his identity is yours, his merits are yours, his righteousness is yours—all because you are dead but united to the One who lives.

A New Calling

If you truly understand what it means to be free from the guilt of your sin by your union with the Son of God, the Prince of Heaven, then your new identity gives you an absolutely fundamental new calling in life. Having spent much of the first ten verses of Romans 6 talking about our identity with Christ and reminding us of our security because of Christ, Paul turns from these great indicatives of what it means to be united to Christ to a series of imperatives.

> Let not sin therefore reign in your mortal body, to make you obey its passions. Do not present your members to sin as instruments for unrighteousness, but present yourselves to God as those who have been brought from death to life, and your members to God as instruments for righteousness. (Rom. 6:12–13)

Your calling is to be an instrument for righteousness. You have not a license to sin but a new lease on life, to live as a new creature in Christ Jesus who can be an instrument for the righteousness of God. See the importance of your mission. When the apostle uses the words "Let not sin therefore reign in your mortal body," he is reminding us of what he's already talked about in the preceding chapter, about sin having dominion through Adam. Sin came into the world, and death reigned in our lives. The influence of the Adamic nature touched us and controlled the world, but now the apostle says, "Do not let that nature and influence reign in your mortal body. Instead become instruments"—some of your Bibles use the word *weapons*—"of righteousness."

You are part of a kingdom battle. Sometimes we think the great battles of the ages are behind us, but Paul is saying that all who are united to Christ have his mission. He is saying, "You are part of God's battle, in Christ Jesus, to push back the darkness, and you can't do that by yourself. But you have Christ in you, and in Christ you have a great new calling not to yield to sin." We are not to present our members as instruments of unrighteousness. To that Paul adds positive commands: live for God, present yourselves to God as those who have been brought from death to life, and use your instruments, your weapons, for the kingdom of God.

There is no way the apostle is saying, "Grace leads to licentiousness." He is saying exactly the opposite. Grace, rightly understood, leads you into a kingdom battle for the sake of the glory of God, and it is a glorious calling that you have.

But if you have this calling, what power do you have to bring it about? It's just us, mortal humans. How can we be part of pushing back the darkness for the reign of God in all the world? Because we have Christ's life in us; we have been brought from death into life. Because of these truths, Paul can write, "Sin will have no dominion over you" (v. 14).

Sometimes you have to just believe what the Scriptures say. The Puritans sometimes said that the man of God would have victory only when he began to walk the walk of faith. That means we need to keep on the straight and narrow, read our Bibles a lot, walk the walk of faith, right? Actually they had exactly the opposite idea. It wasn't about works of supererogation and heroism. The walk of faith, they said, was to come to the Bible as a little child and simply believe what it says. You have Christ in you. There was a time when you could not say no to sin, but that old you is dead. You are alive in Christ Jesus. You have abilities such as no person who is without the Son of God can possibly hope to have. Because you are a new creature in Christ Jesus, you are able to resist sin.

I have a very gentle wife, but every now and then she will get some steel in her voice, usually when one of our children is despairing about her abilities. When I've got a teenager who is saying, "I can't do it. I'm so dumb. I've waited too long. I can't do it," my wife will respond, "You listen to me. You can do this. You're smart, and you're my child, and we're going to get this done."

If you don't believe that you can defeat Satan, if you don't believe you can have victory over sin, you've already lost, and so the apostle says, "Just believe the Word. You are united to Christ." Everything in you says, "I can't help it. I can't stop it. It's too much a part of my life. It's too much a part of the culture." In response, the apostle says, "You have the resurrection power of Jesus Christ alive in you. You are united to Christ and in Christ you can do all things." We are talking about something supernatural here that the apostle says is ours because we are united to Christ.

Living before God's Face, Living with Christ's Rescue

We have a calling, and we have power. But what is our motivation to do what we're called to do and have the power to do? We must recognize that we live before the face of God.

Did you catch the apostle's wording in verse 13? "Do not present your members to sin as instruments for unrighteousness, but present yourselves *to God* as those who have been brought from death to life." We have to be clear in terms of how we perceive what it means to live before the face of God. Is God standing above you with arms crossed and a frown on his face, waiting to see when you get out of line? That is not strong motivation. But God is calling you to live for his glory, and he reminds you that you have already been brought from death to life. So present yourselves to God as those who have been brought from death in Adam to life in Christ.

Paul is talking not about the frown of God but instead about God looking on you with the pride of a father looking upon his own child. Here is the face of approval, of love, of affection. In return, you're presenting yourself to God as one who has been brought from death into life. You recognize that if Christ is in you, there are certain places you don't want to take him. Servicemen, especially in uniform, behave in a way that befits their pride in their country. When John Owen, the great Puritan writer on sanctification, talked about the mortification of sin, he said that you must recognize that some aspects of your life do not befit a Christian. There are certain things unbefitting to your mouth and your mind and your eyes if Christ is in you. You live in ways that befit the child that you are: the child of God that God has made you by the grace of Jesus Christ in you. United to Christ and living before the face of God, you want to live with the honor of that reality. God is not frowning, because there is therefore now no condemnation to those who are in Christ Jesus. That's dead. You are living before God as one who is alive through the work of Jesus Christ and with the identity of his own child.

But you not only have the motivation of knowing you live before God's face, you have an understanding of Christ's rescue. You have been brought from death to life. You were going to hell. The wrath of God could justly, legitimately have fallen upon you, but you have been brought from death to life. A great rescue has occurred, and when you contemplate that rescue, particularly as you focus upon the passion of Christ—crucified, dead, and buried in your behalf—that focus upon his passion should create something in you: love.

John Owen wrote that sin at its core is always lack of love. That's an interesting thought. Why, ultimately, does sin have power in your life? Because you love it. If it did not attract you, it would have absolutely no power over you. We sin because we love it, at least in the moment. If the power of sin is love for it, how do we overcome love for sin? With a greater love. Remember Thomas Chalmers's *Expulsive Power of a New Affection*? Why is the apostle reminding us that Christ was crucified, dead, and buried on our behalf? Because focus upon the passion of Christ fills us with love for Christ, and there's a necessary consequence. Jesus said, "If you love me, you will keep my commandments" (John 14:15). If you are filled up with love for Christ, you will keep his commands, because that will be your greatest love, your greatest desire.

Do Not Be Enslaved

Now the apostle is saying, "You have a new calling, and in that calling you recognize you have power to do what God is calling you to do. And you have motivation to do it because you live before God's face, wanting to live with honor before him. Knowing the passion of Christ on your behalf, you actually want to love him back." There is one more motivation to live for God: so that you are not a slave. For what does your sin do to you? It enslaves you. "Sin will have no dominion over you, since you are not under law but under grace" (Rom. 6:14). Paul repeats that thinking in verse 16: "Do you not know that if you present yourselves to anyone as obedient slaves, you are slaves of the one whom you obey?"

In our culture, you won't get much of a hearing when you say to people, "You need Christ because what you are doing is morally wrong. You are bad if you do it." That doesn't win much of a hearing because the culture does not recognize the law. It does not recognize the moral code. But you know what our culture does recognize? How awful it is to be enslaved. Freedom is more important than morality. I'm not saying that's right; I'm just saying that's where our culture is right now. Take somebody like Amy Winehouse, the English singer who died in 2011. She was highly respected in the pop music world and even adored because of a notorious lifestyle as she thumbed her nose at traditional culture. But do you know when her fans began to turn on her? When her addictions to drugs and alcohol made her start cutting concerts short or not showing up for them at all.

Finally, in the great sadness at the end of her life, as she tried to detox herself from alcohol too fast, the detoxification process killed her as the alcohol reached out to enslave her again, even as she was trying to escape it. Paul is honest enough to say, "Listen, now that you know the grace of God and have the life of Christ in you, know your calling. You are called to push back the darkness. He's giving you the power to do that; you have the power of Christ to be an instrument of the reign of Christ in your life and the lives of those around you. The reason you should do that is because it is befitting of one who is a child of God, who has the identity of the Prince of Heaven, because you love him so much that you want to live for him, and finally because you do not want to be enslaved to the alternatives."

Having said all these things, the apostle declares, "Now that you know the greatness of God's love for you, live for him because that is your calling and your identity in Christ Jesus." You are united to Christ, so all that you hate about your old self is dead, and your true identity before the King of the Universe is to be his favored child. As that child, you have the weapons of heaven at your disposal to do God's will and to keep from being enslaved to the one who would destroy you. What does that do for you?

I think of the monk who asked one of the ancient saints, "How can you actually live the Christian life?" In return, she asked, "What do you think your calling is?" The young monk said, "Every day I do administration and book work, prepare the food, and wash the dishes."

The saint said, "What do you think your calling really is?"

The monk answered, "I'm supposed to take care of the poor."

Said the saint, "No, your calling is to know how much you are loved, because when you remember how much you are loved, you will live for him who gives you the power to do so."

You are united to Christ. The past is dead. Your identity is his. Live for him.

PART 2

God the Son

6

The Glory of the Son

D. A. CARSON

DOES GOD HAVE A SON? We're Christians; of course we're going to say yes. But what does that mean? In world religion, the concept of God having a son varies enormously. Among Muslims, the notion is bizarre. At a street level, many Muslims believe that Christianity holds that God had intercourse with Mary to produce Jesus and that the Trinity consists of God, Mary, and Jesus. They find such a concept bizarre, and I agree with them. Of course, informed Muslims know that's not how we understand the Trinity, but they find our understanding of the Trinity equally bizarre. There I disagree with them. Hindus have no difficulty confessing that Jesus is the Son of God, but then, aren't we all?

Even within the Bible, when we start probing a bit, the notion of "son," even "son of God," is not univocal; it does not mean the same thing in every place. After all, the first distinctively metaphorical usage of the term *son* is found as early as Exodus 4:22–23: "Israel is my firstborn son, and I told you, 'Let my son go, so he may worship me.'" So Israel is God's son, corporately. This eventually gets tied to Jesus through the prophet Hosea, who, in the eighth century BC, pictures Israel as God's own son as he looks back to the exodus. "Out of Egypt I called my son," God says (Hos. 11:1). That is picked up in Matthew 2 with respect to Jesus—Jesus being the fulfillment of this trajectory of Israel as God's own son.

But it's not just Israel. Sometimes the Davidic king is called God's own son. That's not only true in well-known psalms such as Psalm 2 and Psalm 110, but ultimately it's anchored in 2 Samuel 7:14, where God calls the Davidic dynasty into being. "I will be to him a father, and he shall be to me a son," God says in that passage.

Sometimes "son of God" is applied to angelic beings, both good and evil. In Job we read how the sons of God approach God, and among them is Satan himself.

In the New Testament, Christians are called sons of God. Yes, it's true that every New Testament writer who dwells on this theme distinguishes in some sense between Jesus' sonship and our sonship, but nevertheless the term is used. In John's gospel, Jesus is the Son and we're the children of God. In Paul's writings, Jesus is the Son and we're the adopted sons. But the language of sonship and children of God is common. So what precisely do we mean when we profess Jesus to be the Son of God?

Of all the passages we might refer to in this respect, I suspect none includes so much explanatory material as John 5. A lot of passages deal with Jesus' sonship, and we'll pick up a few of them, but this passage is quite remarkable.

The preceding verses depict the healing of a paralyzed man by the pool of Bethesda. After Jesus has healed him, he tells the man to pick up his mat and go home. This miracle is done on the Sabbath, so whether it's the miracle or the carrying of

110

a burden on the Sabbath that causes offense among the Sabbatarians is not quite clear. Eventually we read, "So, because Jesus was doing these things on the Sabbath, the Jewish leaders began to persecute him" (v. 16). In the resulting exchange we are told four things about what it means to confess Jesus as the Son of God.

This is a very tight passage. Some narrative passages flow easily; it's easy to follow the drift. Certain parts of these verses are tightly organized, and we can follow their thought only by taking them apart, clause by clause, and then putting them back together.

First, the Son insists he has the right to do whatever the Father does, and in particular, just as the Father does, the Son works on the Sabbath. We see this in 5:16–18. The authorities are beginning to persecute him, and in his defense Jesus says to them, "My Father is always at his work to this very day, and I too am working" (v. 17).

That's a remarkable response. Jesus might have answered with simple debates about how to understand Sabbath law. He might have said, for example, "The Sabbath law does not envisage a prohibition toward miraculous cures. It's not as if I'm the medical doctor trying to put in a little extra overtime on the Sabbath to increase my income, when I could have told the poor chap to come back the next day. Nor is it that this man whom I have healed is making a living carrying his bed mat around. It's not as if he's a professional bed-mat–carrier, and now he's carrying his bed mat on the Sabbath for a little extra income on the sly. It was a miracle. You are interpreting the law in much too narrow a fashion."

If Jesus had responded along those lines, there would have been a nice little theological debate, but no one would have taken umbrage. Oh, they would have disagreed with him, but there would not have been the kind of offense that arises here. For what Jesus does, as is common in his response to questions, is to divert attention to himself. He makes the issue fundamentally christological: who is the Christ; who is he? He makes it intensely personal. He says, "My Father is always at his work to this very day, and I too am working."

Cutting to the Heart of the Issue

We need a little background here to understand just how pointed this was. There is very good evidence that in the first and second centuries, there was a long-standing debate in Jewish circles as to whether or not God keeps the Law. The individual law with which they had the most difficulty in this respect was the Sabbath. For some people pointed out that if God stopped working on the Sabbath, then every Sabbath the universe would fall apart, because he upholds all things by his providential sway. If God stops doing that part of his work, what happens to the order of the entire universe? The other side said, "No, no. God really must keep the Law. There must be some sort of explanation."

It was common in the first century, and codified in the second century, to break down all categories of prohibited work into thirty-nine different categories. Among the categories of prohibited work on the Sabbath were two in particular: First, you may not carry a burden on your shoulder. You might carry something around, but nothing so heavy that it is on your shoulder, because that suggests that you really are exerting yourself and carrying some sort of burden. Second, you may carry something in your own home, but you may not carry it from house to house. That's a prohibited category of work.

In the debate of whether or not God works on the Sabbath, some responded, "Since God is so big, even if he's moving chunks of the universe around, nothing is bigger than he is, so it never goes higher than his shoulder. And the whole universe, after all, is his, so he never moves anything from one domicile to another. Even though he is in this sense working, God is not *really* working in the sense of contravening any of the prohibited categories of work. Thus God does not work on the Sabbath." Others kept saying, "That's not quite right. God's providence must still prevail." So this was part of the debate in rabbinical circles in the first century.

Jesus cuts through all that. He doesn't discuss what it means to work. He says, rather, "Whatever God has the right to do, I have the right to do too. In some sense, my heavenly Father is working continuously to this very day, and if he has the right to do it, I have the right to do it."

Now, many Jews referred to God as *Father*. That was not a Christian invention. But when the Jews referred to God as *Father*, it tended to be in a plural context: "our Father" or "the heavenly Father." Never "*my* Father." Jesus comes along and says, "My Father is always at his work to this very day, and I too am working."

Now Jews understood, as Christians understand today, that there are domains in which we ought to imitate God. After all, God says, "Be holy, for I am holy" (1 Peter 1:16). We are commanded to love, for God is love. But nowhere in Scripture does God say, "Be omnipotent, for I am omnipotent" or "Be omniscient, for I am omniscient."

Christian theologians have long distinguished between what they call the *communicable attributes of God* and the *noncommunicable attributes of God*. The communicable attributes of God are the attributes of God that he shares—that he *communicates*,

113

to use old English—with his image bearers. We can be holy in some measure. We can love in some measure, though never as inexhaustibly as God. We nevertheless can enter into the same experience, and we are commanded to do so.

But there are incommunicable attributes of God, attributes of God that belong exclusively to him. These we are not commanded to communicate. It would be futile to try to do so, and it would be arrogant and sinful on our part to think that we could. What do you do with God working on the Sabbath?

The Jews understand that Jesus is not making the sort of claim that ordinary human Jews would make. They understand that he is claiming a prerogative that belongs only to God. For however you answer the question, "Does God work on the Sabbath?"—even if you say that the answer is bound up with how high he lifts a burden toward his shoulder or whether the whole universe is God's domicile—all those arguments, however good or foolish or serious they are, really belong only to God. You cannot argue them for individuals such as you or me.

But Jesus says, "My Father is always at his work to this very day, and I too am working." Jesus is saying, "Whatever God's rights are in this respect, I have the same rights." In short, the Son insists that he has the right to do what the Father does, and in particular, just as the Father, the Son works on the Sabbath.

It is important nevertheless to see that what the Jews mean by "equal with God" in the charge that they bring against Jesus is not quite what he means. Verse 18 says, "For this reason they tried all the more to kill him." Not only was he breaking the Sabbath, which was bad enough, but he was even calling God his Father—not the way the Jews did but in the sense that gave him the rights of God himself, making him equal with God.

What they meant by "equal with God" is not quite what Christ would mean. In their minds, there's God, there's Jesus making himself equal with God, so now Jesus is trying to establish two God-centers. That means you have *ditheism*, belief in two Gods: God and this fake, blasphemous Jesus-god. But that is not what Jesus has in mind. Jesus does not have in mind any type of ditheism. What we find in the next verses is just what is meant by saying that Jesus is the Son of God with the rights and prerogatives of God. We find the defense of the peculiarly Christian understanding of *monotheism*, belief in one God.

Here is the beginning of what comes to be called the doctrine of the Trinity.

Equal, but Subordinate, to the Father

That brings us to a second point: the Son insists he is subordinate to the Father, but it is a uniquely defined subordination, as we see in verses 19–23. "Jesus gave them this answer: 'Very truly I tell you, the Son can do nothing by himself; he can do only what he sees his Father doing'" (v. 19). In other words, far from claiming there are two God-centers, Jesus says that whatever his sonship means, nevertheless Jesus, as God, with the rights of God, can do only what God does because he sees what the Father is doing.

This may be making you nervous. You may say, "Yes, but how are we going to defend the deity of Christ in this sort of context?" Before we raise that question, we need to recognize that John's gospel is very insistent both on the deity of Christ and on this kind of subordination of Christ to the Father. We read the very first verse of John's gospel: "In the beginning was the word, and the Word was with God [God's own fellow], and the Word was God [God's own self]." We read, "Before Abraham was born, I am!" (John 8:58). Not simply "I was," which would have established his preexistence, but "I am," taking upon himself the very name of God. In the farewell discourse we read, "Don't you know me, Philip, even after I have been among you such a long time? Anyone who has seen me has seen the Father" (John 14:9). In the resurrection account, in the matter of Thomas's doubt, Thomas comes eventually to exclaim, "My Lord and my God." The affirmation of Jesus' deity is repeated, and overtly so, in John's gospel.

Yet the notion of the functional subordination of the Son is not rare either. In addition to seeing it in verse 19, you see it in 5:30: "By myself I can do nothing; I judge only as I hear, and my judgment is just, for I seek not to please myself but him who sent me." Or again, in John 8:29: "The one who sent me is with me; he has not left me alone, for I always do what pleases him." Never is that made reciprocal, as if the Father turns to the Son and says, "Yes, and I always do what pleases you too." These statements function in only one direction. In John 14:31 we read, "He comes so that the world may learn that I love the Father and do exactly what my Father has commanded me." It is never the other way around. It's not as if the Father says reciprocally, "Yes, and I do whatever the Son commands me too." There is a sustained argumentation of a kind of functional subordination in John's gospel that is every bit as strong as the affirmation of his deity. This excludes any notion that Jesus is a second God, a second God-center.

In our main passage, the remainder of the argument (vv. 19–23) turns on four "for" clauses that increasingly unpack the argumentation. The first is introduced in verse 19: "Very truly I tell you, the Son can do nothing by himself; he can do only what he sees his Father doing, *because* whatever the Father does the Son also does." That is staggering. Once again Jesus claims that his activity is coextensive with that of God. Does

God create the universe? So does the Son. Again, note how John's gospel begins:

> In the beginning was the Word, and the Word was with God, and the Word was God. He was with God in the beginning. Through him all things were made; without him nothing was made that has been made. (John 1:1–3)

That affirmation recurs elsewhere in the New Testament. Indeed, Paul writes to the Colossians, "All things have been made through him [Christ] and for him [Christ]" (Col. 1:15). In that sense, I'm not the son of God at all. I've never made the universe. I doubt anyone reading this book has either. In that sense, Jesus' sonship is unique.

Now we're getting closer to a fundamental understanding of sonship that we need to come to grips with. In the Western world today, what does *sonship* connote? We watch *CSI* on TV, and one of the first things we pick up from a program such as that is that sonship depends on DNA. Any number of rather predictable plots turn on discovering who really is the true father. Paternity tests. You can't beat DNA. But that wasn't the notion of sonship in the ancient world. They didn't worry about DNA.

Like Father, Like Son

Let me come at this from a slightly different perspective. How many men in the West today are doing what their fathers were doing at their age? How many women are doing what their mothers were doing? I would think it isn't a large number.

In the ancient world, it wasn't like that. In the ancient world, if your father was a carpenter, you became a carpenter. If your father was a baker, you became a baker. If your father was a cabinetmaker, you became a cabinetmaker. If your father's name was Stradivarius, you made violins. That's the way it worked. In any age before the industrial revolution, in an agrarian society your identity was bound up with a family business in some sense. That's why Jesus can be referred to as the carpenter's son.

In Mark's gospel, apparently after Joseph dies and Jesus keeps the business going until he begins his public ministry, he himself is referred to as "the carpenter" (Mark 6:3). His work is enough to identify him.

Out of this identification comes a lot of further reflection. Although Jewish boys in the first century went to synagogue school to get a bit of basic writing and reading, nevertheless their trade was not learned at the local university or junior college. There were no junior colleges or universities. If you were a boy, your trade was normally learned from your father; that's where you learned when to plant the seed and how to do irrigation and what sort of fences you needed and so on—whatever you needed to do for your father who was a farmer. That's where you learned your trade. That's why you could be identified with the family business.

A number of biblical metaphors come out of this basic understanding. Sons of Belial, for instance. *Belial* really means "worthlessness." *Sons of worthlessness.* That's not saying that your father is worthless; it's saying that you are such a disgustingly worthless individual that the only ultimate explanation is that you come from the worthless family. The metaphors can be positive as well. Jesus says in the Beatitudes, "Blessed are the peacemakers, for they will be called children of God" (Matt. 5:9). For the record, he is not saying how you become a Christian. He is simply saying that God is the supreme peacemaker. So, insofar as you make peace, you are acting like God. You act like part of the God family because God is the supreme peacemaker.

When Israel in the Old Testament is called "son of God," that means that Israel is supposed to reflect God insofar as human beings are capable of reflecting God's character and behavior. To show that they belong, so far as human beings can, to the God family.

This is why, in John 8, another interesting idiom is based on these reflections. The Jews say, "We're sons of Abraham." "No you're not," Jesus says. "Abraham rejoiced to see my day; he saw it and was glad. You don't even recognize me. You can't possibly have Abraham as your ancestor." Jesus is not denying the DNA connection. They are, after all, Jews. But his point is that they are not acting the way Abraham did, so they can't really be his sons. They up the ante and say, "Actually, we're sons of God." "No," Jesus says, "I come from God. I know God. God knows me. I'm his Son. He's my Father. You don't recognize me. You can't be sons of God. Let me tell you who your daddy is. You are of your father the Devil and you will follow the lusts of your father. He was a murderer from the beginning, and you're trying to bump me off. He was a liar from the beginning, and you're not telling the truth about me." This is not presupposing the bizarre notion of the Devil copulating with their mothers. It's a functional thing. They're acting like the Devil, which shows that they are children of the Devil.

Paul picks up the same argument. Who are the true sons of Abraham? Those who have Abraham's faith. Behavior, not genetics, is important. So this way of thinking is common right through Scripture. There is functionality in the notion of sonship that identifies where you belong. It depends on how you act. What Jesus says is stunning: "The Son can do nothing by himself; he can do only what he sees his Father doing, because whatever the Father does the Son also does" (v. 19). That is, Jesus grounds his functional subordination in his claim to coextensive action with God, and that marks his sonship as utterly unique.

This is very important. Whatever the Father does, the Son also does, and that makes his sonship absolutely unique. No one else can ever say that with a straight face.

The second "for" is found in verse 20: "For the Father loves the Son and shows him all he does." In the same agrarian world, this makes sense. You don't get a father on a farm saying, "I'll show him how to plant, I'll show him how to plow, I'll show him how to harvest, but I'm not going to show him a thing about fertilizer." Rather the father wants to pass on all his knowledge to the next generation. This is part of family solidarity and in particular the love of the father for the son. So intimate is the divine relationship between Father and Son that there is nothing the Father does that the Son does not also do. For out of the love of the Father for his Son, absolutely everything the Father does as God, he makes sure the Son also does as God. Then the argument is actually flipped the other way. The Son perfectly obeys his Father out of love. That's remarkable too.

Several passages support this, among them John 3:35. "The Father loves the Son," we're told. In John 3:34 we are told that the Father "gives the Spirit without limit." To the rest of us he gives the Spirit in some degree, but to the Son he gives the Spirit without measure. And in John 5 he loves the Son and shows him all he does. That grounds the coextensiveness of the action of the Son and of the Father.

The Son loves the Father and always obeys him. We see this as well in John 14:31: "The world may learn that I love the Father and do exactly what my Father has commanded me." When Jesus is in agony in Gethsemane, what does he pray? Does he pray, "Heavenly Father, this is so difficult, but I love those benighted sinners so much. Give me strength, I pray, to go through with this"? That would express his love for us, which is true enough, all right. But that's not what he prays. He prays, "Not my will but yours be done."

Two extraordinarily important conclusions flow from this observation. First, the Son by his very obedience acts in such a way that he reveals the Father. That is, the Father commands and does, and the Son obeys and does exactly what God does. Whatever the Son does is what God does. Whatever the Son says is what the Father gives him to say. And all this the Son does out of obedience, out of love for his Father. What follows from the fact that the Son loves the Father perfectly and does whatever the Father gives him to do? What follows from the fact that the Father loves the Son perfectly and so arranges things that all that the Father does the Son also does? One thing that follows is that every word and action of the Son is the very revelation of God.

There's a second implication that I'm going to overstate a bit, and then I will back off. It is something I think you have to see. The marvelous self-disclosure of the Father in the Son turns in the first place not on God's love for us, but on God's love for his Son. The world must know that the Father loves the Son. In 5:23, the Father utters his resolutions that all must honor the Son even as they honor the Father. That's God's plan.

I'm not denying for a moment that God loves us, but even in the best-known verse that affirms God's love for the world—"God so loved the world" (John 3:16)—the standard is the Father's love for the Son. That's the presupposition. When it comes to arguing for Christian unity out of John's gospel, especially in the passage we sometimes call the High Priestly Prayer in John 17, it is the peculiar relationship of love in the Godhead—the Father loving the Son and showing him everything, the Son loving the Father and perfectly conforming to it—that becomes the very nature, model, and standard of what it means for Christians to be one and to love one another.

We are approaching immeasurably holy ground. We're talking about the Godhead. Although the categories are functional, inevitably you cannot help but see that there is reality behind the function; there's what the philosophers would call *ontology* behind the functionality.

This is a functional demonstration of love, but it presupposes that this is what God is like too. You're supposed to understand the oneness of the Father and the Son in these terms. In other words, we are too quick to think of our salvation almost entirely with respect to its bearing on us. Please do not misunderstand me. Of course salvation has bearing on us, and we ought to rejoice in God's love for us. That is all true. And yet, if we understand our salvation exclusively with respect to its bearing on us, we're not listening to this passage of Scripture. We're not listening to a lot of John's gospel, to what it says with respect to the Godhead.

"All whom the Father gives me," Jesus says, "will come to me" (John 6:37). That's an arrangement in the Godhead. Jesus adds in verse 39, "And this is the will of him who sent me, that I shall lose none of all those he has given me." The reason why none then will be lost is because the Son is determined to do his Father's will, not just because the Son loves us. Do you see? These are functionalities that grow out of the very nature of the Godhead. It goes even further in John 5:20–21. "Yes, and he will show him even greater works than these, so that you will be amazed. For just as the Father raises the dead and gives them life, even so the Son gives life to whom he is pleased to give it." In other words, here is the exemplification of how the Son does all that the Father does. Yes, God makes the universe, but we've already seen the opening verses of this gospel insist that the Son likewise is God's agent in the making of the universe. Who gives life, finally? That's a prerogative of God. That's a big theme in the Old Testament.

My earliest memory is sitting in the bathtub as a child, being washed by my father. When my mother bathed me, she was efficient. When my father bathed me, he told Bible stories. He always reviewed the last one and told the next one. I got narrative after narrative after narrative from the Old Testament and the New Testament while I was being bathed. Some stories are very effectively told in the bath. One is the account of Naaman, who was dunked seven times in the Jordan River—a very effective bath-time story.

In the course of wanting to be healed of leprosy, Naaman has a major misunderstanding with the king of Israel. Receiving a request to cough up the prophet Elisha—who apparently has wonderful miraculous powers—so that he can heal Naaman, the king tears his clothes and says, "Naaman is just looking for an excuse to start a fight with me. That's all this is. Who am I? Am I God that I can kill and make alive?" There it is: the assumption that only God has the authority to make alive.

If in the Old Testament prophets bring a child, such as the Shunammite's son, back to life, these prophets are themselves the first to insist that this is the work of God. They are nothing more than God's secondary figures—God's emissaries to perform a miraculous deed—but it is God who does it.

But listen to Jesus' words. "For just as the Father raises the dead and gives them life, even so the Son gives life to whom he is pleased to give it." That puts Jesus in a very different category from Elisha. He has the prerogatives of God, and this by the determined will of God. God has given these things to the Son to do—and the Son does them. He has all the authority of God in creation at the front end and in life-giving and even resurrection at the back end. It's all his. Whatever the Father does, the Son also does.

All Judgment to the Son

Further explanation is given. A lot of our translations have "moreover" or some other connective. It's really another "for."

> [For] the Father judges no one, but has entrusted all judgment to the Son, that all may honor the Son just as they honor the Father. Whoever does not honor the Son does not honor the Father, who sent him. (vv. 22–23)

When this text says, "The Father judges no one," it's not saying that God does not have the right to judge anyone or that he is functionally incapable of judging anyone. After all, at the end of the text when Jesus says that he is the Judge, he says, "I judge only as I hear, and my judgment is just, for I seek not to please myself but him who sent me" (v. 30). That is, he is judging in line with God's own judgment.

When we are told that the Father judges no one, we have to understand it in this same model of an agrarian handcraft society. Stradivarius Senior makes new violins, chooses the best woods, measures perfectly to get all the ratios exactly right, makes sure the wood is properly kiln-dried and shaved down to exactly the right thickness and thinness in the various parts and bent and held appropriately. All this carefully accumulated knowledge from centuries of violin making is passed on to Stradivarius Junior. Eventually Stradivarius Senior says to Stradivarius Junior, "From now on, I'm not going to make the varnish anymore. That's your job."

In summary you might say that Stradivarius Senior does not make varnish. Stradivarius Junior does. It's a delegated responsibility. That doesn't mean that Stradivarius Senior can't do it or doesn't have the right to do it. It means that in the Stradivarius family there are some delegated responsibilities.

So also in the Godhead. God is the supreme Judge. He's the Creator of all. He's the final Judge of all. Many Scriptures depict that point. But there is a sense in which he delegates the judgment peculiarly to the Son. The Son can do anything the Father does. He does everything the Father does, but in particular there is a delegation of judgment to the Son, which is something that Jesus elsewhere picks up on. Do you remember what he says at the end of the Sermon on the Mount?

> Many will say to me on that day, "Lord, Lord, did we not prophesy in your name and in your name drive out demons and in your name perform many miracles?" Then I will tell them plainly, "I never knew you. Away from me, you evildoers!" (Matt. 7:22–23)

There's Jesus acting as the ultimate judge on the last day. Jesus knows that is part of his role, but that belongs to God alone.

All this serves to make one point: there is a kind of functional subordination in the Son's relationship to the Father, yet it is a carefully defined subordination in which the action is coextensive with the Father. Elsewhere Jesus says, "The Father is greater than I" (John 14:28). If you discuss these matters with any friendly neighborhood Jehovah's Witness, he or she will be quick to quote this verse and say, "Do you see that Jesus must be some sort of inferior God, for Jesus himself says 'The Father is greater than I'?"

But I am quite prepared to acknowledge that Barack Obama is greater than I. He's greater in political savvy, greater in military potential, greater in media coverage. But he's not more of a human being than I am. He's not more of a man than I am. When I say that Barack Obama is president and deserves the honor that presidents are due, and that he's greater than I, this is not some sort of intrinsic affirmation of an ontological superiority on his part, some higher level of being. We're long past the divine right of kings. So when Jesus says, "The Father is greater than I," we must ask what he means. Does he mean, "The Father is more of a god that I am"? There's not a hint of that notion anywhere in Scripture. Not a hint. And there are many affirmations that insist, "My Lord and my God," "before Abraham was born, I am." Yet there still remains a functional subordination in the Godhead itself.

Note the third "for" clause: the Son insists that, just as the Father, he has life-in-himself. (Yes, I want the hyphens there.) "Very truly I tell you, whoever hears my word and believes him who sent me has eternal life" (v. 24). Even that statement is fascinating, merely from the point of view of the relationship between the Father and the Son. You might think Jesus would say, "Whoever hears my word and believes me." That's not what the text says. "Whoever hears my word and believes him who sent me." That's because all Jesus' words are the words of him who sent him.

If you hear Jesus' words and believe them, you believe God's words and trust him, for the two are tied up together. You cannot really believe Jesus without believing God. If you really do believe God, you will believe God's witness to who Jesus is.

The Focal Point of Salvation Itself

"Very truly I tell you, whoever hears my word and believes him who sent me, has eternal life and will not be judged but has crossed over from death to life" (v. 24). Jesus is at the very focal point of salvation itself: who is saved and who is not saved. Believing Jesus and his words, believing Jesus and his truth, believing Jesus and his teaching—believing Jesus is equivalent to believing God.

Note verse 25: "Very truly I tell you, a time is coming and has now come when the dead will hear the voice of the Son of God." There's the "Son" language returning. Whether this is talking about the end times, the final resurrection, or eternal life gained now, I am not sure. I suspect it is eternal life gained now. But by the end of the chapter, it is generally resurrection from the dead that is the issue. Now we hear the voice of the Son of God, and at the end we hear the voice of the Son of God, in a final sense, and the dead will live. "For"—and then this very difficult verse, one of the most difficult verses in John's gospel—"as the Father has life-in-himself, so he has granted the Son, also, to have life-in-himself."

This is a very difficult verse, because when we speak of God having life in himself, we mean that his life is uncaused. We often say that God is self-existent. My existence depends on others—my parents and so on—all the way back to God. The universe itself is not self-existent, despite the best efforts of Stephen Hawking to explain otherwise. It is a created order. It does not have life in itself; only God has life in himself. Thus we speak of the self-existence of God.

If the text said, "As the Father has life in himself, so the Son has life in himself," there would not be any logical difficulty, but it would be very difficult to avoid the notion of two Gods. The Father (God Number One) has life in himself, and the Son (God Number Two) has life in himself. But that's not what the text says.

If the text said, "As the Father has life in himself, so he has granted the Son to have life," we could make sense of the word *grant.* The Father alone is self-existent, and he grants the Son to have life, but that means the Son really is inferior. He's like any other created order. That's what Jehovah's Witnesses want us to think. The Son does not have life in himself; that belongs to God alone, and God has granted the Son to have life.

But what Jesus says mashes these things together. He says, "As the Father has life-in-himself, so he has granted the Son to have life-in-himself." If he has life-in-himself, how is it granted? And if it's granted, how is it life-in-itself, which presupposes self-existence and no dependence upon another? Do you see? That is why Christians across the centuries have found this verse very difficult to understand.

The best formulation was worked out very carefully in the fourth century AD, but it is one that we sometimes overlook. Christians spoke of this as an eternal grant. It is not something that took place sometime in eternity past—as if there was a time when it hadn't taken place, and then in eternity past at some point it did take place, and then after that it was done. An eternal grant transcends time. There was not a time when it had not yet occurred. It is the very nature and order of things. These are the relationships between the Father and the Son.

In the fourth century, Athanasius liked to push the expression, "The eternal generation of the Son." Here the connection, it seems to me, is right in the text. If you ask me what "an eternal grant" means, the short answer is, "I don't have a clue," but because I'm a professor, there is a longer answer as well. The reason I don't have a clue is that I scarcely know what time is. Yes, I earned a degree in science and so I've read into that sort of thing a bit, but I scarcely know what time is. I really don't know what eternity is. Is eternity time stretched both ways? That's difficult when all our notions of time are bound up with the movements of the celestial bodies. Is eternity another dimension? I don't know.

But as the Father has life-in-himself, so in the very structure of the Godhead it is granted that the Son have life-in-himself. That's an eternal arrangement, an eternal grant. There is no God Number Two. There is no inferior God. There is a relationship of love between the Father and the Son that is such that the Father discloses everything to the Son and the Son does all that the Father gives him to do, and does so perfectly. And that's what the sonship of Jesus looks like.

Nor should we think this refers only to the limitations of the Son in the incarnation, because sometimes sonship language is used of the preincarnate Son—the Son as he was in eternity past. The very next verse after John 3:16 reads, "For God did not send his Son into the world to condemn the world." God sends the Son into the world. The Son is already with the Father before the world begins. And quite a few verses in John's gospel make the same point. This sonship stretches back into eternity, into the very being of God.

Finally, the Son also insists that he is not only Son of God but also Son of Man. As such he is the God-sanctioned Judge of all: "He has given him authority to judge because he is the Son of Man" (v. 27). Not "the Son of God" but "the Son of Man." What does that mean? Just like "son of God," the expression "son of man" can mean different things in different contexts. One has to read that very carefully. We saw that in Exodus 4 "son of God" can refer to Israel. In 2 Samuel 7, "son of God" refers to the king. "Son of God" can refer to Christians. "Son of God" can refer uniquely to Jesus, depending on the context.

When I was a boy growing up, my father used to tell me that a text without a context becomes a pretext for a proof text. To understand exactly what "son of God" means, you always have to look at the context. The same is true also of "son of man." For example, in Ezekiel God addresses the prophet Ezekiel about eighty times saying, "Son of man, stand up and do such and such." It clearly means something like, "You human being, you and your mortals fear."

Sometimes it's parallel to "human being." "What is man that you are mindful of him, or the son of man, that you remember him?" (Ps. 8:4). That's Hebrew poetry, two lines saying roughly the same thing. *Man* more or less equals "son of man," or "human being." But in Daniel 7:13 one like a son of man approaches the Ancient of Days to receive a kingdom from him. He is one like a human being, but now in a messianic context in which the promised kingdom of God is dawning. Do you see? It depends on the context.

Here in John 5:27 we are told that God has delegated this final function of judging to Jesus the Son of God in particular because he is Son of Man. Why? What does that mean?

For those of you who are interested in such intricacies, this is the only place in all the Gospels where the expression "Son of Man" occurs without an article. In Greek there is an article like the English *the*, and it's always "the Son of the Man." Greek articles don't function the way ours do, but everywhere else in all four Gospels, that's the way Jesus the Son of Man is referred to. Here no article is present, and what that means in Greek is that the quality of this title is being emphasized. God has given Jesus the authority to judge human beings because Jesus is a human being. That's what it means. Because he's Son of Man. He knows all things. He knows the secrets of our hearts. He knows even what could have been under different circumstances. He knows what has been, what is, what will be. He knows what we would have done under different circumstances. He takes it all into account. His justice is absolutely

130

perfect, for his knowledge is perfect, his goodness is perfect, his righteousness is perfect.

Nevertheless, there is one thing the Father does not do. He does not share the experience of human beings. That doesn't mean that he would be an unfair Judge, because his knowledge is perfect. This is not, in any sense, a slight against God. But in the mystery of God's plan of salvation, it is the Son who is not only one with God, but who has also become a human being. And God delegates the judgment to the Son, who does not take an independent course in judgment.

"Now that I'm going to be the Judge, well, I won't consult my father; I'll just do it my way." Then you're back to two Gods again. The text immediately goes on to say that Jesus does not judge according to his own will; he judges only as he hears from his Father. It is still the Father's judgment, but it is the judgment of the One who has become a human being and who speaks, not only out of the perfection of the knowledge of God, but out of the perfection of his identity with human beings. Hebrews says he was tempted in all points as we are, yet without sin (4:15). Jesus knows what it is to be tempted, yet without sin. It is a mark of God's most amazing forbearance and condescension that although all that the Father does the Son also does, the Son does only that which the Father does. The revelation is perfect, yet there is a kind of special delegation to the Son of the function of judgment, in line with the will of the Father, precisely because he's the Son who has become a human being. In the context of all John's gospel, Jesus then goes to the cross and bears—in his own body on the tree—the sin of all whom the Father has given to the Son.

Let me tell you why this is important. First, this passage is important for putting your Bible together. Just as a temple thread runs right through the Old Testament until Jesus is the

Temple, just as a priesthood thread runs right through the Old Testament until Jesus is the Great High Priest, just as a Davidic king thread runs right through the Old Testament until Jesus is the great Davidic King, just as a lamb thread runs right through the Old Testament until Jesus is the Lamb of God, so there is a son thread. Jesus is the ultimate Israel, the ultimate Son, the ultimate Davidic King, the ultimate reflector of God himself. He is the Son. The passage is important for putting your Bible together.

Second, it's important for evangelistic decisiveness. This is pretty difficult because the passage is so condensed—and we're dealing with God, after all. Yet the passage drives toward verse 24: "Very truly I tell you, whoever hears my word and believes him who sent me has eternal life and will not be judged but has crossed over from death to life."

The older I get, and the more enmeshed I am in teaching theology and Scripture, the more I am convinced, passionately convinced, that the ultimate test of our theology is whether we're doing evangelism. Maybe one-on-one, maybe in small groups, but the test of this theology is not having a better understanding than some other Christian in the church, because I can outsmart him and outwit him in my articulation of the eternal generation of the Son. The test of it all, at the end of the day, is whether this moves us to share this self-disclosure of God in Christ Jesus with others so that they might believe and be saved.

Third, this passage is important because this functional way of approaching the sonship of Jesus is especially useful in our efforts to evangelize many contemporaries. I have used this passage with Muslims and seen some of them converted. I've used this passage with secularists in Los Angeles and seen some converted. It is important for explaining what we mean by confessing in our creeds, "I believe in Jesus Christ, the Son of God."

Finally, perhaps above all, it is important because if we are to worship God aright, we must see God as he is. This is God as he is. This is as close as you get in the New Testament to some of the most moving, revealing depictions of the relationship between the Father and the Son. This is our God, and I believe in Jesus Christ, the Son of God.

7

The Incarnate Word

JOEL R. BEEKE

JESUS CAME AS the teacher, and teaching is hard work. Jesus got into a boat one day after he taught, and he fell asleep. The gently rocking waves of the Sea of Galilee probably were about to lull the disciples to sleep as well, but suddenly a huge storm arose, coming through the deep valley lined by cliffs on the southern end of the Sea of Galilee. Even today wind can come roaring down that valley and whip the sea into a storm. Andrew, James, Peter, and John, experienced fishermen, had seen these storms numerous times.[1]

But they had never seen a storm like this one. The wind howled; the waves crashed. The boat began to take on water and ride lower in the water, each wave threatening to fill it. Fear gripped the men. The boat was sinking. Were they going to die? They turned to Jesus, who was still sleeping, and they shouted over the waves, "Teacher, do you not care that we are perishing?"

1. See *The Reformation Study Bible*, ed. R. C. Sproul (Orlando: Ligonier, 2005), 1422.

Jesus stood up and rebuked the wind. In an instant the wind and sea were calm. But the men were even more terrified. "Who is this," they said, "that even wind and sea obey him?" (Mark 4:35–41).

Why was Jesus asleep in the storm? Why did the storm not awaken him? The obvious answer is his humanity. He was tired; he was worn out after a day's work. He needed to recharge his batteries. How did Jesus calm the storm? The answer is again obvious: his deity. He had such power over creation that his word instantly changed the weather. He didn't use technology, magic charms, or rituals. He didn't even pray. He just said "Be still" to the storm. He has the power of God, and his disciples recognized it when they said, "Even wind and sea obey him."

But that leads us to a mystery, doesn't it? Was he tired, or was he all-powerful? Was he drained of energy, or was he full of energy? Was he limited so that he needed restoration, or is he infinite in ruling over creation? Which is it?

The answer in Scripture is both. Jesus is limited in his humanity; he is infinite in his deity. That's what John 1 teaches us: "And the Word was made flesh, and dwelt among us, (and we beheld his glory, the glory as of the only begotten of the Father,) full of grace and truth" (John 1:14). John has a wonderful way of taking the simplest words and conveying the deepest truths. Christ is incarnate. Jesus became flesh. Has the wonder of this ever impressed itself upon you?

Incarnation is actually a Latin word that means "becoming flesh." In the incarnation God became flesh. Contrary to Rudolf Bultmann, this is not "the language of mythology." John says it is the language of eyewitnesses who are reporting what they know to be true: "We have seen his glory."[2] The reality of God-

2. Robert L. Reymond, *John, Beloved Disciple: A Survey of His Theology* (Ross-shire: Christian Focus, 2001), 180–82.

made-flesh was experienced by the apostles and portrayed in the Gospels, and no one can take that from them or from us, we who believe it by faith.

It's the Bible that compelled the church to state at the Council of Chalcedon in 451 that Christ is one person with two distinct natures, human and divine. The Westminster Confession (8.2) picked up on that in the 1640s: "Two whole, perfect, and distinct natures, the Godhead and the manhood, were inseparably joined together in one person, without conversion, composition, or confusion. Which person is very God and very man, yet one Christ, the only Mediator between God and man."

We might compare the incarnation to grafting. In the process of grafting, a person cuts a living twig off a tree and cuts it into another tree—sometimes of another species—presses the twig into the tree, and seals the two together with wax or wrapping. Over time the twig and the tree grow together into one unity, one living organism. Both twig and tree retain their unique genetic codes, their own distinct natures, but now the twig draws its life and bears its fruit from the roots of the tree.[3] In a similar but much more profound way, God grafted human nature into his divine Son. The result is not a hybrid demigod, such as Hercules, or some kind of superman: both the divine nature and the human nature retain their individual, essential properties, but now man is joined to God. We take it so for granted, but it is truly amazing. In one living person, Jesus Christ, man is joined to God, not as two people but as one person.

In the denominational theological school that I attended in Canada when I was twenty-one years old, the very first question my professor asked me was, "Jesus was tired and weary. In what

3. Ray R. Rothenberger and Christopher J. Starbuck, "Grafting," *University of Missouri Extension*, accessed September 14, 2010, http://extension.missouri.edu /publications/DisplayPub.aspx?P=G6971.

person did he suffer these things?" The answer is that he's only one person. He's not two people. His human nature is grafted to his divine, and in him, believers draw life from the divine root and bear fruit for God's glory. In botanical grafting, two plants of the same genus or of like nature are combined, but in the incarnation the miracle is that God grafted the finite into the infinite. How unsearchable are his ways! The gospel is too amazing for the greatest thinker and the greatest novelist even to imagine.

God was manifest in the flesh. We can only stammer a bit about it. We see through a glass here, darkly. Describing the incarnation in human language is like trying to paint a mountain on a grain of sand. We stand before this abyss of glory, and we know we can never reach the bottom.

We also must remember that John wrote his gospel not merely for our understanding but for our faith in Christ (John 20:31). The immediate context in John 1 makes it clear that John wrote so that sinners will receive Christ, which requires believing in his name (John 1:7, 11–12) and beholding his glory (John 1:14; 2:11). In this chapter we will exercise our minds about John 1:14 in order to move our hearts to trust in Jesus Christ. No matter whether you are an unbeliever needing to trust in Jesus for the first time or a believer needing to grow in your faith in your Savior, ultimately it's all about trusting in him, having a relationship with this incarnate Savior.

I will expound upon two simple thoughts here: first, "the Word," and second, "flesh." Trust in the Word made flesh for your salvation.

The Eternal, Beloved, Divine Word

"The Word became flesh." The Father didn't become flesh. The Holy Spirit didn't become flesh. The divine nature didn't become flesh. God's essence did not change the Word as if he had lost his divine attributes, but the eternal and only begotten Son of God became flesh.

The Holy Spirit did not choose to say, "The Son became flesh," though that was true, but the Spirit chose to say, "The Word became flesh." The Spirit uses "the Word" to express the greatest thought of the Father's heart. "The Word" is the greatest revealer of God. God calls us to trust Christ as the Word of God.

That means that we must listen to him. By nature, we are not good listeners. When someone else speaks, our minds often run ahead to what we want to say in response, and to our shame, we realize we've missed what the other person has said. When John begins his gospel with "the Word," he's saying right away, "Listen to the Father's Word. Give Christ your full attention. Trust him; trust his Word. Acknowledge his authority above all others. Cultivate quietness before him. The Word was God. The Word became flesh. You must be silent before the Word. So listen. Let God speak. Let God speak in Christ. He's God's Word."

The idea that Christ is God's Word leads us back to John 1:1: "In the beginning was the Word, and the Word was with God, and the Word was God." Here we find three truths about this Word who became flesh, three teachings that illuminate what it means to trust in Christ. If we are going to understand the teachings of John 1, there are three words we must grasp and remember: *eternal, beloved,* and *divine.*

Christ Is the Eternal Word

"In the beginning was the Word." This Word existed when God created the heavens and the earth in the beginning. The

Word was not created.[4] There was never a time when the Word was not. He is the eternal Word. He is "from everlasting to everlasting" (Ps. 90:2). Christ did not begin in Mary's womb; he existed as the Word prior to creation, and so Jesus could rightly say, "Before Abraham was, I am" (John 8:58). He is the "I AM THAT I AM." It's the same language the Lord used to Moses when he declared, "Thus shalt thou say unto the children of Israel, I AM hath sent me unto you" (Ex. 3:14).

We must trust in Christ as the great eternal Word. We must stand in awe before him, trembling in reverence. Psalm 33 says,

> By the word of the LORD were the heavens made; and all the
>   host of them by the breath of his mouth.
> . . . .
> Let all the earth fear the LORD: let all the inhabitants of the
>   world stand in awe of him.
> For he spake, and it was done; he commanded, and it stood
>   fast. (Ps. 33:6, 8–9)

We're in the presence of the Word of God, by whom the mighty mountains were made. Christ was ancient when the galaxies were born, so when we trust in him, we trust in an eternal Word, the eternal I AM. The stars in the night sky make you feel small and insignificant, don't they? The ancient mountains remind you that you were born only yesterday and you'll be gone tomorrow. Looking at Jesus should fill you with reverence, awe, and trembling. He is the eternal Word.

4. Note the contrast between the imperfect of the verb "to be" (John 1:1), and the aorist of the verb "to become" (John 1:3, 10, 14). The latter is clearly associated with creation, including the world and humanity. The former then indicates an already continuing existence apart from the creation of the world and mankind. When the world began, God already was. "In short, the Word's pre-existent *being* is antecedently set off over against the *becoming* of all created things." Reymond, *John, Beloved Disciple*, 35.

Christ Is the Beloved Word

John 1:1 also says, "The Word was with God." Jesus enjoyed personal communion with God the Father and God the Holy Spirit from the beginning. John 1:18 says he was "in the bosom of the Father," at the place closest to his heart.[5] The Father sent us his eternal companion and friend. In the gospel, he sends us the best he has, his own beloved Son, for the worst he could find, sinners such as you and me. What a gospel! God gave us the beloved Word, about whom he loves to speak, and in whom he delights to hear. That is why we read that Christ is called by the Father his "only begotten" (John 1:14, 18), which in Greek refers to a son or daughter with a unique relationship to his or her father, such as that of an only child—a special relationship.[6]

My marriage has been blessed with three children. My wife and I love them all and delight in them, though neither they nor we are perfect. Jesus is the only begotten Son of God. This is the one whom the Father sent, the Son who was in his bosom from all eternity, the One whom he loved with perfect love, the One whom he never had to correct or change or say no to. Christ is the one who always said yes to him, and the One who always said, "I delight to do thy will, O my God: yea, thy law is within my heart" (Ps. 40:8). God sent this beloved Word to the ungodly, to sinners and rebels. That's amazing.

I've had the privilege of being married for nearly twenty-five years. I thought I really loved my wife when I married her, but I love her much more now. It's wonderful to have a good

5. Luke 16:22–23; John 13:23–25.
6. Luke 7:12; 8:42; 9:38; John 1:14, 18; 3:16, 18; Heb. 11:17; 1 John 4:9. Cf. LXX Judges 11:34; Tobit 3:15; 6:10, 14; 8:17; Aquila on Gen. 22:2; Prov. 4:3; Jer. 6:26; Symmachus on Gen. 22:12, Prov. 4:3; Jer. 6:26. Especially significant in the Greek Old Testament are the times in Genesis 22 that Isaac is called the "only son" of Abraham.

marriage, to have that love grow and grow, and to become closer and closer over the years. But think of the Father and the Son, forever and forever, their loving companionship from eternity past. They have always done everything together. Their hearts are one. They are one even in essence. And the Father gives His Word: "For God so loved the world, that he gave his only begotten Son" (John 3:16).

No book in all the New Testament focuses on this love relationship between the Father and Son as much as the gospel of John; John includes more than 120 references to the Father/Son relationship, and eight times the book expressly says that the Father loves his Son. He is the beloved of the Father. This love, John says, is the preeminent motive for all God's divine activity (John 3:35; 5:20).[7] God's preeminent motive is not our salvation, as precious as that is. His preeminent motive is the glory of his own Son.

When your children see affection between you and your spouse in the home, it's not a threat to them. They don't think, "Because my dad and my mom have a special relationship, they don't love me." No, it gives a child security to see that love and affection between parents, for it leads them to say, "My mom and dad really love each other." When my youngest was in kindergarten, she found a picture at school of two swans with their beaks together. They looked like they were kissing each other. She brought it home, pasted it on the refrigerator door, and wrote beneath it, "This is Mom and Dad." She felt security with the love my wife and I have for each other. Love provides security.

If salvation depended on us in any way, or on our love for him in return for his love for us, we would have no security. We'd

---

7. See Bartel Elshout, "The Father's Love for His Son," in *The Beauty and Glory of the Father*, ed. Joel R. Beeke (Grand Rapids: Reformation Heritage Books, 2013), 3–19.

fail. We'd stumble. We're fickle. Yes, we do love him because he first loved us, but our love is so inconsistent. Our security is this: he is the beloved Word. He is always the beloved Word.

Even when Jesus cried out, "My God, my God, why hast thou forsaken me?" (Matt. 27:46), as the Father had to turn away from him as he bore our sin, even at that same moment, he was never so much loved, even by his own Father, as when he was doing the Father's will (Isa. 53:10). There is security in this: that God the Father, God the Son, and God the Spirit share perfect, intratrinitarian love, and in that unbreakable intratrinitarian love is the solidity of my salvation. Jesus asks the Father "that the world may know that thou hast sent me, and hast loved them, as thou hast loved me" (John 17:23). That's got to be one of the most wonderful things in the gospel: we actually enter into a share of that love that he gives to his only begotten Son. So trust in this love. Trust in the gift of God's love. Trust in this wonderful, wonderful Savior. Trust in this gospel. He gives the best for the worst, for the sake of his beloved.

Christ Is the Fully Divine Word

John 1:1 says that the Word who became flesh "was God." That's not to be translated as "a god" or "godlike," as the Jehovah's Witnesses say, but as Christ being God.[8] The word *God* is also used without the Greek definite article ("the") in John 1:6, as well as in verses 12, 13, and 18. Even Jehovah's Witnesses don't say "a god" in all those different verses. So John 1:1 plainly refers to God Almighty, not "a god," even without the article *the*. In fact, Greek grammar teaches us that the absence of the article

8. *The Kingdom Interlinear Translation of the Greek Scriptures* (Brooklyn: Watchtower Bible and Tract Society of New York, 1985), 401, 1139. On the grammar of John 1:1 and Colwell's rule, see Reymond, *John, Beloved Disciple*, 36, esp. footnote 19.

the only intensifies the noun, making it a categorical assertion. Christ was and is God, as fully divine as the Father.

The parallelism is striking between Genesis 1:1—"In the beginning God"—and John 1:1: "In the beginning was the Word." It places the Son at the very center of the Father's work as Creator. As verse 3 affirms, "All things were made by him."

Christ is therefore the full and comprehensive revelation of his Father. Every attribute we affirm of the Father is true of the Son. That's why Jesus could say to Philip, "He that hath seen me hath seen the Father" (John 14:9). That's why Isaiah could prophesy that Christ is "The mighty God, The everlasting Father, The Prince of Peace" (Isa. 9:6; cf. 10:20–21). Truly we behold in Christ "glory as of the only begotten of the Father" (John 1:14).

The conclusion is that if he is fully divine and fully eternal and fully beloved, we must trust him by worshiping him as the Son of God. We must trust him in a way that stirs us up to adore him.

There are many different ways you can say, "I trust you." You can have historical faith, as the old divines called it: merely believing that someone is telling you the truth, as with a reliable news report. You can have functional faith, confidence that someone will do a job for you, such as putting siding on your house—you trust he'll do it. You can have relational faith, trusting that someone will be a faithful friend or a faithful spouse. But none of these things is sufficient. The Lord calls us to trust Christ as fully divine, to trust him as God, to adore him with awe, and to lean upon him with all that we are—to put all our hope of salvation in him, to throw all our weight upon this: the Word is God.

Once a missionary couldn't find a word for *faith* in a native language. He didn't know how to explain the gospel, and it became a real problem: "How can I explain faith?" One day he was walking with a couple of natives, and they came to a bridge over a deep chasm. One native walked straight across, although the bridge was rather shaky. As the other went to cross, the first, who had already completed the passage, shouted to the second, "Just lean on the bridge." In other words, if you try to go across without leaning on the bridge, you will fall, but if you throw your weight on it, it will hold you. When he heard the word *lean on*, the missionary said, "That's it. That's what I'm going to use for *faith*."

Faith means to lean on Jesus, to trust him, to give full confidence to him, to worship him by surrendering all to him, abandoning yourself totally to him as your all-in-all. Is that what you're doing? Are you trusting in this beloved, eternal, divine Word?

There's a similar story about a Scottish pastor counseling a woman who was struggling with assurance of faith. He couldn't seem to get through to her, and he was quite discouraged until he discovered a river running through her backyard toward his home. Across the river was a little bridge. He thought maybe she was watching him out her back window, so he came up to the bridge, looked at it, and then jumped back. He looked again at the bridge, reached forward to touch it, and again jumped back. Observing what he was doing, the woman leaned out the window and shouted, "Lean on the bridge." He turned around and said, "Lean on Jesus Christ." God used that to break the woman's doubts and to bring her to the liberty of the gospel.

We have begun our meditation on "And the Word became flesh" by considering that Jesus is the Word of God. On the basis of the Bible, we confess with the Westminster Confession (8.2) that Jesus is "the Son of God, the second Person in the Trinity, being very and eternal God, of one substance, and equal with the Father." This profoundly shapes our faith in him. We must give our full attention to this Word. Sit at his feet in reverent awe. Rejoice that the loving Father has sent to us his most beloved. Bow down and worship our great God and Savior, Jesus Christ. Trust fully in Jesus Christ, the Word of God. That's why John wrote the gospel of Christ. "But these are written, that ye might believe that Jesus is the Christ, the Son of God; and that believing ye might have life through his name" (John 20:31).

The Word in Mortal, Human Body and Soul

John doesn't just write about "the Word"; he also says "the Word became flesh," meaning that Jesus entered completely into the human condition. How we take that for granted today! We're so used to hearing the gospel and hearing it said of Jesus that the Word took on human nature, the nature of a servant. Thomas Watson said, "Christ incarnate is nothing but love covered with flesh."[9] John Norton said, "The incarnation is the miracle of miracles."[10]

The Son of God embraced all that it means to be human, "for in him," Paul writes, "dwelleth all the fulness of the Godhead bodily" (Col. 2:9). Without ceasing to be God, Christ became flesh. The incarnation is an astonishing act of beautiful humility. When a person becomes great and powerful, yet treats you with kindness and respect as if you were on the same level as him, you're touched, aren't you, by his humility? Christ's incarnation displays infinitely more humility than if the president of the United States took his place as a lowly private in the US Army.

9. Thomas Watson, *A Body of Divinity* (Edinburgh: Banner of Truth, 1983), 194.
10. John Norton, *The Orthodox Evangelist* (London: by John Macock for Henry Cripps and Lodowick Lloyd, 1654), 38.

God displayed his greatest glory in Jesus Christ, with his greatest act of humility. The incarnation overthrows all glory seeking and calls us to be servants as we trust in the Lord Jesus Christ. That's what Philippians 2:5–13 is really about. It is not just a doctrinal statement about the humiliation and exaltation of Christ. The motivation behind what Paul writes in that great chapter is the admonition, "Let this mind be in you, which was also in Christ Jesus" (v. 5). It's as if he's saying, "You Philippians, you've been in the church for years. You want credit. You're seeking glory among yourselves. Quit your trivializing at the foot of the cross. As Christ emptied himself and was willing to become a servant, even to the death of the cross, so you must trust in Christ and learn to follow him. You must learn to be emptied of yourselves and do away with glory seeking. You must be willing to be servants." For the Word became flesh.

This word *flesh* is a scandalous word. It was scandalous for the Jews, who didn't want to believe that the finite could be taken on by the infinite. But it was even more scandalous for the Greeks. The Greeks resonated with the term *Word*. In the culture of their day, *Word* or *logos* was the principle that ruled the world and brought order out of chaos—it conveyed something like "logic" and the laws of nature viewed as a divine spirit.[11] The Greeks would have been shocked to hear that the Word became flesh, for they sharply divided the spiritual world of ideas from the physical world of things. The two can't mix, they said. It's like fire and water.

In the Greek order, our spirits are imprisoned in our bodies much as a bird is trapped in a cage. Paul had to overcome that kind of reasoning in 1 Corinthians 15, because the Corinthians didn't want their bodies to be resurrected. To their minds,

---

11. Leon Morris, *The Gospel According to John (Revised)* (Grand Rapids: Eerdmans, 1995), 102–3.

that was to put the spirit back into the cage. Paul had to show them that "if Christ is resurrected from the dead, he's the head and you're the body, so you've got to be resurrected, otherwise our preaching is vain, and your faith is vain, and everything is vain." Saying that the divine Word became flesh was very, very offensive to the Greek mind.[12]

Before we judge the Greeks, we should realize that our culture also thinks the world is split into two parts: the subjective and the objective. On one hand, we recognize the personal and private realm of spirit, feelings, values, faith, and religion. On the other hand, we affirm the public realm of science, facts, measurable results, and visible things. Many people say these two realms can't mix. As a result, many live schizophrenic lives, with faith in one compartment and daily life and work in another compartment.[13] But God does not have a divided mind. God is an infinite Spirit. He created and rules the finite world, which consists of spirits and physical matter in close relationship with each other. In the incarnation, the eternal Spirit joined himself with matter and human spirit. "The Word was made flesh."

Three words must be conveyed when we consider this word *flesh*—*body*, *soul*, and *death*.

Christ Took a Human Body

When Christ spoke of his flesh, he meant "flesh and blood" (see John 6:51–56). When the Word became flesh, he became

---

12. "If the Evangelist had said only that the eternal Word assumed manhood or adopted the form of a body, the reader steeped in the popular dualism of the Hellenistic world might have missed the point. But John is unambiguous, almost shocking in the expressions he uses." D. A. Carson, *The Gospel According to John* (Grand Rapids: Eerdmans, 1991), 126.

13. See Nancy Pearcey, *Total Truth: Liberating Christianity from Its Cultural Captivity* (Wheaton: Crossway, 2004).

physically human. One of the first heresies the Christian church faced was Docetism, which denied Christ's true physical humanity. John wrote against it in 1 John 4:3 and 2 John 7. This heresy said the body of Jesus is only a fantasy. It's not historical, not touchable, not woundable, not flesh and blood. John makes abundantly clear that the incarnation of Christ brings together God and the flesh and blood of our humanity, contrary to Greek cultural assumptions.

The incarnation also challenges our cultural assumptions. The gospel is concerned not simply with ideas but with facts and objects. It enters the world of physics, biology, and history. God's Son became as physical as you are. His hands were roughened by the wood of the carpenter's shop. His back was torn by the lash of the scourge. He was truly man. He really died. His pulse stopped. His brain activity ceased. When he rose from the dead, his physical body arose to new life. He spoke. People touched him. He ate fish.

Jesus came to regenerate all creation, including our bodies. Like a diver descending into the depths of the sea to bring up lost treasure, Christ came to earth in a body so that he could raise our bodies into glory. His resurrection is the beginning of a new creation that rises like a phoenix from the ashes of the old fallen order. That's what we see in Philippians.

> For our conversation is in heaven; from whence also we look for the Saviour, the Lord Jesus Christ: who shall change our vile body, that it may be fashioned like unto his glorious body, according to the working whereby he is able even to subdue all things unto himself. (Phil. 3:20–21)

Trust in the Savior; he is the resurrection and the life. Faith in Christ is not just looking forward to an afterlife. Paul is insistent in 1 Corinthians 15 that faith looks forward to the resurrection of the body. If we really believe this, we won't fear death half as much as we do. We won't fear cancer or a car wreck 10 percent as much as we do. The Son of God has taken your flesh into glory, and one day he will glorify your flesh with his.

I know of a man who was mugged in Latvia. He was beaten up and tied up. A knife was brought up and down against his back as his assailants cried out that they were in the Mafia. He had been told that if you're in the hands of the Mafia, you'll never come out alive. Lying on the ground, blindfolded and gagged, with a knife going up and down his back and slapping his face, he didn't even think about coming out alive. It didn't enter his mind. But one thing did enter his mind, and that was the grace of God. He thought, "Christ bled for me, rose for me, and his flesh is in heaven for me. If I die right here on the floor, I'm going to be with him." The peace he had in those moments was unspeakable.

The point is this: when you are in Christ, you're safe and secure forever, and you're able to rise above the problems of this life. There's a future, and the best is yet to be. God's people have the best of both worlds. They've got true peace here and everlasting glory thereafter.

Oh, what a future we have! Christ died to rise again, and he is in charge of heaven, Emmanuel's land, glory. He is in charge of earth. He is in charge of hell. He is in charge of everything. We will meet him, and we will be sin-free. What a glory! No more sin in my body, my flesh. No more sin in my soul. He will look upon us as his perfect bride. Why wouldn't I want to be with him? As an old divine said, he who does not hanker to be with Christ forever has made little progress in the Christian life.

We're so time-bound, so possession-bound, so flesh-bound. Jesus said, "I took a human body to deliver you, to make your body glorious so you could worship me in soul and body forever in glory." This is the first thing we learn from John's great statement, "The Word became flesh."

Christ Took a Human Soul

Flesh refers to the entire human person. Hebrews 2:16–18 tells us, "In all things it behoved him to be made like unto his brethren" (v. 17), though Hebrews 4:15 adds, "without sin." Jesus was like us even in our sufferings and in the temptations of our souls. This was rejected by an ancient heresy called Apollinarianism, which denied Christ's human mind and heart. It said the Word took over a human body as if it were an alien force operating an android of flesh. But Jesus has real human thoughts, real human experiences, real human feelings. He is human from the inside out.

In the Bible, the word *flesh* can refer to the human way of thinking (John 8:15). Scripture tells us that Jesus grew intellectually from a child to an adult (Luke 2:40, 52). It tells us that Jesus in his human mind did not know the day of his second coming (Mark 13:32). That shouldn't shake our confidence in Jesus' teachings, for the Holy Spirit filled Christ's human nature with truth that was without error. Jesus had a human mind that developed. There was some mental limitation in his human nature. If you don't believe that, how can you accept that he died? God's nature is immortal. Jesus was truly God, but he's also truly man.

In Scripture *flesh* can also refer to human feelings and desires (John 1:13). Jesus wept; he displayed sincere grief (John 11:35). He rejoiced as a godly man (Luke 10:21). He ordinarily experienced the peace of his Father's presence and love (John 8:29). And yet, as surety of his people, he went farther into the black hole of sorrow and despair than any other human being. At Gethsemane he was overwhelmed, he was encircled with grief, he crawled as a worm and no man. He cried out, "O my Father, if it be possible, let this cup pass from me" (Matt. 26:39). He was terrified of his impending encounter with the wrath of God, and on the cross he went deeper into darkness than any of us has ever known or shall know. He was no stoic; he has real human feelings, and at the center of it all is his heart of feeling to come to save sinners.

There was a man who wanted to improve his relationship with his wife. He read 1 Peter 3:7: "Likewise, ye husbands, dwell with them according to knowledge," and he wondered, "What does that mean?" So he thought, "My wife loves horses. I know nothing about horses. We own a couple of horses. I'll learn about horses. I'll learn to know her better." He started helping his wife in the barn. She laughed at him because he didn't know anything about horses, but he kept helping her. He discovered that he really got to love horses, and in doing so, he got close to his wife. Sharing their commonality about horses provided another form of intimacy in their marriage. He entered her world, and they drew closer in understanding.

Multiply that infinitely. The Lord entered into our smote-with-sin world. He pursues emotional intimacy with us more than any person near to us. He has become like us in all things. There's no temptation you will ever face where he hasn't been and which he hasn't gone through. Trust in that. When temptation comes, say, "Lord, you've been here. I'm going to trust in you to give me strength to get through it, looking unto you." Be filled with gratitude and joy in his love. He took a soul, not just to save us from sin, but also so that he could be our soul mate.

Christ Took a Human Death

Jesus became flesh to unite God and sinners in his death. In the Bible, *flesh* implies being mortal, transient, here-today-and-gone-tomorrow, given over to death.[14] We see this in Jesus' reference to himself as the living bread: "I am the living bread which came down from heaven: if any man eat of this bread, he shall live for ever: and the bread that I will give is my flesh, which I will give for the life of the world" (John 6:51). The Word became flesh to give his flesh for the world, so that he could give life to the world: his death for our life, his hell for our heaven. His righteousness became unrighteousness, so that we, in our unrighteousness, could become righteous in him. He took our corruption to give us his holiness. It's the glorious gospel exchange.

The broken covenant between God and man could not be restored until the demands of God's justice were satisfied. Jesus had to do the two things of the gospel that we could never do for ourselves. He had to pay for our sins; we call that his *passive obedience* to the bitter death on the cross (Gal. 3:13). He also had to obey the law perfectly for us; we call that his *active obedience*—loving God above all, loving his neighbor as himself (Rom. 5:19; Gal. 4:4). The net result of active and passive obedience is that the offended justice of God could be propitiated, so that God can now look upon us as sinners and see, between us and him, Jesus Christ, in the same way David looked at Mephibosheth and saw Jonathan. When by grace we believe in him, God the Father looks from his throne, looks on poor sinners such as us, and sees his Son. Those two things are imputed to us, reckoned to our account, never to be taken away, so God "might be just,

---

14. Pss. 73:26; 78:39; Isa. 31:3; 40:6; 1 Cor. 15:50.

and the justifier of him which believeth in Jesus" (Rom. 3:26). But he had to die. Justice could not be satisfied in any other way.

To be our Savior, Jesus had to experience that the wages of sin is death. He came to deal with sin. The only way our sin could be dealt with was by his agony and his bloody sweat, by his suffering the wrath of a sin-hating God—the equivalent of going to the bottomless pit and entering into the lake of fire for us, by his dying and burial in the grave.

The unthinkable happened as the God who could not bear the sight of sin looked at Calvary. There the Son of God hung in the naked flame of God's holiness as he bore our sin. And his Father turned away—the Father in whose bosom he lay for all eternity. Have you ever considered what the agony of Golgotha was all about? What do you see when you look at the cross?

If you go to Israel today, you see the supposed site of Golgotha, and it's so touristy, so clean. In reality Golgotha was the absence of all that was pleasant, beautiful, and refreshing. It was the presence of everything ugly, atrocious, revolting, and shaming. Everything about the place was odious. There was no order on Golgotha. No harmony. No decency. It was the place of skulls, bones, and putrid flesh; it was the place of crosses stained with blood, victims writhing in pain compounded by vile insults from passersby. Only one person spoke on Jesus' behalf, and that was a despicable thief. The pure-minded women were silent. The disciples were cowering with fear. His friends had forsaken him. No eye looked upon him with pity. He hung there, rejected by heaven, rejected by earth, rejected by hell. A Father who had always loved him seemed cold and distant. Sin is fearful in the face of Sinai's thunderous lightning, but sin is most bitter in the torn flesh of Christ's suffering.

Have you ever seen what your sin did to Emmanuel? Have you ever realized what your Bridegroom undertook when he took to himself all your liabilities as his bride and paid the wages to the bitter, bitter last swallow of the cup of his Father's wrath, to deliver you from your sin? Has another *for* ever pressed itself upon you like the *for* in 2 Corinthians 5:21, "For he hath made him to be sin for us, who knew no sin; that we might be made the righteousness of God in him"? Do you trust in this salvation? Do you truly believe this gospel? Do you trust in Jesus Christ who became flesh?

What a distance Christ had to go to save us! Some friends of ours flew thousands of miles to get to Asia, spent thousands of dollars, filled out complicated legal paperwork, made several trips, worked through translators, and on and on, all to adopt one child, just to take one orphan into their home so they could love this child forever. That's what God does for each believer, and far more.

He traversed this world for thirty-three years and went all the way to the cross. Jesus, having loved his own, loved them to the end and paid the price even of death. If he hadn't gone the whole way, if he had stopped just short of death, your sin wouldn't be paid for. You would be an eternal orphan, cut off from God's family. But he satisfied all the demands of the law. He died that you might live, might be adopted into God's family, might be welcomed into the Father's home here and forever.

No wonder John says, "Behold, what manner of love the Father hath bestowed upon us, that we should be called the sons of God" (1 John 3:1). What kind of world does this love come from? This is alien to our world. What kind of love is this, that the Father should so love us that we should be called the sons of God? Adoption by God through the death of his Son?

It's unparalleled. John is astonished by this amazing love. God brings us into his family, gives us family privileges, family rights, family blessings? It's amazing!

A few years ago I was preaching on the theme that none of God's people are ever alone because we belong to the largest family the world has ever known. Afterward a woman came to me weeping. She said, "I'm an orphan. I don't have a father or mother. I don't have any brothers or sisters. I have one uncle who lives in Australia, and he never writes to me. I was feeling sorry for myself all week long. But tonight I've heard something that has never dawned on me before. I belong to the biggest family on earth. I belong to God's family. When I'm adopted by Jesus Christ, I receive millions of brothers and sisters." You never need to be lonely. You've got Christ, and you've got horizontal relationships. Thank God for what the death of Jesus Christ does.

I have a brother who has thirteen children; they are all married, and they all love each other. This family is amazing; they never need any outside entertainment. Their entertainment consists of going to visit each other as married brothers and sisters—twenty-six of them in all! They're always communing, and they're so close, one big happy family.

Can you imagine what the death of Christ will do when it brings every adopted son and daughter together one day in glory? When you walk into a church, how would you feel if you were the only worshiper there? The whole chemistry, the whole pathos would be different, wouldn't it? But when you enter a church filled with believers, you get a sense of belonging to this wonderful family of God. This is just a little, temporary foretaste; imagine having millions upon millions of believers praising God, all brought together through the death of Christ, because the Word became flesh. Put your trust in the Word who became dying flesh for the sake of dying sinners, that you might *live in him*.

Trust and Serve the Lord Forever

God offers this God-man Savior to you, not once but a thousand times. When Jesus left Judea on the way to Galilee, he and his disciples passed through Samaria, and he came to a well. The Samaritan woman was shocked as Jesus initiated a conversation. She asked him about the living water he was talking about and was so amazed by what he told her that she ran off to tell her friends about the Savior. She said, "Come, see a man, which told me all things that ever I did: is not this the Christ?" (John 4:29).

In the same way, Jesus Christ comes to you. He comes lowly in his human nature, understanding what it means to be weary, hot, thirsty, and in need of a helping hand, and he offers himself as the living water. But he also comes to you as God. He comes to you as the Almighty One. He knows you completely. He knows all about your sins, all about your bad record, all about your bad heart, and he offers himself freely. He offers you full pardon, the peace of God, access to the fountain of living waters, because he is the Word made flesh.

As a man, Jesus, like us, was an empty cup that needed to be filled by God. As God, he is the river of living water that can satisfy our souls forever. God took the cup of Jesus' humanity, filled it with himself, and now offers this cup to you. God offers himself to you in Jesus. Trust this offer. Receive this cup. Drink the living water by faith. Through the straw of faith, God's grace brings the water to your mouth. Trust Jesus. He is the incarnate Word. Once you trust him, go out and live for him forever.

There was a very wealthy Englishman who went to California in the 1850s and made his millions through the gold rush. Now a multimillionaire, he went back to England via New Orleans, and he did what many tourists did in the 1850s in New Orleans: he went to visit the infamous slave-trading block. He came around the corner and saw a young, beautiful African woman being sold on the block. Two men in the audience were trying to outbid each other to buy her, and they were talking together, right in front of the Englishman, about the terrible things they would do to her if they got her.

The man was incensed. He got the auctioneer's attention and shouted, "I'll give twice the price anyone gives for this slave." The auctioneer stopped. "Twice the price? No one has ever given that much for a slave. Do you really have the money?" The Englishman reached into his pocket and waved the money, and the auctioneer said, "Sold."

The man walked forward, took the young woman off the block, brought her down to his level—and she spat in his face. He wiped the spittle from his face, took her a few blocks away, went into an office, argued with the man behind the desk, and finally said, "I have a right to do this." The Englishman got some papers, signed them, turned them around, handed them to the young woman, and said, "These are your manumission papers." And she spat in his face.

He wiped the spit away and said, "Don't you understand? You're free." She stared at him for a moment, then collapsed at his feet, hung onto his boots, and began to weep. She wept a good long while, but finally she looked up at him and said, "Sir, do you mean you paid more than anyone ever paid for a slave? You bought me just to set me free?" He said, "Yes." She began to weep again. Then finally she looked up at him

158

and said, "Sir, I have but one request. Can I be your slave forever?"[15]

That's how a Christian responds. Jesus Christ, the incarnate Word, paid more to buy you than anyone has ever paid for a slave. Once you're set free, you'll want to serve him forever.

15. Paris Reidhead, "So Great Salvation," *SermonIndex*, accessed November 26, 2013, http://www.sermonindex.net/modules/articles/index.php?view=article&aid=16849.

8

The Life and Ministry
of Jesus

IAIN M. DUGUID

"FOR EVEN THE SON OF MAN came not to be served but to serve, and to give his life as a ransom for many." Mark 10:45 shows us the person and work of Christ in very succinct form, and I want us to see three things here, three things that are not altogether distinct but are merged together: who Jesus is, what he came to do, and the significance that these truths have for you and me—the difference it would make if we really understood these things in our lives.

First, Mark 10:45 shows us who Jesus is. You see that Jesus designates himself by the title he uses most often for himself in the New Testament, which is "the Son of Man." Jesus did not invent that title. The Hebrew equivalent, *ben adam*, would or should immediately have conjured up two very different Old Testament connotations in the minds of Jesus' hearers.

On the one hand, there's the normal, regular use of that phrase, which emphasizes a difference between mere mortals and almighty God. So in Numbers 23:19, Balaam says, "God is not a man that he should lie, or a son of man [*ben adam*], that he should change his mind." In the book of Isaiah, the Lord gently chides his people; why are they still "afraid of man who dies, of the son of man who is made like grass," even though the sovereign Lord is the one who comforts them (51:12)? Of course, the most common use of the term "son of man" in the Old Testament is in the book of Ezekiel, where the prophet is addressed in those terms by the Lord, as a way of reminding the prophet of his weakness and insignificance in comparison to the holy almighty God.

On the other hand, the term "Son of Man" as used in Mark 10 would also have reminded Jesus' hearers of Daniel 7, that glorious vision of "one like a son of man" coming with the clouds of heaven, approaching the Ancient of Days, being given authority, glory, sovereign power over all peoples and nations and languages (vv. 13–14). This *ben adam*, this son of Adam, is far more than a mere human. In fact, he seems to combine in one person both human and divine traits. Insofar as he is one like a son of man, he is clearly a mortal human being.

Earlier in the vision, the Ancient of Days is also described in anthropomorphic form: he sits on a throne, he wears clothing, he has white hair. But only the second figure is described as one "like a son of man," which suggests already that there is more to his humanity than God simply appearing in human form. At the same time, this son of man rides on the clouds, which is a clear claim of divine authority. In the Old Testament, God is the only one who comes riding on his cloud chariot (see Ps. 68:4; Isa. 19:1). And when this son of man comes into the presence of the Ancient of Days, he is given authority, glory, and sovereign power over all peoples, nations, and languages, and they are instructed to bow down and worship him.

One of the Aramaic words used here, *palach*, elsewhere always refers to homage shown to deities. So here we have the son of man given an everlasting and indestructible dominion and sovereignty that everywhere else, the book of Daniel is clear to show us, belongs to God and to God alone, in contrast to the temporary kingdoms and temporary glory that the sovereign God gives to the empires of this world. What would Daniel have made of that? It must have boggled his mind.

From our perspective, looking backward, we can see how "Son of Man" was thus the perfect title for Jesus to bear on his mission to earth, because it combines in itself incongruous ideas of mere humanity with the unparalleled glory of God himself. Very often in Jesus' earthly ministry, it is the mere human aspect of the Son of Man that is prominent. Eugene Peterson says, "This Son of Man has dinner with a prostitute, stops off for lunch with a tax collector, wastes time blessing children, when there are Roman legions to be chased from the land, heals unimportant losers while ignoring high achieving Pharisees and influential Sadducees."[1]

Ultimately Jesus hung pierced and bleeding upon a cross. He died and was buried in a tomb. Isn't that the most un-godlike of acts? Sons of Adam all die, and so must this one. But his majesty as the Son of Man was still present, although veiled while on earth. Jesus taught as one who had unparalleled authority, not like the rabbis who hedged their statements by saying, "Well, Rabbi So-and-So says this, but Rabbi Such-and-Such says that." Jesus says, "You have heard that it was said, but I say to you."

Moses ascended to bring the people God's law, but when Jesus stood on the mount, he gave the people *his* law. As God in human flesh, he didn't need to preface his statements with

---

1. Eugene Peterson, *Reversed Thunder* (San Francisco: Harper and Row, 1988), 30.

"Thus says the Lord" to give them authority as the prophets regularly did, because he himself was the Lord. He forgave people their sins, a prerogative that God reserves for himself. And he claimed to have the authority to judge as the Son of Man. John 5:27, in which Jesus says of the Father, "And he has given [me] authority to execute judgment, because [I am] the Son of Man," is a clear reference to Daniel 7.

At his trial before Pilate, Jesus spoke of possessing a kingdom of his own, and he declared that no one had the power to take his life from him. He could lay it down, and he could take it up again. On the Mount of Transfiguration, the veil was drawn away for a moment, and the three disciples who accompanied him saw with their own eyes the glory of God shining in the face of Jesus Christ. Both humility and glory are present in Jesus because he is the son of man and also Son of Man. Very man and very God.

Jesus . . . the Servant

Jesus is not just the Son of Man; he's also the servant. It's clear from the context in Mark's gospel that when the disciples heard the phrase "the Son of Man," they made the connection to Daniel 7 but not to the broader Old Testament context. They were ready for Jesus to be the Son of Man riding on the clouds, entering his kingdom in glory, and giving places on either side to his favorite disciples. What they still had to learn was that our salvation does not come through the advent of a triumphant heavenly figure bearing a sword and blasting his enemies with fire from heaven, rewarding his friends with positions of power and influence. Our salvation comes through the advent of a baby in a manger, who lived as an ordinary carpenter and progressed to wearing a crown of thorns and bearing a cross. The Son of Man did not come to be served, as you might have expected from Daniel 7; he came to serve and to give his life as a ransom for the many.

This aspect of the Messiah's life was also anticipated in the Old Testament. The title "servant of the Lord" is an exalted one. Moses and David are among those who are called "my servants" by the Lord: men who were singled out for unique honor in God's eyes. So too at the end of Isaiah 52, the prophet speaks of a coming servant of the Lord who will be high and lifted up, a servant who will act wisely—that is, who will act in such a way that his plans will succeed. He starts out announcing the glory of this servant of the Lord and the certainty of his victory.

Then, in one of the most astonishing twists in the whole Bible, in Isaiah 53 we cut from celebrating the exaltation of the servant's victory to suffering the agony of the servant's apparent defeat. The servant must suffer a fate that is so awful that it will leave observers at a loss for words. Astonished by his total disfigurement, his own people will not recognize this servant as God's envoy because his appearance will be marred beyond human semblance. His form is disfigured more than any other among the sons of man, the *bene adam*.

This servant will grow up like a young shoot, but whereas God's people were expecting the blossoming shoot of Jesse promised in Isaiah 11, this servant will instead be a shriveled stump, growing up out of dry and parched ground. He will have no form, no beauty, no majesty to commend him to them. Instead the servant will take onto himself all the negative consequences of Adam's curse—and so he will be despised and rejected by men, a man of sorrows, acquainted with sickness and disease. Why must there be this terrible sorrow, this terrible suffering for the faithful servant of the Lord? Why should God's chosen one meet such an awful fate? The answer Isaiah gives is that this is our sorrow. This is our suffering that he bears, the fruit of our sin and our transgression, because we have all gone astray like sheep. The Lord placed the penalty on him in our place, so that he was slaughtered like an animal sacrificed as a sin offering.

The Lord laid the punishment of our iniquity upon him so that his chosen servant would be deprived of justice, deprived of descendants, and buried with the rich, and would share the fate of those who will be judged because of their oppression of God's people. Yet Isaiah tells us it was the Lord's will. No, stronger than that; it was the Lord's *delight* to crush his servant, because only in this way could the Lord's sovereign purpose prosper in his hand—through the suffering death of the servant.

That would not be the end of the story. Through his suffering, after his suffering, he would see the light of life and be satisfied, because through his work the servant would make the many to be accounted righteous, and he would receive his reward, because he bore the sin of many and made intercession for transgressors.

Christ's Work: A Ransom for the Many

You can see in Isaiah's description of the servant that we've already moved from describing the person of Jesus to outlining his work. When Jesus said that the Son of Man came not to be served but to serve, he wasn't just talking about his humble manner of life. He was alluding as well to the form of death he had come to die. It's the same progression that Paul makes in Philippians 2. Jesus Christ took the form of a servant, which means not just humbling himself but humbling himself to the point of death on the cross. The Son of Man's role in coming to serve was not just to set an example of how you and I should live our lives as the servants of the Lord. No, Jesus came to serve by giving his life as a ransom for the many.

In a profound sense, you cannot separate Jesus' person and his work. Jesus came to be the ultimate Son of Adam, the perfect servant of the Lord, the new Israel, so that he could live the perfect life that Adam should have lived, that Israel should have lived, and so that he could die the agonizing death that their sins deserved. In so doing, just as Isaiah 53:4 foretold, he gave his life as a ransom for the many, the chosen people of the Lord.

A key element, then, of Christ's work was to give his life as a ransom. But what does it mean to ransom someone? In the simplest terms, ransom means freedom from bondage. In the middle of the month, you might take your beloved guitar to a local pawnshop, where they'll give you a few dollars to help you make ends meet. When your next paycheck arrives, you'll go back and redeem your guitar; you'll ransom your guitar back from its bondage. In the Old Testament, if you fell on hard times, you could go that route with your own person. You could sell yourself into slavery in order to survive, but there was someone in your family—your kinsman redeemer—whose job it was to purchase you back, to ransom you.

The grandest, the most amazing ransom in the Old Testament took place when the Lord redeemed his people out of Egypt, the land of their bondage. That became the paradigm example of ransom, the pattern for our redemption from our bondage to sin. You remember that in the time of Joseph, Israel's ancestors went down into Egypt when there was famine in the Promised Land. At first they were treated well, and Egypt was a refuge for them. But they became enslaved when over the course of time a new pharaoh arose who didn't know what Joseph had done for his people. Their lives in Egypt became increasingly bitter, and they found themselves in bondage, oppressed by a harsh master.

In the same way, we too were once in bondage to sin. We don't enter this world as neutral parties, able to decide for ourselves whom we will serve. On the contrary, we are all born in sin's grip and under its power, just as the Israelites were born into the grip and under the power of the Egyptians. Jesus said, "Everyone who commits sin is a slave to sin" (John 8:34). In Romans 7, Paul declares that we've all been sold into the power of sin, which is why we are utterly incapable of keeping God's holy law.

If you're a parent, our bondage to sin should not be a hard concept to grasp. I remember teaching my children many things. I remember teaching them how to read. I remember teaching them how to tie their shoelaces—thank you, Velcro. I remember teaching them how to build towers out of Duplo. I don't remember sitting down with them and saying, "Now, kids, here is how you sin." Somehow they all got that lesson on their own and at a very early age. We're all born knowing how to sin and not being able *not* to sin.

We may have different patterns of characteristic sin from each other, so that perhaps one person struggles with anger while another person overeats. One person is stingy, another is proud and boastful, while still another engages in sexual sin. Such is the subtlety of sin: it is not limited to the worst things we do. Very often it is at work in the best things we do. So you may go down to the inner city and build a house with Habitat for Humanity. It's a good thing to do. But maybe your motive is to demonstrate to your friends and family what a good person you are. It's all about your glory, not the Lord's, in which case that good thing becomes sin. Maybe you're not concerned about your friends and family; you don't worry about what other people think about you at all, and you're very proud of the fact that you don't depend on the admiration of others. Or maybe you're doing this good deed to build your resume of righteousness to show that you don't really need God's grace and mercy. You're going to earn your own way into heaven by putting God in your debt. That's sin.

What you and I owe God is nothing less than thinking thankful and worshipful thoughts about him every second of every day, as well as loving him with every word we say and every action we do. How's that going for you? If you're anything like me, the moments when you think about God at all are few and far between—let alone times when you actually think about him in that thankful, worshipful way.

The fact is that all of us fall far short of God's glorious standard, and the wages that we earn for that disobedience, the Bible tells us, is death. We are born into sin, and we continue in bondage to sin, just as those Israelites did in Egypt. We need someone to ransom and redeem us.

When the Israelites cried out to the Lord in their bondage, he heard their cry and sent Moses to deliver them. He ransomed them, bringing them out of Egypt, bringing them safely through the Red Sea.

Can you imagine what that must have felt like for the Israelites? One moment you are trapped between the Egyptian army and the Red Sea, facing death on both sides. The next, the Lord has opened up a safe passage for you through the water and has drowned your adversaries in the depths of the sea, leaving you finally free to live your own life out from under the Egyptian yoke. No wonder the people burst into singing and dancing, celebrating their great deliverance.

But what price was paid for their ransom? The blood of the Passover lamb. When the firstborn of Egypt were struck down by the tenth and final plague, Israel, God's firstborn, was kept safe, protected by the blood of all the innocent lambs. They were to commemorate these thereafter by ransoming their own firstborn. While they put to death the firstborn animals of all the flock, their own firstborn sons they were to ransom as a reminder of God's ransoming them out of Egypt.

So too Jesus came to ransom us from our slavery to sin. The apostle Peter reminds us, "You were ransomed from the futile ways inherited from your forefathers, not with perishable things such as silver or gold, but with the precious blood of Christ, like that of a lamb without blemish or spot" (1 Peter 1:18–19). Jesus didn't come just to be our teacher and tell us how we ought to live. Jesus didn't come just to be a good example and demonstrate for us what the godly life ought to look like. Jesus came to pay our ransom. As the perfect Passover Lamb, he came to set us free at the cost of his own death from our own failing efforts to earn God's favor for ourselves. Jesus was God's firstborn whom the Father did not ransom but gave up as a ransom for the many.

This reminds us that our salvation is completely a gift of God, not something we can choose or earn for ourselves. The guitar cannot earn its way out of the pawnshop. The Old Testament slave could not work his way out of bondage. Israel could not just decide one morning, "Oh, I'm going to leave Egypt." If the people were going to be redeemed, it had to be God's work from beginning to end. It is the same way with our ransom from the bondage of sin. Sin is not something from which we can decide to be free. We can't just decide to turn over a new leaf. We are completely helpless, tied up as captives in sin's grasp. Only God can give us freedom. And God has chosen to do that for his people, which is why Jesus came to earth to give his life as a ransom for the many, for all those whom God the Father had chosen to give to the Son before the foundation of the world.

So in Christ we have forgiveness of our sins, reconciling us to God. In Christ, God himself has paid the penalty for our sins, which is death and hell. That's why Jesus had to go to the cross. Since the penalty of sin is death, the only way in which a just God could remain just and still justify sinners was to absorb into himself the just penalty for our sins.

God the Father took every one of the sins of his people—past, present, and future, every one of our sins—and nailed them to the cross with Jesus Christ, declaring at the end of Christ's suffering, "It is finished." With that declaration, you were ransomed. At the cross, Jesus shed his blood for all your sins so that you wouldn't have to. In that way, the righteous wrath of God that stood against sin is completely satisfied, while God is still able to have the people that he chose for himself for all eternity.

Living a Life of Perfect Holiness

God also paid the legal cost of the new relationship with him, which is perfect holiness. God's standard is perfection, not just a blank record. God says you must "be holy, as I am holy" (1 Peter 1:16), not that you must simply do nothing. You have to have perfect holiness to stand before God, which is why Jesus Christ came into this world—not just to die for you but also to live for you. He couldn't be beamed down onto the cross like a president going to visit a combat zone. The president may identify with his troops by being helicoptered in, protected carefully for a few hours, and then helicoptered out. While that may be much better than not doing anything at all, it does not equate to the incarnation of our Lord.

In the incarnation, Jesus Christ came and lived right alongside us in the midst and the heat of the battle, doing so in such a way that he lived the perfect life of unstained obedience to the Father that you should have lived, so that you might not simply have your sins washed away, but that you might receive his perfect righteousness as your own. He thought the God-honoring thoughts that you and I should have thought. He served God wholeheartedly as you and I should have served him.

When you are united to Christ, when you are adopted into God's family as his beloved son or daughter, your sinful record is given to Christ and his perfect record is given to you. He promises never again to bring up against you your record of sins. As the psalmist puts it, "As far as the east is from the west, so far does he remove our transgressions from us" (Ps. 103:12). As Paul reminds us in Colossians 2, the record of our debt has been permanently set aside, nailed to the cross once and for all (v. 14). It is finished.

Do you remember the moment when you first believed that truth? For some, perhaps, the realization came as a dramatic moment of insight; for others, a slowly dawning realization. Either way, that truth should bring you intense and dramatic joy today, as deep and profound as the joy the Israelites experienced on the far side of the Red Sea. Did they pinch themselves to see if this could possibly be true? Could they really be safe and free? Can we possibly be safe and free? Oh, the lavishness of God's grace, that he would give his precious, beloved Son to die like that for me.

Does that news thrill you today? I have to confess that often I am very ho-hum about a truth that ought to dazzle me. It ought to amaze me. Even now I wrestle with my own heart, which so often is cold toward the gospel. I understand it in my head as an abstract truth, but do I really soak in it? Do I really experience the joy and the freedom that it ought to bring? I so quickly forget the lavishness of God's grace toward me in redeeming me through his Son, which then leaves my heart wide open to all kinds of fears and all kinds of temptations.

In that I am not unlike the Israelites, who must have imagined that from the Red Sea onward their lives would be smooth sailing. They'd been delivered out of Egypt. The Lord had disposed of the most feared military force of that time. They had experienced grace upon grace, but how quickly they found that real life was more complicated than they had imagined. They found themselves wandering in the wilderness, having to trust God to provide for their needs with daily manna. The Promised Land remained tantalizingly out of reach for an entire generation. They quickly began to grumble and to long to return to their former slavery in Egypt. How quickly they forgot their redemption. How quickly they rebelled against God, resenting the trials they faced along the way. How vividly and how selectively they remembered the good parts of living in Egypt: "Oh, the leeks, the garlic, the cucumbers, the melons. All we have now is manna, manna, manna." How quickly they feared the slightest obstacles and doubted the sincerity of the Lord's promises to them.

The Lord took the Israelites out into the desert precisely for this reason, to show them their own hearts and to demonstrate that his faithfulness to them would continue to be shown in spite of their sinful rebellion and unbelief. In spite of their unfaithfulness, in spite of their grumbling, in spite of their complaining, the Lord would nonetheless faithfully fulfill his promises and complete his promised ransom of his own people in his own time and in his own way, through a path that led through many dangers, toils, and snares.

Perhaps that's where you find yourself today. Like the Israelites, perhaps you are puzzled, fearful, forgetful, resentful in the midst of life's deserts. Haven't you been ransomed by the blood? Set free from sin's bondage through the death of Christ? So why do you continue to struggle with the old sinful nature? Shouldn't that intense struggle be over by now? Shouldn't you be living the victorious Christian life as you move from one triumph to the next? Doesn't Paul say, "Sin will have no dominion over you" (Rom. 6:14)? Then why does sin so often still seem to have you under lock and key? Why is the Christian life often such a battle, not just against your circumstances and outside forces, but against your own heart?

The answer is that, just as the Israelites, you have not yet reached the Promised Land. The road there lies through the wilderness. The Son of Man came to suffer and to serve, and so our lives in this world are marked by the same calling to suffer and to serve. This world is not our home. Yes, we have been ransomed and redeemed, but we have not yet reached our glorious heavenly home. Yes, we have been crucified with Christ and Christ lives in us, but we are still called to live that life, in this world, by faith in the Son of God who loved us and gave himself for us.

The Difference Christ's Ransoming Work Makes

In the face of many trials and temptations, God's purpose is to show you and me more and more clearly the continuing depth of the depravity of our own hearts. Isn't that what so much of the sanctification process is? If God's goal in sanctification is to minimize the total number of your sins, he's doing a lousy job. But if God's goal in the sanctification process is to glorify Christ by showing you that, redeemed and ransomed as you are, you still have a foul heart that would quickly turn back to Egypt and yet God's grace is nonetheless sufficient for you, then the Holy Spirit is doing a wonderful job. He will bring us back by that means, time and time again, to the simple gospel truth that we need to believe: in spite of our continuing sin, we have been ransomed completely by Christ's blood and our sins have been forgiven out of his lavish grace.

The Son of Man came not to be served but to serve and to give his life as a ransom for many. What difference would it make in our lives if we really soaked ourselves in this truth? First of all, I think it would challenge our expectations of the life that God promises us here and now. If the pattern of life that God laid out for his own beloved Son was a life of suffering and service, why would his pattern for your life be any different from that? Jesus calls us as his disciples to take up a cross and follow him. The Christian life is not about gaining the best position for yourself and lording it over others around you. It's not, in short, about your best life now, which is what James and John wanted when they asked to receive seats on either side of the Lord when he came into his kingdom.

The Christian life is about dying to ourselves and to our most cherished ambitions and instead seeing Christ living in and through us, and that feels hard. It feels like dying and not living. But the reason it feels hard is because we have forgotten that Jesus has ransomed us, that he has bought us out of that dark bondage in order that we might have life in all its fullness. Like Israel in the wilderness, we disbelieve the truth that we have been redeemed out of Egypt by a Lord who has a good future for us. Instead we believe the lie that the old life in Egypt was better. We find ourselves remembering the leeks, the garlic, the cucumbers, and the melons and forgetting the beatings and the requirements to make bricks without straw. We remember the temporary satisfaction that our sin gave us, and we forget the shame and the emptiness that it brought, so we dabble with sin and bow down to its demands instead of recoiling from it with horror. We put ourselves first in our own attempts to meet our own desires for security, for significance, for comfort. All that is a lie. Whenever you and I sin, we are believing the lie that the sin will meet our needs and are disbelieving the truth that it will leave us emptier than ever . . . even though, if we stopped for a moment to think about our experience, we would see that our sin has brought us nothing but isolation and pain.

We bow down to our chosen idols. We believe their false promises instead of submitting our hearts to the true and living God. Some people use food to medicate away feelings that are too painful to face, using binge eating to get away from reality. Other people use Internet pornography, idolizing comfort and buying into the lie that a temporary escape from emotional pain is worth the cost of their sin. One of my idols is my desire for respect and admiration, and as a result, often I will monopolize a conversation. I will set myself up as an authority about something I know nothing about. I'm a college professor. I get paid to feed my idolatry. I have a desperate need to prove that I am somebody and that my life matters, and I believe if I talk impressively enough, if I get invited to speak at conferences, I must be somebody. It's a lie. It doesn't matter how many people are impressed by my sermons, my lectures, or my books—it's never enough. And so I feel empty inside, jealous of others who get the attention I feel is rightfully mine. It makes me a driven workaholic who is difficult to work with and difficult to live with, because I'm worshiping a lie.

The feelings that we experience are very real and very enslaving. They feel as if they have tremendous power over us. If you are in Christ, the power of the idols in your life is broken at a deep level, because they are built, at their base, on a lie. The truth is this: the Son of Man came to give his own life as your ransom. There is the true foundation for your security and your significance.

Do I feel insecure, that I don't really matter? Yes, I really feel that, and my idols tell me their version of what I need to do to rid myself of that feeling. But the blood of Christ tells me a different story. It reminds me that at the cross, God declared that I matter to him in an incredible way.

Do you long for intimacy? Yes, you really do, and your idols tell you what you need to do to be rid of that longing. But the blood of Christ tells you a different story. It reminds you that in Christ, God himself has ransomed you; he has given you peace with him. He has called you his own beloved son, his own beloved daughter, and he has adopted you into his family. He shows you his lavish grace, and his gospel arms you with the truth to withstand Satan's lies.

When you face temptation, the answer is not to use the law in your heart and say, "I can't do that because God told me not to." You have to speak the gospel to your heart and remind yourself again of God's ransoming love for you in Christ, a love that is so rich, so deep, and so profound that even when you continue on in sin anyway, as I so often do, you will discover that you cannot outrun the grace of God.

If you're a Christian, Jesus Christ has not only paid the ransom for the sins you've already committed, but he has also paid the ransom for those sins that you are going to commit today and tomorrow and the day after that. Every single sin has been paid for by the lavish grace of God that meets you in Christ. We need to return constantly to those truths. They need to be the center of our worship services and the center of our conversations with our friends, because we so quickly forget. The same gospel also needs to address our hearts after we sin. As you enter temptation, Satan will try to persuade you, "This sin is no big deal." But after you've sinned, he will turn around and magnify its proportion and say, "You cannot come close to God because of your sin." That lie too is answered by the gospel.

If I continue to cling to my guilt, to act as if there could be no forgiveness for someone like me, I'm denying the reality of the ransom that is mine through God's lavish grace. If God declares that the blood of his Son is sufficient to wash away all your sin, who are you to argue? If the Judge of the whole universe declares you not guilty in Christ, are you going to contest that verdict? But when you continue to cling to your guilt over your ongoing sin, you are acting as if it is your verdict that counts, not God's. Psalm 130:3–4 tells us,

> If you, O LORD, should mark iniquities,
>   O Lord, who could stand?
> But with you there is forgiveness,
>   that you may be feared.

In the closing period of his life, the apostle Paul wrote, "The saying is trustworthy and deserving of full acceptance, that Christ Jesus came into the world to save sinners, of whom I am the foremost" (1 Tim. 1:15). Paul lived out of the reality he told the Romans: "There is therefore now no condemnation for those who are in Christ Jesus" (Rom. 8:1). It is finished. Your ransom is paid, and if God says there is now no condemnation for you in Christ, why do you still condemn yourself? God's lavish grace that he has shown to you in Christ is not a trickle. It is a mighty torrent; it is a roaring river; it is a Niagara Falls of mercy, sufficient to atone for every sin of the foremost sinner in the world, which means it is sufficient for you and it is sufficient for me.

Are you still trying to ransom yourself through living the best life that you can? Still trusting in your own efforts to please

God? If so, you are still in utter bondage to your own sin, even if you are living a better life than Mother Teresa ever managed. Only Christ can ransom you from your empty efforts and your vain striving, and only the gospel can give you the rest that you so long for. Come to Christ today and find that rest in his perfect finished work on your behalf. If you know that the Son of Man came to give his life as a ransom for the many, then today the forgiveness that is yours through the lavish grace of God should give you great joy.

It won't instantly solve all your problems, not even your sin problem. You will continue to sin and to struggle as long as you live in this body of death, as Paul tells us in Romans 7:24. That is God's trajectory for you, just as it was his trajectory for the Israelites. But thanks be to God; in Christ we have ultimately been ransomed from this body of death, set free from the condemnation that we deserve, and adopted into God's family. The Son of Man took up this body of death on our behalf so that he could make us into the sons of God. When you grasp the wonder that he truly understands the depth of the bondage from which you have been set free, you will leap with joy.

You're no longer a slave in imminent danger of being beaten for your failures and cast out of the house forever. You've been ransomed, you've been purchased, you've been adopted; you are a son, you are a daughter. The Father loves you in Christ with a lavish grace, and he will not let you go. You've been forgiven of your sins, washed with the blood of Christ, redeemed, accepted in the Beloved, and what more do you need than that, in life and in death? The vast, unmeasured, boundless ocean of God's love and mercy to you in Jesus Christ is your rich treasure and your reward. You've been bought with a price. You've been ransomed. The Son of Man who came from heaven to serve and to suffer and to ransom you has purchased you for himself, and he will not let you go.

179

9

The Cross of Christ

JOEL R. BEEKE

IT IS TWELVE O'CLOCK. The Lord Jesus has been on the cross for three pain-filled hours. Three times he has spoken from the accursed tree. All three occasions have focused on the well-being of others. Out of love, he has prayed for his enemies, promised salvation to a thief, and made arrangements for his mother's welfare. Many in the tumultuous crowd have scarcely heard the words he has spoken. Many who but five days before waved palm branches before him and cried out "Hosanna" now cast a variety of abominable accusations into his teeth.

Then, at noon, something very unusual takes place—something that ends all the noise and clamor at the place of execution. Suddenly it gets strangely dark at Calvary, and in all Judea and the rest of the country. This darkness cannot be explained in terms of natural phenomena. It is more than a thunderstorm, more than an eclipse. By a special miraculous act of almighty God, it becomes midnight at midday.

This supernatural darkness, which lasts for three hours, is a symbol of God's judgment upon sin. God is light and in him is no darkness at all. The Bible often associates sin with darkness and holiness with light. The physical darkness that covers Calvary points to a deeper and even more fearful darkness that Christ himself describes as "outer darkness"—that is, the darkness of hell, where there is weeping and gnashing of teeth.

The sun withholds its light; thick, heavy darkness descends upon Golgotha. The Great High Priest enters Golgotha's Holy of Holies. The curtain is drawn; friend and enemy are excluded. The Son of God is left alone. When Christ was born, the extraordinary bright light of God's glory and of a multitude of angels filled the heavens. When Christ dies, the heavens become extraordinarily black because of his being forsaken of God. Forsaken of God, forsaken of men, he confronts a fearful, dark end.

Christ's first three hours on the cross were packed with intense physical suffering; the accent of the last three hours is on internal suffering. Darkness descends upon Calvary because of him who hangs on the center cross. From noon to three o'clock that Friday afternoon, the Lord Jesus Christ is cast out of God's comfortable presence into outer darkness. What the Savior endures in his inmost soul for those three hours on the cross defies our most profound imagination. No Mel Gibson film can begin to picture it.

The thick, heavy darkness over the land is exponentially magnified in the greater darkness within the soul of Jesus Christ. For three long hours, Christ wrestles with the powers of darkness. He is in the midst of darkness and is experiencing darkness in the depths of his being.

The sacrifice of the Passover lamb in Exodus 12 was preceded by the plague of three days of darkness. Here the great Passover Lamb is sacrificed in the midst of a much more profound darkness. There is darkness within and darkness without. We read of no word spoken in these three hours by Christ or by anyone else around the cross. It was an awesome, eerie, unforgettable scene.

Hear the silence, feel the darkness, and then tell me that Jesus doesn't understand your darkness. He does understand. Here is one Friend who can sympathize with your darkest moment, with your deepest darkness, with your indescribable agonies. Here is One who can draw beside you when you cry out with tears, "Heaven is silent." He says, "I understand; I have been there, and I know what it is like. I can get you through this. Your weeping may endure for a night, but joy will arise in the morning." Here in deepest darkness is the deepest sympathy for you as a Christian when you walk in darkness. Jesus endured midnight at midday.

Christ endured most of his previous sufferings in silence—the spitting, the mock-robing, and the scourging at Gabbatha; the cross-carrying, the nailing to the cross, and the being dropped into a prepared hole, with all the pain that entailed as the nails tore at his human flesh. But when he reached the extremity of all his sufferings in experiencing the full brunt of his Father's dereliction and his Father's malediction, he could not but cry out as he neared the end of his six hours on the cross: "My God, My God, why hast thou forsaken me?" (Matt. 27:46; Mark 15:34).

This fourth word from the cross represents the climax, the apex, the extremity of Jesus' sufferings. Here Jesus descends into the essence of what hell is; here is the most climactic moment of suffering ever endured, an hour of incredible destiny and density; an hour so compacted—so infinite, so horrendous—as to be seemingly unsustainable.

To begin to grasp a little of the profundity of this amazing cry from the cross, which is the essence of the cross, I want to examine three points: the extremity of Christ's sufferings, the reason for his sufferings, and the love behind his sufferings.

The Extremity of Christ's Sufferings

No cry in the world has contained so much suffering as Christ's fourth word from the cross: "My God, My God, why hast thou forsaken me?" We will first look at five principles that remain unmoved despite the dreadfulness of this moment for Jesus. Then we will look at four realities in the experience of Jesus when he uttered those words.

First, Jesus' cry "My God, my God, why hast thou forsaken me?" did not in any way diminish his deity. He did not cease being God before, during, or after this cry. He is God and man—two natures in one person—forever.

Second, Jesus' cry did not divide his human nature from his divine person. His person was not split down the middle so that the hypostatic union between his natures was broken. These two—God and man—never ceased to be united. Christ's desertion was not in his divine nature but in his human nature. Nor was this desertion mutual. His Father temporarily deserted Christ, but Christ did not desert his Father.

Third, Jesus' cry did not destroy the Trinity. Jesus' cry did not reveal a crack in the Trinity so that Father and Son fell apart. That is utterly impossible. Father and Son were still one in their being and one in all their attributes. The three persons did not become two persons. The Trinity did not become a duality. There was still the Father, Son, and Holy Spirit—three persons in one Godhead—but the awesome fellowship of delight was temporarily severed between the Father and the God-man. Thomas Brooks writes, "The Godhead was not separated, though the working power thereof were for a time sequestered."[1]

---

1. Thomas Brooks, *The Golden Key to Open Hidden Treasures*, in *The Works of Thomas Brooks* (1867; repr., Edinburgh: Banner of Truth, 2001), 5:100.

Fourth, Jesus' cry did not detach him from the Holy Spirit. He did not cease to be filled with the Holy Spirit without measure. He certainly lacked the comforts of the Spirit, but never the holiness of the Spirit. The Spirit was still in him without measure, although the ministry of comfort was not active at this time.

Fifth, Jesus' cry did not cause him to disbelieve his mission. Both Father and Son knew from all eternity that he was to become the Lamb of God who would take away the sin of the world. Acts 15:18 says, "Known unto God are all his works from the beginning of the world." Jesus had been walking with destiny up until the very moment when the hour of laying down his life finally came. There he, by himself, accomplished the redemption of sinners by being made a sacrifice for their sin. It would be unthinkable to imagine that the Son of God could question what was happening on the cross or be perplexed as to the reason for the absence of his Father's loving presence. Jesus had refused the wine mixed with myrrh at the very beginning of crucifixion so that his senses would be as alert as possible to the end. All his feelings were serving this one redemptive end.

Taken collectively, these five principles teach us that even here, yes, especially here, we must bow down and worship the Lord Christ. If here Christ had ceased to be God, this would be a moment in time that worship of him would be idolatry, for it would break the first commandment. We would be worshiping a mere creature. Surely if we are Christians and we come to this verse, we don't worship up to this point, and then worship after this point—we worship in verse 46 as well. In fact, surely here is the ultimate reason for worship. When Jesus cries out to God, we feel instinctively the need to fall down in worship and say, "My Lord and my God!" Jesus' fourth word from the cross should evoke worship and adoration in our hearts.

Though we cannot grasp the emotional and spiritual content of what the forsakenness of God was for Jesus, we know that it was far more awful that we can ever envisage. We can at least stammer a little of our thoughts concerning four things, among many others, that it involved.

First, Jesus experienced here the agony of seemingly unanswered supplication. That is made plain from Psalm 22:1–2.

> My God, my God, why hast thou forsaken me? Why art
>   thou so far from helping me, and from the words
>   of my roaring?
> O my God, I cry in the day time, but thou hearest not; and
>   in the night season, and am not silent.

What Jesus prayed for is hidden from us. Was it, once more, that the cup might pass? Or that he might be given one token of his Father's light, or smile, or benediction? Whatever it was, there was no answer—only the echo of his own voice and the cruel taunts of hell. The heavens were silent.

Second, Jesus experienced here the agony of seemingly unbearable stress. Stress and distress so overwhelmed him that he cried with a loud voice. Psalm 22, we have just seen, calls it a "roaring." Perhaps you have seen the famous painting *The Scream* that depicts a huge mouth uttering an awful scream. The idea of the painting was to depict that, typical of stressed humanity, most human beings will experience "the scream" at some point in their lives. They cry out; they shriek; they roar! But however horrific such a painting is on an earthly level, it pales in comparison to this roaring cry of the Lord Jesus. No cry in human history has matched this cry. This cry pierced the darkness, as it were, as a cry from the bottomless pit. It "was like the *perpetual shriek* of them that are cast away for ever," John

Flavel writes. "It is as much as if Christ had said, O my God, no words can express my anguish: I will not speak, but roar, howl out my complaint; pour it out in vollies of groans: I roar as a lion."[2] This is the cry that is experienced in hell when the wrath of God overwhelms the damned. This cry is heart-piercing, heaven-piercing, and hell-piercing. What agony!

How do children feel when they fall and cry and run quickly to their fathers for help, but their fathers are not there? Their stress levels rise in a moment, and they begin to scream and wail and sob, "My dad is gone!" Even that is nothing compared to Jesus' excruciating stress and distress in the presence of a withholding, silent Father. What must the angels have thought when they heard Jesus cry and roar, and the Father remained stationary and unresponsive, yes, turning his back on his own beloved Son?

We have to hold two things together here. On the one hand, never did the Son know so much of the Father's just wrath as at this moment. It was deluging him with no restraint. The whole of divine justice rained upon him, wave upon wave. Never had he been so much the object of wrath! Yet, though he could not experience it at that moment, was there ever a time when the Father was more pleased with him than then? Never. The Father loved him because he laid down his life for his enemies. Never was anything so much approved of, and admired, and yet never had Jesus experienced so little of that love. He knew nothing of it.

Does this not frighten you if you are not a believer? This cry of hell—does it not disturb you and make you tremble? Do you know that these will be your words if you remain unrepentant? This is what you will experience! Unbearable stress, wrath, abandonment, forsakenness—and not for three hours but forever! Do

2. John Flavel, *A Fountain of Life*, in *The Works of John Flavel* (1820; repr., Edinburgh: Banner of Truth, 1968), 1:412.

you not need this Savior for your soul? Will you not embrace him, believe in him, trust in him, and be saved?

Third, Jesus experienced here the agony of seemingly unmitigated sinnership. All the sins of all the elect of all ages, and all the hell that they deserve for eternity, were laid upon Christ in a compressed manner. Without being supported by his deity, he never could have sustained the burden. Since he was divine and human in one infinite person, his sufferings carry infinite value in the presence of an infinitely holy God. That's how Christ could bear our justly deserved eternal hell, dear believer, in such a short compass of time.

I once saw a picture in *US News & World Report* of a man standing in front of the Sears Tower. He held two large boulders in his hands. The caption beneath the picture explained that some stars are so dense that if compressed to the size of the boulders the man had in his hands, they would weigh as much as the Sears Tower. I have no way of proving that to be true, but it is a faint picture of how God compressed upon his Son all the agonies of sinnership in a short period of time.

Jesus' cry includes such a profound sense of sinnership that his sense of sonship seemed temporarily to recede to the background to some degree in his own consciousness. That receding does not mean, of course, that Jesus doubted his own divine sonship or lost a sense of it altogether. That would amount to a failure to receive in faith the Scripture's testimony as to his very identity. He had spoken often to others about what the Scriptures said concerning himself. He had displayed a consciousness of his divine identity and had appealed to the Scriptures as testifying to it. Since he believed these things during the course of his ministry, it would not be compatible with his impeccability or with faith in the Word of God if he had fallen into doubt or uncertainty regarding his divine identity.

Let me explain. Though Christ has a divine consciousness and a human consciousness, he has only one self-consciousness, which belongs to his divine person. His divine personhood is the foundation on which his theanthropic constitution is erected. Though he experienced change and development in his human consciousness so that he could pass into deeper sorrow and heaviness when he entered the Gethsemane experience, yet his self-consciousness never changes because it is an aspect of his personhood and that personhood is divine. That being the case, how could he ever altogether cease to be conscious of himself in his identity as the eternal Son of the Father? Would that not be postulating a self-consciousness seated in his humanity rather than in his divine personhood? In his human mind he is conscious of human experience, and in his divine mind he is conscious of realities that his human mind cannot comprehend, but when he reflects on his individual identity, he at all times knows but one self, the self who is the I Am That I Am, who was with the Father before the world was, and who was sent by the Father to come into the world as a man.

Nevertheless, in Jesus' consciousness in these moments, it appears that a sense of sinnership dominates his consciousness to a frightening degree. In Gethsemane, and in the first and last words from the cross, Jesus was able to call on God as his Father. But now the cry is "Eli, Eli" (Hebrew), or "Eloi, Eloi" (Aramaic)—"my God, my God." He is aware of God—the goodness of God; the otherness of God; the power and holiness of God—but in that dread moment, in his self-image, he feels sinnership more intensely than sonship, though the sonship is by no means obliterated. He feels your and my sin, dear believer. Paul says that God the Father "made him to be sin for us, who knew no sin" (2 Cor. 5:21). In his self-image, he feels at this moment not so much that he is the Beloved in whom God is well pleased, but he feels himself to be the cursed one: vile, foul, repulsive—an object of dread. This is the essence of the dereliction, the essence of what God thinks of sin, the essence of the price the God-man had to pay for sin.

Yet in the midst of this agony of sinnership, Jesus exercises unassailable faith. He cries, "Eli, Eli," or "Eloi, Eloi"—the *El* meaning "strong one." In the midst of this sense of no possession, he *is* possessing. His feelings say, "No God," but his faith says, "*My* God." His feelings say, "No strength, no strong one," but his faith says, "*My* strong One." He is appealing to the One who has always supported him in his troubles. Though every fiber of his feelings says, "No God," yet his faith says, "My God, my God." His feelings say, "You have been left alone," yet faith says, "Impossible. No matter what my feelings tell me or what taunts are thrown in my face, my Lord and my God." Calvin says, "Still in His heart faith remained firm, by which He beheld the presence of God, of whose absence He complains."[3]

"Eli, Eli." Great faith is shown here, and a great example: to abandon our feelings when our feelings say, "God has abandoned me." Oh, to flee to faith in the Strong One instead of feeling in myself, the weak one! Too often as Christians, and particularly as ministers, we are governed by our feelings rather than our faith. We need, especially as ministers, to model for our people how to live by faith in the midst of our darkest hours and our deepest trials. At such times, our people, and others beyond our congregations, are watching us more closely than ever to see if Christianity is worth its salt.

Then too we see Jesus' faith in the question he asks: "Why hast thou forsaken me?" Sometimes we ask "Why?" in a bold

3. John Calvin, "Commentary on Matt. 27:36," in *Commentary on a Harmony of the Evangelists*, trans. William Pringle (1846; repr., Grand Rapids: Baker, 1996), 3:319.

way. "Why has this happened to me?" This was far from Christ's spirit. This was not a bold or impudent question. Neither did it come out of a sense of puzzlement, as if he had always known his mission, yet here he wonders, "What am I doing here?" We must banish these thoughts from our minds. It is impossible for Christ to lose all consciousness of his reason for existing. This is not the "Why?" of impudence or bafflement. It is the "Why?" of submissive faith. It is not wrong to ask "Why?" in submission to God. It all has to do with the spirit in which we ask.

Jesus is asking "Why?" here that the Father of heaven would bring to his faith in a very vivid way the reasons why. He knows why, but he wants the reasons made memorable, made such that he can hold on to them for sustenance in these hours of darkness. "Father, remind me why this is necessary. Yes, it is necessary for me to be God-forsaken in order that God-forsakers may know union and communion with God. Here it is necessary, yes. And look at the end—is it not glorious?" This is what the Lord is doing—he is asking in faith that his human nature might be strengthened as he exercises faith—the reason of his doing this, and the end of his doing this. Here again is a wonderful example to follow.

Finally, Jesus experienced here the agony of seemingly unassisted solitariness. Jesus endured an incomprehensible, inexplicable abandonment by God. He is saying, "Why hast thou forsaken me, deserted me, abandoned me?" This was a new experience for the Lord Jesus. Before he came to this earth, he was the eternal Son of God in heaven, and there he knew nothing but the Father's love lavished generously and continuously upon him. As he said in Proverbs 8, "I was daily his delight, rejoicing always before him" (v. 30). That was his experience in heaven. But it was also his experience on earth.

As the eternal Word, Jesus had always been with God. As the incarnate Son, the Father had always been with him. Jesus said in John 16:32, "I am not alone, because the Father is with me." Jesus knew continuously the Father's love and support and nearness. He felt a oneness with the Father. There never was a sweeter Father, and there never was a more loving Son. They had gone up from Bethlehem to Calvary together, just as Abraham and Isaac went up the mount in Genesis 22. Even in moments of severe trouble and sorrow, heaven sent help. In Matthew 17, "This is my beloved Son" was declared from heaven (v. 5). In the garden of Gethsemane, an angel was sent to strengthen him.

But now in the hour of greatest need, Christ experiences a new, unique pain: the Father is not there. This is uncharted territory for him. When he most needs encouragement, no voice cries from heaven, "This is my beloved Son." When he most needs reassurance, no one says, "I am well pleased." No dove descends on the holy mount to convey and symbolize peace; no angel is sent to strengthen him; no "well done, good and faithful servant" resounds in his ears. No rod and staff are given him as he walks through the valley of death. No grace is extended to him, no favor shown, no comfort administered, no content of the cup removed. He is in a far country, a strange country, hanging in the naked flame of his Father's wrath, with no eye gazing upon him in love, saying in its look of compassion, "We understand." The pure-minded women are silent. The disciples, coward and terrified, are far away. He treads the winepress alone.

God is present only as one apparently displeased, as one bearing down upon Christ in every detail of Golgotha with profound wrath. Instead of love, there is wrath. Instead of affection, there is coldness. Instead of support, there is opposition. Instead of nearness, there is distance. This didn't happen all of a sudden. This happened over a period of three hours.

What Christ is experiencing could best be imagined like this: Here is a son with his father, and the son suddenly realizes the father is gone. He sees him not too far away and goes after him, crying out, "Dad," but the father keeps going and gets farther away with greater strength. The son's cries do not bring the father back; he keeps running, and the son keeps crying out. There is no change in the demeanor of the father, and the son is crying louder, and the father goes farther away and eventually disappears. The son cries out one last time, "Father! Why?"

That is what we have here. The Son is pursuing the Father as he distances himself farther away. There is an indescribable pursuit going on here, yet the Father is purposefully going farther and farther away. No amount of pursuing will catch up with the Father, and eventually there is nothing left but abandonment! The Son cries out, "My God, my God, why hast thou forsaken me?" This is what he feels and senses—abandonment and forsakenness. Not one kind look; not one kind word; no consolation and no comfort, and no encouragement. He is alone! Deserted! Forsaken!

Every detail shouts to you and me, "This is what God thinks of your and my sin!" Every detail declares the irrationality, the heinousness, the dread character of sin.

This fourth word from the cross takes us over our heads. We can understand how David could come to this heart-rending cry in Psalm 22, but we find it impossible to comprehend how these same words could be uttered by Jesus Christ, the Son of God! How could he endure unanswered prayer, the fading of filial consciousness, the abandonment of his Father, which for him is the hell of hell, when he too is God of God?

How could God forsake Christ as though he were Cain and not Christ? How could God the Father forsake God the Son? Martin Luther, after meditating on this fourth word from the cross for hours, exclaimed, "God forsaken of God! Who can comprehend it?"[4] What this has meant for Christ cannot be adequately explained, not even by Christ himself. Although he utters these words in human language, they reflect an experience to which human beings are strangers. These words of Christ are spoken in time and space, but they come from another world. No son of Adam ever went through what Christ went through. Many people have felt forsaken of God, but no human beings, not even the reprobates, are completely forsaken by God while still in this life.

Nevertheless, being abandoned, even outwardly, is a fearful state. Outside the emergency room in a California hospital, there is a drop-off box with a picture of a baby on it. The thought of abandoning one's baby, akin to dropping mail in a mailbox, makes us shudder to the core of our being. Yet when believers feel forsaken, it is no more than that—a feeling that does not correspond with reality. They lose the sense of God's presence, but not his presence itself. With Christ it was both a feeling and a fact. He felt forsaken because he *was* forsaken. He faced the real thing; we face, at our worst times, only the shadows.

The Reason for Christ's Sufferings

But why? Why was Christ forsaken by God in the absolute and real sense of that word? We cannot hope to find a

---

4. Quoted in Friedrich W. Krummacher, *The Suffering Savior*, trans. Samuel Jackson (Boston: Gould and Lincoln, 1859), 410.

completely satisfying answer to this question. If even Christ himself asked, "Why?" and received no answer, how then shall we find a solution to the greatest riddle of all time, to this terrible darkness, this appalling situation, this unfathomable depth in human history?

Yet this does not mean that Scripture leaves us completely in the dark as to why Christ was forsaken. Isaiah 53 unlocks part of the secret when it tells us that he was smitten of God and afflicted. Verse 10 says, "It pleased the LORD to bruise him." It is God who does not spare him but delivers him up for us all. It is God the Father who in his love for this evil world gives his own Son. But why? Why does God so deal with a sinless One, with his own divine Son whom he loves? Why does God bruise him? Why does God place him under the anathema, under his own wrath, and under his own curse? All the shallowness of contemporary atonement thinking derives from a failure to stand before the magnitude of this anomaly. He is sinless; he is divine; yet he is accursed by God. Why? There are only four possible explanations for the actions of God the Father.

The first possibility is capriciousness. That is, the Father, out of caprice, simply out of a mood change that came into his mind, anathematized his Son. That is, of course, an untenable, unthinkable answer. God could never bruise and desert his Son out of mere arbitrary sovereignty. He knows no mood changes. He is not capricious. His love is steady; it is *agape* love.

The second possibility is that God the Father bruised his Son in malice; that he despised his Son and held him in contempt; that in malevolence the Lord Jehovah crushed and bruised and extinguished the life of his own Son because of the evil that is common to his nature. This too is absolutely impossible, for it would be a criminal act on the part of God. If

195

you saw a father bruising and extinguishing and anathematizing his son, you would not conclude from that bare fact that this father loved his son, but quite the contrary. Yet many who have no understanding of the atonement stand before the cross and foolishly say in shallow sentimentality only this, "Here is proof of the love of God."

The third possibility is didactic: the Father wanted to teach the Son profound lessons about suffering, so he laid harsh judgment—especially the judgment of desertion—upon him. This possibility is drawn from how God treats his people at times by bruising them with painful desertions of various kinds. God appears to leave his people at times. He doesn't actually leave, just as he never actually left Calvary. Christians can have a sense of God's presence, and at times feel a sense of God's absence, even if their feelings are not accurate. Hezekiah was deserted, but the Lord never really left him; he still heard and dealt with Hezekiah.

Sometimes the Lord will withdraw as a disciplinary measure, because you have offended him, as was the case with Hezekiah. Sometimes the Lord will withdraw as a precautionary measure. He sees you heading into dangerous territory morally and spiritually, and he withdraws as a precaution, making you aware of the direction you are heading. Sometimes he will withdraw as a test, not because you have done wrong. "Will you stay with me if I take away the sense of my staying with you?"

But God never had reason to teach his Son for the Son's own profit because his Son is perfect already. The Father had no need to bruise him for his own sake as a test, a discipline, or a precaution.

The fourth possibility for the Father's bruising of his Son is penal. That is, we find the source of the sufferings of

Jesus not in the capriciousness of God, nor in malice in God, nor in the didactic heart of God, but in the righteousness of God. There is something in the nature of things, something in the position that Jesus occupies, that made it the right thing for God to bruise him. God had made his Son to be sin on behalf of sinners, therefore he was dealt with as the righteousness of God demands that sin should be dealt with. The Father's bruising was judicial wrath. It was a just infliction of punishment for sin that he had not committed but was carrying for his people.

The Father's bruising is rooted in judicial substitution. The logic of this judicial substitution is found most clearly in 2 Corinthians 5:21: "For he hath made him to be sin for us, who knew no sin; that we might be made the righteousness of God in him." The whole logic of Calvary lies in the *for*. He is made sin for us. He died for us; he bore our sin; he was made accursed for us; he gave his life as a ransom for many. When all the anomalies and mysteries of salvation pile on top of one another, this little word *for* demolishes them all. In that *for* the whole darkness is illuminated, because that little word unites Jesus Christ and sinners. In other words, only one thing can explain why God inflicted punishment upon his own Son, and that is that his Son stood in an intimate connection with sin and sinners. If Christ was not in connection with sin and sinners, then Calvary was the darkest moment this world has ever known. If that is true, then there is no God and there is no meaning; there is only universal illogic and universal paradox. But we join Christ to sin and to sinners by the word *for!*

So what is the content of this *for*? In what sense was Christ *for* his people? The *for* means, first of all, that he was acting on behalf of his people. He was acting for their benefit; he was acting as their representative; he was acting in their interest. That is one of the great strands of New Testament teaching— Christ the Representative, the Advocate, the One who acts in the place of his people. He intercedes for them, he pleads for them, and he looks after their interests. But you must not stop there, because Jesus Christ is more than a representative. A representative acts in the place of or on behalf of his client. But Jesus Christ not only acts on the behalf of his people, Jesus Christ does something more.

Second, Jesus suffers on behalf of his client. In other words, he is not only the Priest interceding and pleading, but he is the Sacrifice in the place of his people. He not only acts for the client but he assumes the liabilities and responsibilities of the client.

The great *for* of substitution is the reason why Jesus bore our sin in our place and obeyed the law in our place, so that God's justice can be satisfied and so that God can be just and the justifier of those who believe in Jesus (Rom. 3:26). The great *for* of substitution moves Christ to assume the guilt of his people and justifies God in treating him as his people deserve to be treated on account of their sin.

Dear believer, do you understand now? *"For us"*—Christ was anathema because he was your substitute. He was anathema because he was your sin. Therefore God bruised him penally and did not spare him. Therefore he was made a curse for you, to redeem you from the curse. He was your condemnation so that there is no condemnation for you—none whatsoever! He was Son of God crucified, Son of God anathema, Son of God desolate, Son of God forsaken, because he was the Son of Man who must suffer many things. And that "must" is rooted not in human conventions, nor in theological contrivances, but in the great central truth of the heart of God that God delights in mercy (Mic. 7:18) and therefore is in the business of saving sinners.

God loves to forgive sin. He loves to multiply pardon and to make it abound. But God condones nothing. God himself must bear the sin. The God who forgives, the God who bears, the God who exacts, is the God who demands the atonement. But wonder of wonders, the God who provides the atonement *becomes* the atonement. Not only is there a Lamb of God, but God *is* the Lamb. God has found the Lamb in his own flock, in his own bosom. This surely is the greatest reality in the Christian faith—Jesus Christ becomes the sacrifice, the scapegoat.

No one around the cross could answer Christ's profound question. Even the angels had no answer. But back in Psalm 22, Jesus answers his own question in verse 3: "But thou art holy, O thou that inhabitest the praises of Israel." Why did God forsake Jesus? Because God is holy! But isn't God love? Indeed he is! But God's love is a holy love and a pure, sin-hating love. As Habakkuk states, "Thou art of purer eyes than to behold evil, and canst not look on iniquity" (1:13).

This was also true on Calvary. God could not behold evil, even when that evil was found on his own Son. He could not look upon the iniquity that his all-seeing eye detected on Christ.

But surely there was no evil or iniquity found with Jesus? No, not as far as any personal sins were concerned. He had none. But inasmuch as he was the representative of sinners and their surety, he bore much sin. When the Lord Jesus took on himself his people's sins, God treated him as sin-bearer, holding him responsible for their sins. Therefore Jesus was forsaken. God as Judge severed connections with his Son in his human nature. Christ thus received the wages of sin: namely, death. As you know, death means more than physical death; it involves also spiritual and eternal death, the complete separation between God and man. That is what Adam brought upon himself and his descendants. Christ therefore, having taken Adam's sin upon himself, must also bear Adam's punishment. Christ descended into hell, the place of total loneliness and abandonment, crying out, "My God, My God, why hast thou forsaken me? But thou art holy, thou art just in demanding satisfaction for sin at my hand. I know I must answer for all the sins of all my people. Therefore I can but justify thee, O my God. Let thy sword awake against the Man that is thy fellow!"

Christ's penal suffering, therefore, is vicarious—that is, he suffered on our behalf, dear believer. He did not simply share our forsakenness, or take the brunt of it, but he saves us from it. He endured it *for* us, not *with* us. You, dear believer, are immune to condemnation (Rom. 8:1) and to God's anathema (Gal. 3:13), because Christ went into the outer darkness to bear all this for you. As interceding High Priest, he of course also sympathizes with you, but what Golgotha secured for you in the first place was immunity rather than sympathy.

As soon as Christ died upon the tree, there could no longer be the slightest place for one grain of penal suffering to be visited upon any of his people. There is no toehold for it. He endured all the torments and relational distance that we deserve as condemnable sinners. The Savior was once abandoned for me, and so I shall never be abandoned. "Christ . . . suffered for sins, the just for the unjust, that he might bring us to God" (1 Peter 3:18). In other words, Golgotha will achieve all that God intended it to accomplish. Every lost sheep will be brought home to God.

This then is the only explanation for the three hours of darkness and for the roar of dereliction. God's people experience the confirmation of this still today, when the Holy Spirit brings them to stand by the cross in dreaded darkness, coming before the tribunal of the Judge of heaven and earth, there to experience that, as the darkness subsides, we wondrously and miraculously are not consumed for Christ's sake who was consumed on our behalf. We come out of the darkness confessing, "Immanuel— God with us! Because Immanuel has descended into the lowest hell for us, God is with us in the darkness, under the darkness, through the darkness—and we are not consumed!"

The Love behind Christ's Sufferings

I conclude with three applications relating to the triune God's love in Christ's forsakenness.

First, Christ's being forsaken reveals the stupendous love of Christ. If Thomas Watson could say, "God incarnate is nothing but love covered with flesh,"[5] how much more vivid is Christ's love displayed in his cry of dereliction, that the King of Kings is willing to undergo such an ordeal for sinners! "My God, my God, why hast thou forsaken me?" was the cry of the incarnate God whose soul was sinking, sinking, sinking ever deeper into the bottomless pit of divine wrath. Never shall believers be able to fathom the love of him who saved them from perdition. As one hymn writer put it:

> But none of the ransomed ever knew
> How deep were the waters crossed,
> Nor how dark was the night that the Lord passed through,
> Ere He found His sheep that was lost.[6]

5. Thomas Watson, *A Body of Divinity* (Edinburgh: Banner of Truth, 1983), 194.
6. Elizabeth C. Clephane, *The Ninety and Nine* (Boston: D. Lothrop and Co., 1877), no pagination.

As followers of Christ, Christians ought to expect suffering and persecution. Paul writes, "All that will live godly in Christ Jesus shall suffer persecution" (2 Tim. 3:12). And again, in Philippians 2:5–8, the apostle tells us to let the mind of Christ Jesus, the mind of love that is willing to sacrifice for the beloved, dwell in us. Do you remember what Paul is driving at here? The Philippians were claiming their own rights rather than surrendering their petty rights. They wanted to be praised for the service they gave the Lord. They wanted their gifts to be acknowledged and honored. Paul reflects on this mundane problem and says to them, "If you are complaining that you are not being honored for what you do, look to the Lord of glory. Though he is God, he did not grasp at equality with God. He didn't demand to come to this earth in all his regalia. He did not protect his dignity by refusing to be born in a stable. Philippians, let this mind of abandoning your pretensions be in you. Don't say, 'I have been a pastor or elder in this place for twenty years, and it is about time I get some recognition for it.' If Jesus did not grasp at being equal with God, why do you grasp for your so-called rights?"

Is Christ's mind in you? Oh, what practical, profound teaching lies in the fourth word from the cross. If we worship Jesus at the cross, we will relinquish every form of internal, unresolved bitterness. How can we house bitterness against someone who treats us with far less ill than we have treated the Lord of glory?

Let us abandon our petty rights, our mundane complaints, at the foot of the cross. Let us quit our trivializing. How do we dare to trivialize at the foot of the cross?

Second, Christ's being forsaken reveals the stupendous love of the Father. You say, "But where is the love? There seems to be nothing but wrath here!" Look again and remember John 3:16, "For God so loved the world, that he gave his only begotten Son." He gave him; he gave him up to this judgment! True, God had to turn his face away from Jesus, because he found sin on him. But this was all according to his plan and will. Remember, Jesus was made to be sin by God, that we might be made the righteousness of God in him. Jesus was forsaken that we might be accepted of God and never be forsaken of him.

In the gospel, the Father loves sinners lavishly and profusely. He gave everything he had. He held nothing back. When the Father gave his only Son, who had been his bosom Friend from eternity, he took the best he had and gave him for the worst he could find—sinners such as you and me—and committed him to experiencing the worst imaginable humiliation and suffering. He spared not his own Son but gave the supreme commitment of his heart.

Christ's forsakenness of the Father makes plain that the Father held nothing in reserve but was extravagant in his super-abounding love to unlovable sinners who were at enmity with him. Dear believer, the fourth word from the cross preaches God's unchangeable love for you. That love has conquered you. You are caught up in love that has broken down all the prejudices of your evil mind and heart. Sovereignly and graciously, that love has brought you into its own domain and caused you to swim in its infinity. The love of the Father is overflowing; it flows from his very heart and being. Who can stop the forth-gushings of God's love? No one anywhere has ever loved the way this God has loved. And this love is made transparent at the cross—yes, most vividly in the cry of dereliction. Amazing grace! God is willing to turn a deaf ear to his Son's agony in order to turn a hearing ear to your needs as a poor sinner.

Reverently speaking, the love of God appears to be almost foolish. I wouldn't dare to use that word if God hadn't used it first. When we know our sinfulness a bit, we are prone to cry out, "O God, how foolish thou art to love such a creature as I am! Lord, depart from me, for I am a sinful man." Then, knowing others a bit as well, we ask, "Lord, dost thou not fear that if thou dost pour out thy heart for sinners, making thyself vulnerable to them, they will throw thy love back in thy face by trampling upon the blood of thy Son?" The wisdom of men is foolishness with God, Paul says, but "the foolishness of God is wiser than men; and the weakness of God is stronger than men" (1 Cor. 1:25). The "foolishness" of God's amazing, giving love can never be comprehended by human wisdom. Had others treated us the way we treated God, we would offer them no hope, no mercy, no forgiveness. We would refuse to cast our pearls before such swine, but God dared to cast the Pearl of great price in the pathway of the kind of filthy, wretched, sinful swine that we are. God was "foolish" enough, in his infinite wisdom, to decide to bring glory to himself and the Son of his love by making his Son the Mediator and Savior of a great multitude that no man can number.

Finally, Christ's being forsaken reveals the stupendous love of the Spirit. After Christ drank the cup of his Father's wrath to its bottom, bitter dregs, we read in Mark 15:37–39 that three veils were rent. The Father rent the veil in the temple (v. 38), the Son rent the veil of his flesh (v. 37), and the Holy Spirit rent the veil of the human heart (v. 39). The Spirit caused the scales to fall from a centurion's eyes and worked so mightily on his heart, convincing him of the real identity of Jesus, that he could not help but cry out in the midst of a Christ-rejecting crowd, "Truly this man was the Son of God" (v. 39). The Holy Spirit used

Christ's forsaken and loud cry of victory in death to persuade the centurion that Jesus Christ was the Messiah.

Still today, the Holy Spirit is in the veil-rending business. Thank God he is, so that the scales can fall from our eyes, our hearts can be opened, and we can embrace the Son of God. We never would do it on our own. The Spirit manifests his incredible love in working patiently yet irresistibly in the hearts of sinners such as we, applying to us the wonderful truths of the cross. When he lovingly and persuasively shows us that Christ was forsaken of the Father that we might never be forsaken of the triune God, and that all our sufferings that entail feeling forsaken are the fruit of merely walking in his shadow but are a far cry from the reality of forsakenness that he endured, our hearts flow over with love in return. In response, we cry out, "We love him, because he first loved us" (1 John 4:19). Oh, the precious love of the Spirit in dealing with us as stubborn sinners, applying to our souls the truth of Christ and the truths taught by Christ (John 16:13–15)!

How patient the Holy Spirit is! When you have children, you never have to teach them how to sin. But you need a lot of patience, don't you? You have to say things to your children a thousand times. A thousand nos. A thousand reasons why. A thousand repetitious lessons. What patience a parent needs! But think of the patience of the Holy Spirit, teaching you the same lesson a thousand times when you should learn it by one look at the cross, followed by walking in obedience. He's so patient in dealing with stubborn sinners.

I went through a rough time in my life some years ago. I often called one of my brothers for advice, sometimes nearly every day. One time I said to him, "My dear brother, do you not get weary of me calling you? You're always so patient. Tell me if you get tired of me, and I won't call you again."

He said, "My brother, I love to help you. I'm always here. When you call, I never once think, 'I'm sorry it's my brother calling.'"

That's how you can go to the Holy Spirit—twenty-four hours a day, seven days a week. He's never tired of you coming again with your sins, with your same old repetitious prayers. He's patient with you because he loves you. From all eternity he loves you for Jesus' sake. How beautiful is the love of the Holy Spirit!

One day I was thinking how tired God must be of my prayers. My son came up the steps right at that moment and said, "Good morning, Dad." Then it hit me: *You know, he's said "Good morning" to me the last two thousand mornings in a row, and I'm not tired of it. In fact, I'd miss it if he didn't say the same thing. Why? Because he's my son.*

Jesus Christ is not tired of you, dear believer. The Holy Spirit's not tired of you. The Father's not tired of you. They love you with an everlasting love. Enjoy the love of the triune God and cry out in response, "We love him, because he first loved us" (1 John 4:19).

A Scottish highland shepherd boy bedded down his sheep one evening just before a ferocious storm raged through his valley. He awoke in the morning to discover to his horror that the viaduct running over the valley had been broken. The train track lay broken in the valley! The shepherd boy quickly ran up the embankment to stop the train. He arrived just as the anticipated train was coming and waved to the conductor to stop, but the conductor waved him away. So the boy threw his body across the track. The conductor slammed on his brakes, ran over the boy, and stopped just before the train descended into the valley's abyss. Most of the people were sleeping on the train. They got out and ran to the valley. They looked at the broken track, then at the mangled remains of the boy. No one said a word for a few minutes.

Finally one old man spoke: "That boy there, he saved my life."

Dear friend, Jesus Christ, who gave his life as a ransom, who gave it all away to the cross, is throwing himself across the track of your life. Will you stop your busy train and get out and gaze on the cross? Will you say, as you gaze upon the cross by faith, "That God-man there, he saved my life"?

If we are believers, let us meditate on this love the next time we feel forsaken of God. Think then of what your Savior experienced. No matter how terrible your affliction may be or may become, remember: Jesus has been there before you, and therefore he understands your feelings. He can sympathize with your fears and anxieties, for he has experienced them too—and infinitely worse. Do not conclude that because you feel forsaken and depressed, this implies you cannot be a child of God and may well be a reprobate. Many believers have been assaulted with this satanic insinuation.

A minister was standing by the deathbed of one of his members who had been in deep depression for many years. The servant of God tried to find something to say that might comfort this man who had given evidence of being a Christian in the past. But no matter what he tried, the reply was, "It's no use." What can you say to a man who is dying and who feels God has forsaken him? Suddenly the pastor said, "What became of that Man who died whom God did really forsake? Where is he now?" The dying man was able to cling to that and replied, "He is in glory, and I shall be with him where he is!" Light came to this dying man who had been so long in the dark. He saw that Christ had been just where he was and could hope that he might soon be where Christ was, yes, even at the right hand of the Father.

In Christ's cry of dereliction, of God-forsakenness, under the anathema of God, there is real hope for discouraged and despondent believers. Perhaps today you too feel abandoned and forsaken. Internally, you question: Where is my God? Friend, your feeling of spiritual abandonment is only a feeling. I know that is bad enough. But your abandonment is not a fact. Flee to the once-forsaken but never forsaking Savior, cast yourself upon him and his mercy, and you shall experience the fivefold Greek negative of Hebrews 13:5, best translated as "He will never, no never, no never forsake you."

Praise be to God, there is no abandonment for us because Christ has ended our estrangement. There is perfect reconciliation. We can look into the beautiful face of Jehovah in heaven and say, "My Father," and he says, "My own dear son! I cannot and will not leave you or forsake you. You are too precious to me because the Lamb of God has made you my own forever."

This is the gospel: Jesus forsaken under the judgment of my sins and I never forsaken under the warmth of God's love. Experiencing this, we can say, "I live; yet not I, but Christ liveth in me: and the life which I now live in the flesh I live by the faith of the Son of God, who loved me, and gave himself for me" (Gal. 2:20).

We ought not be half as concerned, however, about the believer who feels but is not forsaken as about those who are really without God in the world and don't seem to care. We can feel sorry for needy children of God who are thirsting for God and his communion, but at the same time we can rejoice, because such people will not perish. They will see God's gracious countenance. But we must be gravely concerned about the self-deceived, about those who profess to know the Lord and yet never have close communion with him, who don't even seem to know the difference between his presence and his absence. What else can this mean than that they are still strangers to God and his grace?

If you can live without a sense of the Lord's presence and if you are satisfied with mere outward Christianity, you are still lost in your sins, and the wrath of Almighty God rests upon you. If you die like that, you will be forever where Christ was in essence for those three terrible hours on Good Friday. Hell is utter forsakenness of any favorable presence of God.

Whether self-deceived or knowingly unsaved, the fourth word from the cross warns you to flee from the wrath to come. You must be born again. Repent of your sin, believe in Christ alone for salvation, and submit to the Savior's lordship with your entire being. Don't rest until you too believe in him who was forsaken in wrath that you might be accepted in mercy. Receive the admonition of Hebrews 2:2–3: "For if the word spoken by angels was stedfast, and every transgression and disobedience received a just recompense of reward; how shall we escape, if we neglect so great salvation?" Amen.

10

Our Risen Savior

D. A. CARSON

IT IS A REMARKABLE FACT that one of the most striking of the resurrection accounts in the canonical Gospels begins in apostolic doubt. How should we talk about the resurrection of Christ? While we could turn to many passages, let us focus on the account of Thomas and then branch out to connect with other biblical passages.

If we are going to begin here, we must begin with Thomas's doubt, and so here I must say something by way of preface: There are many kinds of doubt. Or, better put, doubt can have many points of origin.

When I was pastor of a church in Vancouver quite a number of years ago, we had a lot of college-and-careers and young adults in the church. One young woman named Peggy was a student at the University of British Columbia, with all the vivacity, color, imagination, energy, and zeal for Jesus you could imagine. She didn't think linearly. She would have made a horrible engineer, but in her own discipline she was fine, and in personality, she was a charmer. She came to me one day and said, "Pastor Don, there's a guy at the university called Fred, and he wants to take me out and talk to me about Jesus."

I said, "Uh-huh."

"No, no. I'm not going to compromise. I'm not interested in him romantically or anything. I want to talk to him about Jesus. Don't you think that's all right?"

"Uh-huh."

We had two or three cycles of this, and finally I said, "Fine. Go out with him. Talk to him about Jesus and then bring him to see me." So she did.

That Saturday night—I was still single in those days, so I was in the church office at 10:30 p.m., studying away—there was a knock on my door, and in bounces Peggy, followed by Fred, who was a football hunk and as dure and as linear as she was vivacious. She bounced in and said, "Pastor Don, this is Fred. He wants to talk with you." Well, I could see that wasn't true. I was merely a barrier on the way to Peggy. But we went out to an overnight restaurant, one of those twenty-four-hour places, and sat down. I tried to get him to relax and open up and talk a bit. We were there for a couple of hours, but it didn't go anywhere. He was clearly a biblical illiterate. He didn't know anything, and he didn't believe anything, and he doubted everything.

The next Saturday night at 10:30, there was another knock at the door. Peggy and Fred had gone to see a movie, and then they had come by. Out we went to the restaurant again, and this time Fred had a list of questions. We talked through everything on his list of questions, and I gave him some things to read. He was still very dure and very linear. Next Saturday night, another movie, then back to the same restaurant with more questions. Fred had read everything I'd given him to read.

This went on for thirteen weeks. Often I got to bed about 2 a.m. What this was doing for my Sunday morning sermons, I have no idea, but at the end of thirteen weeks Fred looked at me and said, "All right. I'll become a Christian." Just like that. Of all the people I've seen converted over the years, this is the only one I've ever seen converted quite like that. The man had doubts everywhere, especially in our first meeting—but they seemed to spring from the fact that he was just bone ignorant.

Many Kinds of Doubt

Some doubt is grounded in sublime ignorance, and you address it with instruction and information. Some doubt is grounded in a philosophical stance. That is, a person has self-consciously adopted a position that orients the whole life against the gospel. Here, for example, is the famous atheist Aldous Huxley in his book *Ends and Means*:

> For myself, the philosophy of meaninglessness was essentially an instrument of liberation. The liberation we desired was simultaneously liberation from a certain political and economic system and liberation from a certain system of morality. We objected to the morality because it interfered with our sexual freedom. We objected to the political and economic system because it was unjust. The supporters of these systems claimed that in some way they embodied the meaning (a Christian meaning, they insisted) of the world. There was an admirably simple method of confronting these people and at the same time justifying ourselves in our political and erotic revolt. We would deny that the world had any meaning whatsoever.[1]

1. Aldous Huxley, *Ends and Means* (New York: Harper & Brothers, 1937), 270–71.

Huxley abandoned that philosophy eventually, but I found very similar passages in the postmodern thinkers—Michel Foucault, for example, and one or two others.

Sometimes doubt is based on sheer fatigue. You can't keep burning the candle at both ends without it affecting you. For Christians, perhaps this shows up first of all not in systematic doubt but in a sort of cynicism. Instead of a charitable outlook toward others, you begin to have a snarky outlook toward others. Pastors are good at this when they're tired. Sometimes the godliest thing in the entire universe that you can do is go to bed and get some sleep, not stay up and pray all night. There is a place for that, believe me, but sometimes the godliest thing you can do is go for a walk, come home, go to bed, and get a snooze.

Sometimes doubt is fostered not so much by deliberate philosophical and systemic choices as by unconsidered, morally obtuse, atomistic choices: thousands of them, all bad. Occasionally you see a man or a woman who has been faithful in the church for years, maybe high up in the church, having genuinely made a profession of faith; perhaps he served on the deacons' board or she served on a women's committee. The children are growing up, and as life goes on a little further, perhaps he rises to middle management in his company. He's putting in long, long hours at work. There's now a mortgage to pay; there's college education; his kid is in an expensive school; he can't let down the side at the company. Pretty soon if he shows up for church once a week on Sunday, even that's a bit much, and he's never at prayer meeting, and never at anything in any sort of self-sacrificial way. There's no testimony. There's no joy in the Lord anymore. Five years down the road, he wakes up one day and discovers that he's waking up in bed with the wrong woman. He gets up and looks at himself in the mirror in the washroom and says, "I don't believe all that anyway."

How did that come about? Was there some deep philosophical crisis? No. Was there a formal adoption of philosophical materialism? No. Has he been convinced by some of the contemporary atheists? No. It's come about by ten thousand little decisions, all of them bad . . . step by step, step by step.

I could give you more descriptions of the causes of doubt. Why have I taken this space to address this? Because you must see that when the Thomas passage addresses doubt, it is not addressing every kind of doubt. We must understand Thomas's doubt.

All the kinds of doubt I've talked about are depicted somewhere in the Bible. When you think of fatigue, for example, think of an Elijah. Think of where someone such as Demas ends up after a lot of little decisions, or think of someone such as the high priest at Jesus' trial, who got there in terms of a philosophical structure.

But in Thomas's case, may I remind you that Jesus has been crucified. Quite frankly, his own disciples had not expected Jesus to die, and then they didn't expect him to rise again. They did not expect the resurrection to take place, even though Jesus had announced it again and again and again. Every time he spoke, they didn't have a category for a crucified and risen Messiah. They thought in terms of a conquering king. So when he spoke that way, they thought to themselves, "Deep . . . deep . . . more enigmatic utterances from the Master. We'll understand someday." But they didn't have a clue. Not a clue. The proof positive, of course, is that once Jesus was in the grave, they were not in the upstairs room saying, "Oooh, yes. I can hardly wait until Sunday." They had no expectation of the resurrection. None.

And then Jesus appears, to the women, to Peter alone, at the empty tomb, on the Emmaus road, eventually to five hundred in Galilee. There are at least ten or eleven separate occurrences that we know about, in addition to however many appearances there were that we don't know about.

The Cry of a Disappointed Skeptic

But on the evening of that first Resurrection Sunday, Jesus appeared to the apostles—at least to ten of them. Judas had committed suicide, and Thomas wasn't there. So we pick up the narrative, and we learn, first, of the cry of a disappointed skeptic:

> Now Thomas (also known as Didymus), one of the Twelve, was not with the disciples when Jesus came. So the other disciples told him, "We have seen the Lord!" But he said to them, "Unless I see the nail marks in his hands and put my finger where the nails were, and put my hand into his side, I will not believe." (John 20:24–25)

What kind of doubt is that? That's not the doubt of a philosophical materialist—that is, a person who believes that there is nothing else but matter and energy and space and time. Thomas was, after all, a first-century, devout Jew. He was a monotheist. He believed in one God. Moreover, he was a monotheist in the Jewish heritage, who believed the Bible, what we call the Old Testament. He was a monotheist who believed that there is one God, the Creator, who made everything; he believed that there is a final coming end, a judgment that we must all finally face. He believed in the difference between right and wrong. He believed in the importance of the sacrificial system at the temple.

He had read and memorized the Ten Commandments. He was a first-century, devout, pious Jew. So what kind of doubt was it? It wasn't the doubt of somebody who had made ten thousand wrong decisions and ended up in bed with the wrong person. It wasn't even the doubt of someone who is exhausted, though he may have been tired at this juncture.

No, this is the doubt of someone who wants to distinguish between faith and gullibility. He had really believed that Jesus was the Messiah, just as all the other apostles had, but his expectation of what the Messiah was like did not include a suffering servant theme, a death and resurrection theme. A conquering king, yes. But executed in shame, ignominy, and horrible suffering on a cross? Messiahs don't die, especially if they can do the kinds of miracles Jesus did. They win, and they transform the nation. They don't become martyrs.

So deep was Thomas's disappointment that you can almost hear the gears in his brain going around. *I will not be snookered again. It may be that some of these fellow apostles of mine have talked themselves into this. They want Jesus back so badly they're denying the inevitable . . . it's a group hallucination. Who knows what they saw, but I can't believe this, and I'm not going to commit myself to something that is ephemeral and wishy-washy and based on the testimony of others. What I need is solid evidence that the body that went into the tomb is inescapably bound up with the body that came out, no twin brought in at the last moment. Hmm . . . maybe Jesus had an identical twin somewhere. But if he suddenly showed up, where are the marks of the nails? Or maybe they saw somebody who looks an awful lot like him. A really, really close counterpart. They say that high-flung politicos sometimes have doubles who take their places. Maybe Jesus has a high-flung double somewhere. Or maybe they saw somebody who had been crucified but somehow escaped?*

No, no, no. In the ancient world, when you were crucified, you hung tied or nailed to the cross, and you pushed with your legs and pulled with your arms to keep your chest cavity open so you could breathe. The muscle spasms would start, and you'd collapse. Then you couldn't breathe, so you'd pull and you'd push, and you'd breathe. Then you'd collapse, and this could go on for hours, even days. This is why, when the Romans wanted you to be taken down a little sooner, sometimes because of a local custom such as Passover, they'd come along and smash your shinbones. Then you couldn't push anymore, and you'd suffocate in a few minutes.

But when they got to Jesus, the account says, the soldiers found him already dead. One of the quaternion of soldiers took his short javelin and shoved it up under Jesus' ribcage and pierced his pericardium. That was an unusual wound. The others crucified with Jesus were not wounded that way. In fact, in all the ancient documents that have come down to us, or that we've read about, or that we've heard about from archaeological sites, we know of only one other case in which someone was wounded that way. There may have been others, of course, but we have evidence of only one other case in which someone was pierced with a javelin in crucifixion. So what does Thomas say? "Unless I see the nail marks in his hands and put my finger where the nails were and put my hand into his side, I will not believe."

This is the doubt of someone who does not want to be snookered by wishful thinking. That's not a bad kind of doubt. Oh, there's a sense in which, if he had been more insightful, had believed in Jesus' words, and had had a better grasp of biblical theology, he would have had a category for a crucified Messiah. In that sense, his doubt was bad. Here then is the cry of a disappointed skeptic.

The Adoration of an Astonished Skeptic

Next we come to the adoration of an astonished skeptic, and we come very close to the heart of this passage in verses 26–28:

> A week later his disciples were in the house again, and Thomas was with them. Though the doors were locked, Jesus came and stood among them and said, "Peace be with you!" Then he said to Thomas, "Put your finger here; see my hands. Reach out your hand and put it into my side. Stop doubting and believe." Thomas said to him, "My Lord and my God!"

Jesus greeted Thomas with what was probably the Hebrew *shalom* or the equivalent in Aramaic. Like the modern Arabic *salaam*, *shalom* can be used to mean nothing much more than "Hi there" or "Good-bye." But the word itself means "peace"— not just psychological well-being but well-being before God. There is no doubt that, both in the first week when Jesus used this expression and in this week, Jesus means it to be invested with huge theological weight. On the tail end of his death and resurrection, he is saying, "Peace be with you"—the *shalom*, the well-being before God that is presaged now and will come to fulfillment in the consummation is yours because he is here in his resurrected existence.

> Then he said to Thomas, "Put your finger here; see my hands. Reach out your hand. Put it into my side. Stop doubting and believe." Thomas said to him, "My Lord and my God!" (vv. 27–28)

What are we to make of this confession? Let me begin by mentioning how Jehovah's Witnesses and some other skeptics take it. Jehovah's Witnesses believe that the Bible is the inerrant Word of God, which means they can't simply say, "I don't believe this. This is rubbish." They have to have another interpretation. What sort of interpretation do they offer? They offer one of two. I'll mention only one here. Some say that what Thomas said when he saw the resurrected Christ was, "Uh! My lord, my god!" which would mean that Thomas's response was blasphemy.

Now, every culture has vulgarity and blasphemy—every culture. But to imagine that a first-century, pious Jew would choose as his form of blasphemy, at this point of sublime experience, the particular blasphemy that takes God's name in vain is simply historically inconceivable. It just wouldn't happen. Worse yet, Jesus then blesses him for getting it right. But the most difficult element of this interpretation is the little word *and*, because even if you could, in some wild stretch of the imagination, imagine that Thomas was blaspheming and saying, "My lord, my god," how do you turn that into "my lord and my god"? The other explanation offered by Jehovah's Witnesses is equally incredible, so much so that I will not recount it here.

But the question you and I must face when we stop to think about this passage in the flow of the narrative in John's gospel is this: why does Thomas confess so much? Why doesn't he simply say, "You're alive!" or "Oops, I was wrong" or simply "Jesus?" Why does he confess so much? "My Lord and my God!" The only way you can answer that question, it seems to me, is if you remember where it comes in the whole sequence of the book. You have a whole week between Jesus' appearance to the ten disciples on the first Sunday and his appearance to the eleven, including Thomas, on the second Sunday. There's no passage that says, "The following items were going through Thomas's head." But you are expected to read the narrative with a certain kind of sympathy. I can imagine, without any distortion of what you find in John's gospel, that he was thinking things like this:

These guys can't be right. It doesn't make any sense. I mean, it's just wishful thinking. Supposing they are right. No, no. It can't be. I've got to see. I've got to have good evidence. I don't want to get snookered. But supposing they are right. If they are right, what would that mean? He did say some awfully strange things. Just a few nights ago, the night that he was betrayed, he said things like, "Don't you know me, Philip, even after I have been among you such a long time? Anyone who has seen me has seen the Father."[2] We thought that was pretty strange when he said it that night. But suppose he was telling the truth. Does that make any sense at all? No, it can't be. This is ridiculous. I've got to see the evidence. But that's what he did say. He said some other strange things too. He said once, "Before Abraham was, I am."[3] We thought that was pretty over the top too. I mean, he's the Messiah, so of course we accepted it. He's saying enigmatic things all the time. We didn't always understand, but that was a bit over the top. You know? And he insisted that the Father's will was that "all may honor the Son just as they honor the Father."[4] That's pretty high too. If Jesus did rise from the dead, then maybe in some sense those things are really to be taken literally. Wait a minute. Wait a minute. What's the messianic passage from Isaiah? "For to us a child is born, to us a son is given."[5] He's going to be Davidic, you know. He will reign on the throne of his father David. "And he will be called Wonderful Counselor, Mighty God, Everlasting Father. . . . Of the increase of his government and peace there will be no end."[6]

2. John 14:9.
3. John 8:58 (ESV).
4. John 5:23.
5. Isaiah 9:6.
6. Isaiah 9:6–7.

He might have remembered other passages that aren't mentioned in John's gospel but are mentioned in the Synoptic Gospels. For example, Mark's gospel records how on one occasion Jesus was preaching in a crowded house with everybody standing, packed in like sardines. A paralyzed man heard that Jesus was nearby. He couldn't walk, but his four friends carried him on some sort of makeshift bed and tried to make a way into the house. "Excuse me. Excuse me. We've got a sick man here." "Wait your turn. The Master's talking. Don't be so pushy. Just wait your turn."

But they wouldn't wait, so they went up the outside stairs. So many of the houses in Jerusalem and in Galilee in those days had flat roofs where people went to catch the evening breeze, to cool down in days before air conditioning. They went up on the rooftop and listened until they got to the place over where Jesus was talking, and they started picking up the tiles. Then they lowered their friend down on rope. If the crowd wouldn't back out because of sympathy, maybe they would back out because a bed was coming down on their heads. Eventually the paralyzed person was in front of Jesus, and Jesus said, "Son, your sins are forgiven" (Mark 2:5). Immediately the theologians who were present said, "Who can forgive sins but God alone?" (v. 7).

We need to think about that utterance. Supposing, God forbid, a mugger and his gang stop you and beat you up badly. Maybe they gang rape you, and you end up close to the precipice of death in the hospital. Then I go to the ICU to see you and say, "I have some good news for you. I have found out who those muggers were, and I have forgiven them." What would you say to me? You would have an apoplectic fit, probably a heart attack right on the spot. Wouldn't you be spluttering, "What right do you have to say things like that? You aren't the one who was gang raped. You aren't the one who was mugged. Only the person who's been offended can forgive. You weren't offended. How can you possibly pronounce forgiveness in the name of somebody who was actually offended?"

At the end of World War II there was a young Jew in Auschwitz by the name of Simon Wiesenthal. His entire extended family had been wiped out. He was the only one still living. As he came in from a work detail at the end of a long day—at the end of the war, just weeks before the Russians came and freed Auschwitz—he was pulled out of the line by his guards, shoved into a room, and told, "Go in there, Jew."

What he found was a young German soldier, maybe nineteen or twenty years old, clearly on the point of death. He had taken some wounds and was not going to make it. On his deathbed, he had asked to talk to a Jew, and in the providence of God the Jew who was shoved into the room was Simon Wiesenthal. The Nazi wanted forgiveness. He said that not only had he been involved in horrible things toward the Jews, but he had come to realize that the whole Nazi scheme was wrong and evil, and he feared meeting God.

After the war Wiesenthal wrote about this in a little book called *The Sunflower*.[7] It's only about eighty pages long, and most of the pages are given over to what was passing through Wiesenthal's mind as he listened to the Nazi beg for forgiveness. Wiesenthal's reasoning, in brief, was this: *Who can forgive but those who have been most offended against? In Auschwitz, those most offended against are dead! I, who survive, do not have the right to pronounce forgiveness. Therefore, there is no forgiveness for the Nazis.* Without saying a single word, he turned and walked out of the room.

7. Simon Wiesenthal, *The Sunflower* (New York: Schocken Books, 1976).

After the war was over Wiesenthal wrote this up and got it published. He sent his book to many, many ethicists all over the world, both Jewish and Christian, and asked the question, "Did I do what was right, or was I wrong?" That generated a huge discussion in ethical circles.

From a Christian perspective, he was almost right. He was very close to right. Only the offended party can forgive. But what he overlooked is that the most offended party is always God. David understood that after his wretched sin with Bathsheba. He had seduced a young woman, eventually having her husband killed in a wretched plot. He thought he had gotten away with it . . . until Nathan the prophet confronted him. After David had become broken over all this, he eventually wrote Psalm 51.

In the context of his public confession in Psalm 51, David includes the words addressed to God: "Against you, you only, have I sinned and done what is evil in your sight" (v. 4). At one level, this is a load of rubbish. He had certainly sinned against the young woman; he had seduced her. He had sinned against her husband; he had had him bumped off. He had sinned against the military high command; he had corrupted them. He had sinned against his family; he had betrayed them. He had sinned against the baby in Bathsheba's womb. He had sinned against the people; he was supposed to be the chief magistrate. It's hard to think of anybody whom he *hadn't* sinned against. Yet he has the cheek to say, "Against you, you only, have I sinned and done what is evil in your sight." At a certain level, he was exactly right, because what makes sin distinctively sin—what makes it so heinous, what makes it so damnable—is that it is an offense against God.

If you cheat on your income tax this year, the most offended party is not Uncle Sam. It's God Almighty. If you sleep around, the most offended party, if he or she finds out, is not your spouse. It's God Almighty. If you nurture bitterness, the most offended party is not the one against whom you are bitter. It's God Almighty. This is why, from the Bible's point of view, however much we ought to see personal forgiveness at the horizontal level, what we must have above all is God's forgiveness—or we have nothing. God is the most offended party. That's what the gospel is about.

When Jesus said to the paralyzed man, "Son, your sins are forgiven," the theologians had it basically right when they thought, "Who can forgive sins but God alone?" (Mark 2:7). The paralyzed man hadn't mugged Jesus recently. He hadn't punched him in a drunken brawl at the end of a bar fight. There was no history or personal knowledge of abuse, so far as the record goes. Yet Jesus pronounced the kind of forgiveness that belongs to God alone. Who can forgive sins but God alone? Just so. And Thomas was there.

All these experiences cascaded through Thomas's mind as he had a week to think things over. They're part of the historical narrative, both in John's gospel and in the Synoptic Gospels. When he actually did see the resurrected Christ and the offer was made, "Put your finger here; see my hands. Reach out your hand and put it into my side," he had thought about them enough to know there was only one sufficient acclamation at that point. He said, "My Lord and My God!"

It may be that Thomas had gotten a step farther. It soon dawned on Christians who had not been expecting the death or the resurrection that this was not an accident in history. This was God's plan from the beginning. They found the Scriptures that actually pointed in this direction through great typological threads and trajectories that ran right through the whole Bible. They had to understand that Jesus' death and resurrection were not merely dramatic events or things that attested to who he was as a kind of proof—"I can do this after all"—but things that accomplished something.

What were they doing? Writing these words several decades later and thinking through all these things, John the Evangelist gave hints all through his book of how Jesus had presented teaching all along the line that pointed in the right direction. Whether Thomas understood it at this stage or whether it took a few more weeks before the pennies really dropped, I don't know. Certainly the understanding of these things unfolds in the book of Acts as you watch Christians think through the implications of Jesus' death and resurrection.

In John 10, for example, Jesus is presented as the good shepherd. "The good shepherd lays down his life for his sheep" (v. 11). "I beg your pardon," you might say. "What sort of nonsense is that? A good shepherd might risk his life for his sheep, but he doesn't lay down his life for his sheep. If he accidentally loses his life, fair enough. But he doesn't lay it down. That's ridiculous." But that's what Jesus says. Then, in case anybody misses the point, he says, "No one takes it from me, but I lay it down of my own accord. I have authority to lay it down and authority to take it up again. This command I received from my Father" (v. 18). And he calls that being a good shepherd? Suddenly this metaphor is pushed in a direction that can make sense only in the light of Jesus' voluntary self-sacrifice on the cross and in the resurrection that comes out the other side. But there's no way that at the time the disciples understood what he said about dying as the shepherd *for* the sheep, so that the sheep themselves may have eternal life. The passage is explicit.

Then there's the Bread of Life passage in John 6. You must eat Jesus' flesh and drink his blood. It sounds barbaric. The opponents abandoned Jesus at this point. His own disciples didn't have a clue what was going on. Jesus asked them if they too wanted to leave him. At least they said, following the example of Peter, "Lord, to whom shall we go? You have the words of eternal life" (v. 68). But they weren't saying, "We understand this. This is deep theology, but we've got it." No. They trusted Jesus at this point, but they didn't have it. In retrospect it becomes pretty obvious.

When you dine out, suppose you stop at McDonald's and eat a hamburger. What will you be eating? Dead cow. Dead lettuce. Dead tomato. Dead cucumber, dead pickle, dead barley, dead wheat, dead poppy seeds. Everything you eat in that hamburger will be dead . . . except for a few minerals such as salt, of which there will probably be too much. Everything else is dead. In fact, you might say it all died for you, because, quite frankly, unless it dies, you die. If that cow, lettuce, tomato, and so on all remained alive, you would die because you would have nothing to eat.

We don't make that connection today because most of us no longer live on farms. Our food comes from the grocery store. It's wrapped in cellophane. It's found in boxes. People who were brought up in an agrarian society know that food comes from plants and animals, and either they die or you do. They understand substitutionary death. Not for a moment am I suggesting it's voluntary, but I am suggesting it's substitutionary. Either it dies or you die.

Jesus dares to explain that it's a metaphor. He says, "I am the bread of life"—the one who comes to me and feeds on me will not perish (v. 35). He shows that it's not a question of eating in the literal, cannibalistic sense. When I decide to have a sandwich, I might get the bread out, but I will not stare at the bread and say, "Bread, I come to you." That's not what we do with bread. We just eat it. The reason that Jesus can use this language, "Whoever comes to me" and "Whoever believes on me" (v. 35), is to show that the language of eating and drinking is finally metaphorical. It's metaphorical with a point—namely that the only way you have Jesus' life is because he dies.

There is no way the disciples understood that. But suddenly you not only have the God-man die self-sacrificially in a substitutionary way, vindicated by the resurrection to guarantee that this life is distributed to those whom the Father has given . . . suddenly the pieces of the theology of John's gospel begin to come together. I could go through John's gospel and show you how there are elements in every chapter that point forward to the cross. John has got it by the time he writes his book. Whether Thomas got it all at this early stage I'm not sure, but John certainly got it when he was writing this book.

World War I—the Great War, "the war to end all wars"— was one of the stupidest wars ever fought. I suppose there are some stupidities in all wars, but some are grounded in important principles. That one was grounded in nothing but greed, name-calling, and lust for power. It was horrendous: a twenty-three-hundred-mile trench across Europe with howitzers and machine guns on both sides, mowing each other down. In four years, ten million all told died in an incredibly stupid war. One of those who survived on the British side was C. S. Lewis, part of a small coterie of poets who produced some of the most moving war poetry I have ever read.

One of the poems was "Jesus of the Scars," written by Edward Shillito. Much of the language of that poem is drawn from one particular scene. Earlier in the poem, Shillito describes how the heavens seem bronze and they frighten us; there is no

peace, and there is suffering and noise and terror everywhere.
Then he writes:

> If, when the doors are shut, Thou drawest near,
> Only reveal those hands, that side of Thine;
> We know to-day what wounds are, have no fear,
> Show us Thy scars, we know the countersign.
>
> The other gods were strong; but Thou wast weak;
> They rode, but Thou didst stumble to a throne;
> But to our wounds only God's wounds can speak;
> And not a god has wounds, but Thou alone.[8]

Suddenly this death and resurrection are more than a vindi-
catory act of power. It is now the very climax of God's purposes
in redemption. It is the vindication of God. It is the triumph of
death over life. It is the God-man bearing our sins, vindicated
utterly in the plan of God in such a credible way that God's
wounds speak!

How much Thomas understood at this stage, I don't know.
But John understood it. The reader of this gospel cannot help
but see it, for all the pieces are carefully put in place by Christ
in enigmatic language in the days of his flesh, until you come
to this climactic scene.

We cannot leave this confession without reflecting on
the little word *my*. This is not a liturgical formulation. Then
it would be *our*. It would be first person plural: "Our Lord
and our God, we bow in thy presence." That's not what it
is. It's "my Lord and my God." At the end of the day, this
must be a personal confession with personal faith, personal
testimony, and personal acknowledgment of who Jesus is,

8. Edward Shillito, *Jesus of the Scars*, 1919.

or it is worth nothing to you. The confession is not mere confessionalism.

The Particular Function of a Converted Skeptic

Here again the resurrection is supremely unpacked in verses 29–31. "Then Jesus told him, 'Because you have seen me, you have believed; blessed are those who have not seen and yet have believed'" (v. 29). I suspect that many of us suppose that the meaning of this verse runs something as follows: "Dear old Thomas at least got it right at the end. He had to have an actual sign. He had to have the proof of the miracle, and so he believed. Not bad. But it would have been a lot better if he had just taken Jesus at his word. Blessed rather are those who do not see and yet believe. Why do you have to ask for signs? Why do you have to ask for miracles? Just believe." A lot of Christians understand the verse this way: any faith that demands this sort of sign is a second-class faith. Really good faith, spiritually deep faith, is faith that is independent of signs. It just trusts Jesus' Word.

Is that what's going on? Very doubtful.

First, this view is much too tied to contemporary understandings of what faith is. If you have a roving mike and go to people on the street and say, "What do you think faith is?" what will you hear? Unless you stumble across an informed Christian, what do you think the answer will be? Overwhelmingly in Western culture today, the answers will be along one of two lines. The first is that faith is a synonym for religion. There are many faiths; there are many religions. The second is that faith is a personal, subjective, religious choice. That is, it's abstracted from questions of truth. It's abstracted from questions of revelation. That's why so many people say you can't argue about faith: because it's personal. You have *your* faith; I have *my* faith. What's to be said after that?

This view gets put into remarkable places. Take *The Da Vinci Code* by Dan Brown. That book swept the continent and became a film. Many people enjoyed it immensely, and its view of faith perfectly reflects dominant views in our culture today. At one point Sophie responds to a statement from Langdon by saying, "But you told me the New Testament is based on fabrications." You already know that this is not typical evangelicalism.

"Langdon smiled. 'Sophie, *every* faith in the world is based on fabrication. That is the definition of faith—acceptance of that which we imagine to be true, that which we cannot prove.' "[9]

Even on its own merits, that statement is idiotic. It's idiotic because it is deeply inconsistent. It's one thing to say that faith is based on something we cannot prove; it's a quite different thing to say that every faith in the world is based on fabrication. If your faith is based on fabrication and you know that, then it is not properly grounded. You know that it is false. Langdon wants to destroy Christianity on two separate grounds that are not mutually compatible: On the one hand, it's grounded on fabrication. It's just made up. On the other hand, he softens it a bit and says it's grounded on stuff you can't prove. It's a personal, subjective, religious choice. That view of faith is found everywhere—in the media, in film, in books. It is simply everywhere.

What If There Is No Resurrection?

This view will not square with the New Testament. Consider the apostle Paul, writing about the resurrection in 1 Corinthians 15.

9. Dan Brown, *The Da Vinci Code* (New York: Anchor Books, 2013), 448.

The Corinthians were having trouble with a whole category of resurrection, so Paul teases out the implications of their unbelief. He says, "Okay, suppose for a moment there is no such thing as resurrection. Let's tease out what follows from that assumption."

First, if there is no such thing as resurrection, then Jesus did not rise from the dead. In other words, Paul wants the Corinthians to see that Jesus' resurrection from the dead, which they do believe in, establishes a baseline for a final resurrection. But if there's no resurrection at the end, as they believe, then why do they even believe that Jesus is resurrected from the dead? Okay, so Jesus is not resurrected from the dead.

Second, he says, "You are still in your sins" (v. 17). On the assumption that everything else the Bible says is true—that we're damned before God, that we need a sacrifice, that we can't pay the redemption price ourselves, and that we're all sinners—if Jesus has died without any theological significance as the victim of some vicious, wretched first-century plot at the eastern end of the Mediterranean, then why on earth should you think that his death is, in any sense, a victory for us on the ground of our faith? At the end of the day, you're still a damned breed. You are still lost in your trespasses and sins.

Not only so, Paul says, but the witnesses who claimed they saw Jesus resurrected are all a bunch of liars. The apostles and the other five hundred witnesses Paul mentions are not telling the truth. They've either deluded themselves or they're mass liars. They might be liars who are willing to suffer and even be martyred, but at the end of the day, you can't believe a word they say. They're claiming that Jesus' resurrection is historically real when there is no such thing as resurrection.

On top of that, Paul says, "Your faith is futile" (v. 17). Do you see what that means? Faith is futile if you believe something that is not true. One of the things that marks true faith is the truthfulness of faith's object. That's why the Bible never, ever comes along and says, "Don't ask stupid questions. Just believe. Shut up and believe. It doesn't matter whether it's true or not, just believe. Shut up. Believe." The way the Bible fosters faith is by articulating and defending the truth. That's the way faith is fostered. The Bible never asks you to believe what is not true. It never asks you to believe what may not be true. If it is genuine at all, genuine faith must have as its presupposition the truthfulness of that which is its object.

Of course, I still insist that genuine saving faith is more than that. After all, the Devil himself can believe that Jesus rose from the dead. The Devil himself can believe certain true things, but there is no trust component to his faith. Faith is more than believing that certain propositions are true. The Devil himself can believe these propositions to be true and know nothing of saving faith. Faith is never *less* than having true things as its object. This is so much the case that Paul goes even further in 1 Corinthians 15; he says that if you believe that Jesus rose from the dead when, in fact, he did not rise from the dead, not only is your faith futile, but you are of all people most to be pitied (v. 19). If you build your whole life around the supposition that something is true when in fact it is not true, you're a joke.

This is the common assumption in the whole Bible, so that Christians are encouraged to rest their whole lives—their direction, their priorities, their goals, their marriages, their pocketbook, their priorities, their aims, their hopes, their prayers, what they live for, what they die for—all on the ground of certain things that are true. In that sense we are encouraged to believe and to trust but never, ever simply to take a running leap into the great unknown . . . which may or may not be true, but it doesn't really matter as long as you think it's true. It's good enough for you.

There are many people in our day and age for whom Jesus' resurrection isn't deemed necessary, because they've been taught, and have come to believe, that he "lives within my heart," and that's the only important thing. But that's not what Paul says. Paul says that if Jesus hasn't risen from the dead, you're a joke. Your whole life is ridiculous.

What is going on with Thomas? You can see more clearly if you link verse 29 with verses 30–31:

> Then Jesus told him, "Because you have seen me, you have believed; blessed are those who have not seen and yet have believed."
>
> Jesus performed many other signs in the presence of his disciples, which are not recorded in this book. But these are written that you may believe that Jesus is the Messiah, the Son of God, and that by believing you may have life in his name.

To Thomas it was given to see that sign that was grounded in history. The other apostles were given the same evidences, as well as the five hundred who saw Jesus risen from the dead. Out of this came all the theology of the resurrection, so that Christ's resurrection life is pulsating within us, and one day we have the promise of resurrection existence in the new heaven and the new earth. God has vindicated Jesus, utterly satisfied with Jesus' death on the cross, and that's why Jesus has risen from the dead. So much theology surrounds the resurrection of Jesus, and it is all grounded in the history, in the indubitable space-time history, that Jesus did rise from the dead. This was attested to by witnesses.

These Are Written That You May Believe

Jesus knew full well that he was going back to heaven. In fact, a little earlier in John 20, he told Mary Magdalene to stop hanging on to him. He hadn't gone away *yet*, but that presupposes that he was going away. It was only a few weeks before the ascension. After that, you can be a Thomas all you like; you can ask for signs that Jesus did rise from the dead, ask to put your fingers into the wounds in his hands, ask to put your fist into the wound in his side, and that sign is not going to be given you. Jesus is gone, and he's not coming back until the end of the age. Blessed therefore are all those who are still coming down the road, who do not see but yet believe. That's what Jesus has in mind in verse 29, and the connection between Thomas and all those converts is precisely the witness of Thomas and the other apostles and the writer of this book. "These are written that you may believe" (v. 31).

God has disclosed himself in history. There are all kinds of things we cannot know about God from the merely historical arena. Words must be given; men were inspired by God to put down the words that we have in Scripture. I'm not denying that our knowledge of God comes by direct inspiration of ancient writers who put down these words in a book that we may study and read them and know them. That's true.

But God has also disclosed himself in supreme events—in the burning bush, in the exodus, in the giving of the law at Sinai. These are not just ideas. These are events in space-time history. They really happened. There were people who were there, and the access that we have to those events, since we were *not* there, is through their witness. This is precisely why the witness theme is so strong in John's gospel, in the book of Acts, and elsewhere.

When the apostles are told to shut up about Jesus' resurrection in the book of Acts, their answer is, "We cannot help but speak what we have seen and heard" (4:20). Witness. Witness. Witness. Thomas has been granted by God the privilege of witnessing the resurrection with the consequence that he is incorporated into this book, which itself becomes a written testimony to their historical witnesses. "These are written that you may believe that Jesus is the Messiah, the Son of God, and that by believing you may have life in his name" (John 20:31).

As you think of the risen Christ and of all that the resurrection is bound up with, in terms of vindicating God, in terms of the promise of resurrection existence for us, you see all the anticipation of what is yet to come and you see that it is grounded in what takes place in history. Its purpose is evangelism.

"These are written that you may believe that Jesus is the Messiah, the Son of God, and that by believing you may have life in his name" (v. 31). This commands that you bend your knee and raise your heart heavenward and say, "Lord, I believe. Help my unbelief." For we who already believe, it not only demands that we more greatly appreciate and adore God for what he has done in the space-time resurrection of his blessed Son, but it also impels us to bear witness to this truth, based on what has been reported in his Word as to what took place in space-time history. "The Word was made flesh and made his dwelling among us" (John 1:14). The Word, in flesh, died and rose again, and there were witnesses. We based everything in our lives on the truth of the resurrection of Jesus Christ from the dead. This vindicates all his previous utterances, so that we bow before him and join with Thomas and joyfully say, "My Lord and my God!" and understand that the promulgation of this message is that men and women may believe and have life.

PART 3

God the Holy Spirit

11

Streams of Living Water

D. A. CARSON

FOR MANY YEARS I lived in England—nine or ten years scattered over the last three decades. Scores of times I have landed at one or the other of England's airports. Provided the whole place wasn't fogged in, I always marveled at how much greenery I could see as I landed. Almost always, everything was green. Only two of the eleven or twelve summers that I spent there did I land and see some brown because they were having a bit of a drought.

Now I live in Chicago, and sometimes when I land, everything is white. Even in the summer, it's rare that I land and everything is green. A green strip runs through the whole area—the Des Plaines River system—and of course there are all kinds of green patches from people watering their gardens, but a lot of summers, everything in sight is basically brown. I have some good friends who live in Phoenix, and when I land there, everything is brown for miles around—except from five or six miles up you can see the perfectly circular patches of green, with long irrigation wheels that sweep around very, very slowly, in the Ogallala aquifer.

Such experiences drive home, in visceral ways, the connection between water and life. They're the sorts of experiences that anybody brought up in an agrarian climate knows all the time. But most of us don't come from a farm. When we have a drought, we discover we can't water our lawns every day; it's got to be every second or third day. In most drought situations, nobody's saying we have to share our bathwater. We don't make the same sorts of connections, do we?

Yet John 7 makes the connection between water and life. In a nutshell, that's what this passage presupposes. More precisely, it draws the connection between water and the life-giving Spirit. Yet for all its fundamental simplicity, this passage carries layers of Old Testament allusions, plus one or two disputed points, such that it is well worth our while to follow attentively so that we hear well what God is telling us in this passage.

It will help, I think, to organize our study into three parts.

Setting the Stage for Rivers of Living Water

First, it is important to understand the background of the passage both in the Old Testament and in Judaism. Verse 37 begins "On the last and greatest day of the festival . . ." What festival? And why is this recorded? The festival is the Feast of Tabernacles, or the Feast of Booths, mentioned in John 7:2. The Feast of Tabernacles found the majority of the citizens of Jerusalem putting up little booths, the equivalent of tents, to remember the time when they were not well established in the land. Before they had got into the Promised Land, they had been pilgrims on the way, and this reminded them of that time.

The festival also came to be very much associated with harvest. This is one of two connections between John 7:37–39 and the preceding chapter. The other connection has to do with the mention of Jesus' departure, which is seen in the last clause in verse 39: "Up to that time the Spirit had not been given, since Jesus had not yet been glorified." We'll come back to that.

In the preceding verses we read,

> Jesus said, "I am with you for only a short time, and then I go to the one who sent me. You will look for me, but you will not find me; and where I am, you cannot come." The Jews said to one another, "Where does this man intend to go that we cannot find him? Will he go where our people live scattered among the Greeks, and teach the Greeks? What did he mean when he said, 'You will look for me, but you will not find me,' and 'Where I am, you cannot come'?" (John 7:33–36)

Already Jesus is talking about his departure, a theme that becomes more and more focused and tied to the Holy Spirit, as we shall see as the book progresses.

The Feast of Tabernacles was a seven-day feast; the devout were supposed to spend seven days in the booths. On the seventh day, a golden flagon of water was filled at the Pool of Siloam and then carried in procession by the high priest to the temple. As the procession approached the water gate on the south side of the inner court, there were three loud blasts of the *shofar*, the trumpet of joy, and then the priests marched through the gate and then around the altar with a flagon. The pilgrims watched and choirs sang the *Hallel*, Psalms 113–18. When they got to the last of these, Psalm 118, every male pilgrim shook a *lulav*—a mix of willow and myrtle branches, twigs tied together with a palm. Each waved the *lulav* in his right hand and in the left hand held a piece of citrus fruit, signifying that this was the time of harvest. Give God thanks for all things, because he is the one who gives us the rain, enables us to eat and keep our stomachs full, and supplies our needs. It was a kind of harvest festival as well as a time for remembering the pilgrim years.

At the end of this, all cried three times, very loudly, "Give thanks to the Lord! Give thanks to the Lord! Give thanks to the Lord!" Then the water was offered to God at the time of the morning sacrifice; along with the wine offering, it was poured out before the Lord. In Jewish thought, this pouring out of the water at the Feast of Tabernacles symbolized God pouring out his Holy Spirit in the last days. It signaled a stream of life-giving water poured out and flowing over the whole earth, as was expected in the Messianic Age because of several Old Testament passages.

This water rite was not ordained in the Old Testament, but at the time of the New Testament it had already been observed for about two hundred years and was an annual event at the time of the Feast of Booths. That is the setting for what John reports:

> On the last and greatest day of the festival, Jesus stood and said in a loud voice, "Let anyone who is thirsty come to me and drink. Whoever believes in me, as Scripture has said, rivers of living water will flow from within them." (7:37–38)

Because of the symbolism of the feast, the words have all the more power. That's the first observation on the background.

But we also have to ask, "What is the last and greatest day of the feast?" If it's a seven-day feast, and this takes place on the last day, you would think it must be the seventh day. That makes sense, but by the first century, the eighth day was seen as a special day of celebration as well. On the eighth day, there was a joyful dismantling of the booths, symbolizing that the people of Israel were now in the land. In the first century, many people did speak of this day, this eighth day, as the last day of the feast. For example, when the first-century historian Josephus speaks of the last day of the Feast of Booths, he means the eighth day. This was also a day of rest—a special, additional Sabbath put into the calendar. Again there was the repeated singing of the *Hallel*.

I don't know for sure, but this was probably the eighth day, in which case there may be an additional edge to what Jesus says. He waits until everything is dismantled. They've sung their psalms for the last time. The festival has come to an end. It's the last day. Then he says, "Let anyone who is thirsty come to me and drink." This is certainly in line with one of the major approaches of John's gospel, which shows that Jesus is the ultimate Passover, the ultimate Feast of Booths, and the ultimate Lamb of God. He is the one to whom these Old Testament structures have been pointing all along.

That brings me to the third element in the background. Many Old Testament texts connect water and life or water and the Holy Spirit. Let me list just a handful:

- In Zechariah 14, for example, there is a connection between the Feast of Tabernacles, at harvest, and good rainfall. Zechariah 14 was certainly read in the Jewish liturgies at the time of the Feast of Tabernacles.
- Remember the words of Isaiah 12:3: "With joy you will draw water from the wells of salvation."
- There is the wonderful passage in Isaiah 55: "Come, all you who are thirsty, come to the waters; and you who have no money, come, buy and eat! Come, buy wine and milk without money and without cost" (v. 1).

243

- Ezekiel 47:1–9 pictures eschatological waters of life—that is, waters on the last day giving eternal life to the people of God.
- Ezekiel 36:25–27 promises water and the Spirit. In my view, that passage lies behind John 3 and the promise of the new birth.
- Isaiah 58:11 says, "The Lord will guide you always. . . . You will be like a well-watered garden, like a spring whose waters never fail."

The last element in the background is this: to get at the Old Testament background more closely, we must make a translation decision. You see, in the first century, the manuscripts were written in capital letters and without punctuation, which means that every once in a while you can debate where you should put the punctuation. This is one of those debates. Different punctuation gives you a slightly different reading.

The TNIV text reads, "On the last and greatest day of the festival, Jesus stood and said in a loud voice, 'If anyone is thirsty let him come to me and drink." Period. "Whoever believes in me, as the Scripture has said . . ." And so forth.

But there is the possibility of a slightly different reading. The NIV footnote suggests putting a comma after "to me" in verse 37: "If anyone is thirsty let him come to me, and let him drink who believes in me." That makes a little couplet. It means that the next words, "As Scripture has said," begin a sentence, and if we read that sentence in the NIV, it says, "As the Scripture has said, streams of living water will flow from within him." Because you've begun with "As Scripture says," then "from within him" at the end of the sentence may refer not to the believer but to Jesus. So the flow of the passage in that case reads, "If anyone is thirsty let him come to me, and let him drink whoever believes in me. [After all,] as the Scripture has said, streams of living water will flow from within [Christ]"—within Jesus, who is standing up and speaking these words.[1]

That is why this is sometimes called the christological interpretation. It is certainly in line with things that are said later in the gospel of John, after all. In the farewell discourse, Jesus connects his own going away with the giving of the Spirit: because he goes away, the Father will send the Holy Spirit.

Yet with all due respect, although this is probably the dominant view today, I think it is mistaken. I think the TNIV text has it right. This turns out to be very important. The little phrase "Whoever believes in me," which begins verse 38, is used forty-one times in John's gospel, and in every other passage, without exception, it begins the sentence. That means you really ought to put a period just before it. "Let anyone who is thirsty come to me and drink. Whoever believes in me, as Scripture has said, rivers of living water will flow from within them."

That means that the "within them" refers to the believer, and that too is well in line with what Scripture says in John's gospel. For example, in John 4:13–14, in the interchange between Jesus and the woman at the well, Jesus says, "Everyone who drinks this water [from the well] will be thirsty again, but whoever drinks the water I give them will never thirst. Indeed, the water I give them will become in them a spring of water welling up to eternal life." That's what's being said here as well. "Let anyone who is thirsty come to me and drink. Whoever believes in me,

1. Editor's note: Carson's choice of the TNIV as his preferred translation presents a bit of a problem, in that the TNIV translates verse 38 as "rivers of living water will flow from within them." Here the word *them* is used as a gender-neutral alternative to *him*, the word used in the NIV, the ESV, and most other translations. In the TNIV's rendering, Carson's point about the christological interpretation is less clear, as *them* distances itself from reference to a single man.

as Scripture has said, streams of living water will flow up from within them."

Jesus is not promising that streams of living water will flow up from within the believer and spread to a lot of other people. That may be true, but it's not the point here. The point rather is that this water promised by Jesus, given by Jesus as its source, wells up from within the believer and transforms his or her entire life.

In that case, this little phrase "as Scripture has said" prompts us to look for Old Testament texts that speak of the Spirit of God welling up within us to transform us, to change us, to renew us. I don't think there is one particular Old Testament text in view; I suspect there may be a whole lot of them, such as the ones I've already noted. But there is one other Old Testament passage I should mention, which begins in Nehemiah 8:5 and ends in Nehemiah 9:21. The scene is the reading and explaining of Scripture when Ezra joins up with the returnees at the end of the exile. In this regard he is obeying what Deuteronomy commanded centuries earlier.

> Then Moses commanded them: "At the end of every seven years, in the year for canceling debts, during the Festival of Tabernacles, when all Israel comes to appear before the LORD your God at the place he will choose, you shall read this law before them in their hearing." (Deut. 31:10–11)

We find Ezra doing exactly that in Nehemiah 8:

> Ezra opened the book. All the people could see him because he was standing above them; and as he opened it, the people all stood up. Ezra praised the LORD, the great God; and all the people lifted their hands and responded, "Amen! Amen!" Then they bowed down and worshiped the LORD with their faces to the ground.

The Levites—Jeshua, Bani, Sherebiah, Jamin, Akkub, Shabbethai, Hodiah, Maaseiah, Kelita, Azariah, Jozabad, Hanan and Pelaiah—instructed the people in the Law while the people were standing there. They read from the Book of the Law of God, making it clear and giving the meaning so that the people understood what was being read.

Then Nehemiah the governor, Ezra the priest and teacher of the Law, and the Levites who were instructing the people said to them all, "This day is holy to the LORD your God. Do not mourn or weep." For all the people had been weeping as they listened to the words of the Law.

Nehemiah said, "Go and enjoy choice food and sweet drinks, and send some to those who have nothing prepared. This day is holy to our Lord. Do not grieve, for the joy of the LORD is your strength." (vv. 5–10)

Day after day, from the first day to the last, Ezra read from the Book of the Law of God. They celebrated the festival for seven days, and on the eighth day, in accordance with the regulation, there was an assembly. (v. 18)

In chapter 9 as the Israelites confess their sin, we read these words:

You came down on Mount Sinai; you spoke to them from heaven. You gave them regulations and laws that are just and right, and decrees and commands that are good. You made known to them your holy Sabbath and gave them commands, decrees and laws through your servant Moses. In their hunger you gave them bread from heaven and in their thirst you brought them water from the rock; you told them to go in and take possession of the land you had sworn with uplifted hand to give them. . . . Because of your great compassion you did not abandon them in the wilderness. By day the pillar of cloud did not fail to guide them on their path, nor the pillar of fire by night to shine on the way they were to take. You gave your good Spirit to instruct them. You did not withhold your manna from their mouths, and you gave them water for their thirst. For forty years you sustained them in the wilderness; they lacked nothing, their clothes did not wear out nor did their feet become swollen. (vv. 13–15, 19–21)

All this was in connection with the Feast of Tabernacles once the people returned to the land. Don't forget that John 7 is linked with John 6. What is John 6 about? The bread from heaven. It's the Bread of Life discourse, in which Jesus is shown to be the true manna. Now in chapter 7, he is shown to be the true water. He is shown to be bringing this promised Spirit to fulfillment. So tot up the number of links between these verses and Nehemiah 8–9:

- It is the Feast of Tabernacles.
- The seven days are mentioned.
- The eighth day is mentioned.
- The bread from heaven is mentioned in the preceding chapter.
- The water from the rock is mentioned.
- The good Spirit is promised.
- The thirst of the people is mentioned.

All this is saying, in effect, that however vital, powerful, and moving the moment was as the returnees gathered around the Word of God centuries before the coming of Jesus, now it is fulfilled in this: "Let anyone who is thirsty come to me." This is the background of the passage.

The Holy Spirit in John's Gospel

Now we come to the context of the passage in John's gospel. It may help us here to look at a handful of the passages that mention the Holy Spirit in John's gospel, so that we can see how John 7 fits into this stream of argument.

- In John 1:33–34, John the Baptist is speaking. This particular utterance is one of the rare utterances to be recorded in all four Synoptic Gospels, and in the first chapter of the book of Acts: "'The man on whom you see the Spirit come down and remain is the one who will baptize with the Holy Spirit.' I have seen and I testify that this is God's Chosen One." Elsewhere we read that John "baptized with water, but he comes to baptize in the Holy Spirit" (Mark 1:8). After all, at Jesus' own baptism, Jesus is the one on whom the Holy Spirit rests.
- We are told powerfully in John 3:34 that "the one whom God has sent speaks the words of God, for God gives the Spirit [to him] without limit."
- In John 3 we are told of this new birth of water and the Spirit.
- In John 14–16, in five memorable passages as Jesus is about to go home by way of the cross and resurrection, he promises that when he goes he will send the Counselor, the *Paraclete*, the one who comes alongside, the one who will succeed him in being with his disciples. The Counselor will convict the world of sin, and he will give them life, and he will explain to them what Jesus' words really mean, and he will be with them forever. He proceeds from God—and this all in the wake of Jesus' triumph on the cross. In fact, Jesus goes so far as to say, "It is for your good that I go away, because if I don't go the Holy Spirit will not come" (see John 16:7).

249

So there are huge gospel connections between the Holy Spirit theme in John's gospel and the coming of Jesus, the good news of his coming, what he comes for, what he comes to do—the gospel itself.

Now we are ready to look at the argument of John 7 in its immediate flow.

Let us examine the claim Jesus makes. "Let anyone who is thirsty come to me and drink. Whoever believes in me, as Scripture has said, rivers of living water will flow from within them." That's the claim, and in verse 39 there is the identification. John the Evangelist writes, "By this he meant the Spirit, whom those who believed in him were later to receive." So now, unambiguously, we are told that this water language finds its fulfillment in the gift of the Holy Spirit, who was to be poured out after Jesus had risen again. The explanation for this is given in the second part of verse 39: "Up to that time the Spirit had not been given, since Jesus had not yet been glorified."

It is crucial to see that, for all the continuity in the Bible regarding God's plan of salvation, there is a ratcheting up along the line of redemptive history.

Let me approach this tangentially. Some people say erroneously that in the Old Testament, God presents himself as a God of wrath. Look at all those passages that sanction genocide. Read Ezekiel 4–5, read huge swaths of Isaiah. Read about the wars against the Amalekites. But when you come to the new covenant Scriptures, you find a gentler, kinder God. After all, Jesus says to turn the other cheek (Matt. 5:39). There is no longer a tendency toward genocide, is there? Now we're supposed to forgive our enemies. Vengeance belongs to the Lord alone (Rom. 12:19). So when you move from the old covenant to the new, some argue what you really have is movement from God displaying himself in wrath to God displaying himself in kindness. It's often said that way. Whether it's true is another manner, but I suspect that most of us are slightly uncomfortable when we hear things like that, because we don't want to believe it, but deep down we have a sneaky suspicion that maybe it's not too far from the truth.

Yet it really is deeply mistaken. In the Old Testament God presents himself again and again as one who is slow to anger, plenteous in mercy. He will not always chide . . . and so on and so on. In the New Testament there are passages like this one:

> Another angel came out of the temple in heaven, and he too had a sharp sickle. Still another angel, who had charge of the fire, came from the altar and called in a loud voice to him who had the sharp sickle, "Take your sharp sickle and gather the clusters of grapes from the earth's vine, because its grapes are ripe." The angel swung his sickle on the earth, gathered its grapes and threw them into the great winepress of God's wrath. They were trampled in the winepress outside the city, and blood flowed out of the press, rising as high as the horses' bridles for a distance of 1,600 stadia. (Rev. 14:17–20)

It was not uncommon on a well-to-do farm in the first century to gather clusters of grapes and put them in a great stone vat. The servant girls would kick off their sandals and roll up their robes a bit, and then they would go in and start squishing down the grapes. There were little holes at the bottom of the vat, and the grape juice wandered off into channels and was collected. Then you could make your wine. But in this particular case, what is being pictured is people being thrown in. This is now the great winepress of God's wrath, and as people are being tromped down, their blood is rising to the horses' bridles for a distance of 1,600 stadia, about three hundred miles. Now tell me that the God of the New Testament is a gentler, kinder God.

251

The real reason we think that the presentation of God in the New Testament is softer is because in the Old Testament most of the judgments are temporal, and temporal judgments scare us more than eternal ones. Yet the fact of the matter is that the person in the New Testament who gives us most of the most colorful metaphors for hell is Jesus. The truth of the matter is that as you move from the old covenant to the new covenant, there is a ratcheting up of the pictures of God's grace, and as you move from the old covenant to the new covenant there is also a ratcheting up of the pictures of God's judgment.

Through the Old Testament there are more and more threat and promise of judgment, and there are more and more hope and promise of forgiveness and renewal. These two streams barrel through the Old Testament, and they are not resolved. They are not resolved until finally they collide in the cross. Mercy and wrath kiss each other. For those who stand outside the sweeping effect of the cross, what is left but the judgment to come? That warns us that on many fronts in Scripture there is a kind of ratcheting up in focus as you move from the old covenant to the new.

Let me give you another example. Again and again in the Old Testament, God says something like this: "I will be their God, and they will be my people." God says that in Leviticus, in connection with the establishment of the tabernacle. The tabernacle will be placed amidst the tribes—three on the north, three on the south, three on the east, three on the west. "I will be their God. They will be my people." Then God says it anew, ratchets it up afresh, in the prophecies of the new covenant in Jeremiah 31 and elsewhere. The very tone is that something new is being introduced, until finally you come to the book of Revelation, to Revelation 21 and 22.

What is it that God says in the context of the new heaven and the new earth and the New Jerusalem? He says, "I will be their God, and they will be my people." But now when he says it, he says it in a context where there is no longer any mediation, any footnotes, any exception, any contest. As a result, the lesson is drawn: "There will be no more death or mourning or crying or pain, for the old order of things has passed away" (Rev. 21:4). The new has come, as God says, "I will be their God; they will be my people."

At every step you see this progressive ratcheting up, so when we are told in John 7:39, "Up to that time the Spirit had not been given, since Jesus had not yet been glorified," there are two things we must preserve.

On the one hand, we must preserve the newness theme in the New Testament, because there is a vast newness theme, and sometimes in our desire to preserve the continuity of the one plan of redemption, we lose the power of all the newness passages. In the New Testament we're told of a new age, a new creation, a new order, a new covenant, a new life, a new exodus, a new birth—all of them connected with the gospel itself, coming from Jesus.

That does not mean there is no place for the Holy Spirit in the Old Testament. The book of Nehemiah understands this, as it looks to the return of the exiles to Israel and also looks all the way back to Israel's first entrance into the Promised Land. That was the initial time when God gave his good Spirit to them, when he met them with manna, when he taught them the Word of God, when he forgave them their sin. Now there is a huge ratcheting up. With the Spirit poured out in a measure and way in consequence of Jesus' death, it is a foretaste of the consummation to come. That's why Paul, for example, can see the Spirit as the down payment, the first step of the consummation, something flowing out of Christ's gift, his death, burial, resurrection, ascension. Because of this, the Spirit has been given as the down payment, as the promised inheritance.

All this is triggered, we are told, by Jesus being glorified. "Up to that time the Spirit had not been given, since Jesus had not yet been glorified" (v. 39). Jesus makes the point abundantly clear in John 16 as well: "It is for your good that I am going away. Unless I go away, the Advocate will not come to you; but if I go, I will send him to you" (v. 7).

But what is this glorification? The language first is found in John 1:14–18, the last part of the prologue. It alludes six times to Exodus 32–34. In those chapters, you have the wretched incident of the golden calf. After Moses receives the tablets of stone, he comes back and hears the revelry and sees the idolatry, and the stone tablets are smashed. There is terrible judgment upon the people, and God threatens to wipe the people out, but then Moses intercedes with God and reminds God, as it were, of God's promises. "This isn't my people. This is your people. I didn't volunteer for this job. What will happen to your name if these people are not saved? The nations will say that you can't do it."

Then Moses, now feeling desperately alone since his own brother—his spokesman in the whole business of leadership—has been implicated in the idolatry, cries to God, "Now show me your glory." And God says, "I will cause all my goodness to pass in front of you . . . but no one can look on my face and live."

Moses is hidden in a cleft of a rock so he is not allowed to look out. God goes by and intones certain words, and after God has gone by, Moses is allowed to peer out and glimpse something of the afterglow of the trailing edge of the glory of God. While God goes by, God intones, "The Lord, the Lord, the compassionate and gracious God, slow to anger, abounding in *hesed emeth*." *Hesed emeth* is a very common pairing in the Old Testament. *Hesed* can be rendered "love," but it is God's covenant love. It is the love that is bound up with his own covenantal promises and is sometimes rendered "grace." And *emeth* means "faithfulness," but it has a wide variety of overtones. It can mean "faithfulness in word," but then it also means "truth." Thus, for example, when the queen of Sheba sees all the glory of Solomon, she says, "Everything that was told me was *emeth*" (see 1 Kings 10:6). It was the truth. It was a faithful report. The same words that some translations render as "love and faithfulness" can equally be rendered "grace and truth."

Now you come to John's gospel. "The Word became flesh and made his dwelling [literally, "tabernacled"] among us. We have seen his glory, the glory of the one and only Son, who came from the Father, full of grace and truth" (1:14 ESV). That is only the beginning of the connections.

"We Have Seen His Glory"

Just pick up the word *glory*. "We have seen his glory." What does that mean? That the disciples saw Jesus with a halo around his head all throughout the days of his flesh? Or maybe he was the one in the white kimono as opposed to the people with regular, colored ones on our flannelgraphs? No, the wording is explained for us as the book of John goes on. In chapter 2 the first miracle occurs, the turning of the water into wine at Cana. There we are told, "He revealed his glory; and his disciples believed in him" (v. 11).

A lot of people saw the miracle. The disciples saw his glory. Yet by John 12, the language of glory changes. Jesus is glorified, and we see his glory as he is lifted up on the cross. This lifting up before men and women is now a lifting up on the cross itself, in shame and ignominy. Yet it is precisely through this being lifted up on the cross in shame and ignominy that Jesus has his path back to the Father, to return to the glory that he had with the Father before the world began, as he said in John 17. Thus in John's gospel the glorification of the Son is simultaneously the return to the Father, his death and burial and resurrection, and his placarding before men and women. In the wake of all that, John writes, "We have seen his glory."

John writes in such a way that there are some things you are not meant to see until you have read the book through two or three times. Some books are like that. You're going to get on a flight at Philadelphia International Airport for a business trip to Los Angeles, and you've had it with spreadsheets, so you pick up a whodunit at the airport newsstand. By the time you land in LA, you have figured out who done it. It turns out that this book is not one that you are going to add to your library; it was just a way of killing three or four boring hours and plastic food, that's all. So you leave it in the seat pocket, and it's going to disappear. It's not a great literary feast.

There are some books that you read, however, that are so good you want to read them again and again, and the best of them may even be a whodunit. You read a P. D. James novel, for example, and in part you're driven by plotline. You want to find out who done it. But at the same time the characterization is so good and the use of language is so good that you want to go and read it again. Now you want to catch the richness of it, and as a result, when you read it the second time, you see all kinds of things that you didn't see the first time. Good writers are like that.

John does this again and again and again. For example, when you start reading this glory theme in John, you don't see yet where it's going, but he wants you to read his gospel several times. This isn't a throwaway tract, you know, that you read once and say,

"Done that. Know that." No, no, no. You're supposed to read it again and again, and as you read through John's gospel again and again, you find out what the glory theme is about. As you begin to discover it, you hear the words, "Up to that time the Spirit had not been given, since Jesus had not yet been glorified," and you remember the connection from John 1, and you recognize that Jesus is the ultimate tabernacle, the ultimate meeting place between God and human beings, and you remember that he displayed his glory right through his earthly ministry.

But his ultimate glorification came in his death and burial, resurrection and ascension, and that's tied to all his promises about the Holy Spirit in the farewell discourse in John 14–16. All this comes for one reason: Jesus was God's own sent Son, living and dying to do exactly what the Father had sent him to do—the Lamb of God going to the cross, bearing our sin, rising again on the third day. The gift of the Holy Spirit flows from that glorification.

Isn't that true of all that we finally receive from God—that it all turns on a little hill outside Jerusalem two thousand years ago? Do you have forgiveness of sins? It's because of Jesus' glorification. Do you have the gift of the Holy Spirit? It's because of Jesus' glorification. Will there be a consummated new heaven and a new earth? Yes, because of Jesus' glorification. Will you have a resurrection body on the last day? Yes, because of Jesus' glorification. Is the Spirit already given as the down payment of that ultimate triumph? Yes, because of Jesus' glorification. Is there a communion of saints empowered by the Spirit? Yes, because of Jesus' glorification. Is there a new birth borne along by the Spirit of God, poured out upon us? Yes, because of Jesus' glorification.

On the last day, Jesus will say, "Elizabeth Margaret Mabry, come forth," and my mother will come forth because of Jesus' glorification. He will say, "James Montgomery Boice, come forth," and

Jim Boice will come forth because of Jesus' glorification. This will all be because of Jesus' glorification, already anticipated in a down payment and the gift of the Holy Spirit now poured out upon us.

The old songwriter had it right.

I tried the broken cisterns, Lord,
And, ah, the waters failed;
Even as I stooped to drink they'd fled,
And mocked me as I wailed.

Now none but Christ can satisfy,
None other Name for me!
There's love, and life, and lasting joy,
Lord Jesus, found in Thee.[2]

We need forgiveness, but we need not only forgiveness but also transformation. We need not only justification. Yes, of course, we need that, but we also need new birth. We need regeneration. For a sinner such as I, so deeply engrained in my sin, so in love with myself, so deeply controlled by self-interest, what is powerful enough to change the likes of me?

George Whitfield was asked why he spoke again and again and again evangelistically on the text "You must be born again of water and Spirit." He said, "Because, sir, you must be born again." There is no hope for any of us without this blessed gift of the Spirit, who comes and convicts us of our sin and transforms us and conforms us to Christ and prepares us for glory to come—life eternal coming from God himself. This informs all New Testament notions of spirituality.

Here are streams of living water indeed.

---

2. E. B., "None But Christ," *The Cyber Hymnal*, accessed November 20, 2013, http://www.hymntime.com/tch/htm/n/o/n/nonebutc.htm.

12

The Age of the Spirit

MICHAEL S. HORTON

ACTS 2 IS A WONDERFUL TEXT for addressing the age of the Spirit. Starting there, though, would be like walking into the middle of a movie unless we do some Old Testament review, and so I feel the need to riffle through some passages with the goal of finding a broad sweep of redemption. I want us to see the work of the Holy Spirit in creation, in the calling of Moses, in the exodus of the people of God, in the exile, in the return, in the promises that are ultimately fulfilled in our Lord Jesus Christ, and in this age of the Spirit, in which the church is able to take the gospel boldly to the ends of the earth.

There are different ways of thematizing the Holy Spirit's person and work; my approach is not the only way of doing it. Many metaphors may be used, and various theophanies—appearances of God in the Old Testament—can be ordered in different ways. But I think most of them cluster around three principle themes that can be categorized in a couple of different ways: temple, witness, and glory, or—it just happened to come out this way—earth, wind, and fire.

We find analogies in Scripture because God uses means. God draws on the things he has made in order to bind us to himself, and it's remarkable what evidence God gives us in Scripture about how he is maintaining a presence among his people in a temple, how he is a witness to his covenant, how he is the glory of his people, and how his glory fills the ends of the earth. It is profitable to look at some of these themes.

The temple, witness, and glory pattern can be found in Genesis, in creation itself. In Genesis 1, we see the Holy Spirit in his glory cloud, hovering over the face of the earth. The earth is *tohu wa-bohu*, darkness and void, and the Holy Spirit broods over that. The Holy Spirit hovers over the earth and separates the waters from dry land so that he can create a habitable place, a temple for God to dwell with his people forever.

That separation of the waters from the dry land makes it possible for Adam and humanity after Adam to become a choir, leading the whole creation in triumphant procession before the Creator God, giving him honor and glory forever and ever, and finally entering into that Sabbath rest upon faithful obedience during probation. That was Adam's task. God the Holy Spirit came to create that habitable space to separate the waters so that there would be dry land for a temple and for human beings created in God's image.

You also see the filling of the Spirit. Here he is brooding over the waters with the ultimate goal of filling the whole earth, preparing a temple, preparing humanity for a Sabbath coronation with all creation joining in the great assembly. Creation, the Holy Spirit, and temple presence are all themes that comingle not as much in Genesis itself as in subsequent chapters of redemptive history that look back at Genesis and interpret Genesis in that light.

Not only is the temple prominent—the theme of God's presence among his people—but also the theme of witness, or wind, is central. This is a judicial function: the Holy Spirit as a judge. His judicial function is seen both as good news and as bad news. In creation, we see it as good news as he, along with the Father and the Son, pronounces a benediction on all that God has made. That was a judicial act: the Holy Spirit standing in his glory cloud—the two columns, the two pillars of witness—before all that the triune God had made and pronouncing, with the Father and the Son, that it was very good.

The Holy Spirit represents another kind of judicial sentence in the first chapters of Genesis when he comes after the fall and announces judgment. We read in Genesis 3 that "God [was] walking in the garden in the cool of the day." This has often and understandably been interpreted as meaning that God used to go for walks with Adam and Eve, and this was one more opportunity; he was coming for his daily stroll with the royal couple. But this time they weren't home; this time they had run away, so God went calling on them. That interpretation is certainly plausible in light of the translation, but scholars have pointed out recently that it is probably not the best translation. *Wind* and *spirit* are the same word in Hebrew—*ruach*—and so a lot of Hebrew scholars have argued that what's really happening is the day of judgment. God comes down out of heaven to earth in the *Spirit* of the day. What day? The day of judgment.

He's not coming in the cool of the day, breeze wafting through the palms. He's coming in the tornado of the day. He's coming in the wind that shatters all that human beings have built as a mighty palace. He comes in the *ruach* of the day, the Spirit of the day of judgment, the first judgment day that we have in Scripture. It's judicial. The Spirit is there, judicially approving all that God has made and then judicially sentencing the royal couple, who have now abandoned the covenant God made with them.

The Holy Spirit's Presence as Temple, Witness, and Glory

The Holy Spirit is a temple, he is a witness, and he is glory. Later in redemptive history, looking back at the original purpose of creation, there is this anticipation again that out of the central temple would come concentric circles of God's presence until his glory filled the ends of the earth as the people, the descendants of Adam and Eve, would go out and be fruitful and multiply and be faithful in their covenant promise. This glory is *kabod*, weightiness. That's what glory is. Glory and holiness—the same Hebrew word: *kabod*, meaning "heaviness."

These days it seems nothing is sacred, which is to say nothing is heavy, nothing is weighty. This is increasingly true even in Christian circles. How much do we need to recover this great biblical emphasis on the glory of God, the weightiness of God? The Holy Spirit in the Old Testament is central in delineating that.

Even after creation, we see the Spirit representing himself in these three ways, as temple, witness, and glory. We see it in the exodus, for instance, beginning with the Abrahamic promise before the exodus, when God makes the dual promise of an earthly, temporal, typological land and of a heavenly land, which is everlasting and is the fulfillment of that earthly indication. We see it with Moses appearing at the burning bush:

> Now Moses was keeping the flock of his father-in-law, Jethro, the priest of Midian, and he led his flock to the west side of the wilderness and came to Horeb, the mountain of God. And the angel of the LORD appeared to him in a flame of fire out of the midst of a bush. He looked, and behold, the bush was burning, yet it was not consumed. And Moses said,

"I will turn aside to see this great sight, why the bush is not burned." When the Lord saw that he turned aside to see, God called to him out of the bush, "Moses, Moses!" And he said, "Here I am." Then he said, "Do not come near; take your sandals off your feet, for the place on which you are standing is holy ground." (Ex. 3:1–5)

Here again, the Holy Spirit comes down out of heaven to make a habitable place, a place for himself to be present with his servant Moses and—through his servant Moses—with the people whom he will redeem from Egyptian bondage. Here again, he descends in that cloud alive, rife with winged creatures, the cherubim and seraphim.[1] He brings heaven down with him. If it's actually possible to think of this, that little bush was the cosmic throne of God in the universe. It was heaven in miniature. It was the temple of God among his people. It was a holy place, the holy land in miniature, and there God promises Canaan and a wilderness travel. He promises that he will bring his people right back to the same mountain—here's the witness, the judicial witness—and he will make them his own.

The wind again confirms this presence of the Holy Spirit as a witness, that there will be a new creation. That's how the exodus is represented: both in anticipation and, in the prophets, in retrospection. It's described as a new creation, using the same language of the Holy Spirit coming down and separating the waters to create dry land, so there will be a habitable place for God to dwell among his people. See Exodus 14:21 in that light: "Then Moses stretched out his hand over the sea, and the Lord drove the sea back by a strong east wind all night and made the sea dry land, and the waters were divided."

---

1. This colorful description of the Holy Spirit's presence (and others like it throughout the chapter) are symbolic illustrations, used as poetic license by the author.

That's why it's described as a new creation, as God by his Spirit pulls back the waters that drown Pharaoh and his armies, so that his people can be brought safely through to the other side: a separation of waters from dry land that will ultimately lead to a Sabbath rest for the people of God in the Sabbath land.

See this same judicial witness, both to God's salvation and to God's judgment, in that same chapter. "And Moses said to the people, 'Fear not, stand firm, and see the salvation of the LORD'" (Ex. 14:13). There's that witness, in courtroom language. Isn't it interesting too that the best things happen in redemptive history when God's people just shut up and stand there? Or sometimes when they sit down or when they're asleep, like Abraham on a rock. "Fear not, stand firm, and see the salvation of the LORD, which he will work for you today. For the Egyptians whom you see today, you shall never see again. The LORD will fight for you, and you have only to be silent" (Ex. 14:13–14).

It's as if God is saying to these grumbling people, "The only thing that I'm asking is that you shut up and just stand there. Can you do that? Can you just stand there and watch me save you?"

In the exodus, the Spirit also stands as a witness to judgment, as we see in verses 17–18: "And I will harden the hearts of the Egyptians so that they shall go in after them, and I will get glory over Pharaoh and all his host, his chariots, and his horsemen. And the Egyptians shall know that I am the LORD."

Note the way the Israelites will know that Yahweh is the Lord, but that he is also acting as a judge—when "I will get glory over Pharaoh, his chariots, and his horsemen." The Holy Spirit stands as a witness of good news and bad news, of salvation and of judgment.

One other place to mention in this period of history after God's people made it into the Promised Land is found in 2 Samuel 5. David has been anointed king, and now he defeats the Philistines.

> When the Philistines heard that David had been anointed king over Israel, all the Philistines went up to search for David. But David heard of it and went down to the stronghold. Now the Philistines had come and spread out in the Valley of Rephaim. And David inquired of the LORD, "Shall I go up against the Philistines? Will you give them into my hand?" And the LORD said to David, "Go up, for I will certainly give the Philistines into your hand." And David came to Baal-perazim, and David defeated them there. And he said, "The LORD has broken through my enemies before me like a breaking flood." Therefore the name of that place is called Baal-perazim. And the Philistines left their idols there, and David and his men carried them away.
>
> And the Philistines came up yet again and spread out in the Valley of Rephaim. And when David inquired of the LORD, he said, "You shall not go up; go around to their rear, and come against them opposite the balsam trees. And when you hear the sound of marching in the tops of the balsam trees, then rouse yourself, for then the LORD has gone out before you to strike down the army of the Philistines." And David did as the LORD commanded him, and struck down the Philistines from Geba to Gezer. (2 Sam. 5:17–25)

David is basically told to wait for the Holy Spirit to come upon him and to come upon the army to make them victorious over the Philistines. The Holy Spirit will descend in salvation for his people and in judgment of the nations. When David heard the marching of the armies of heaven in the treetops, that was his heavenly marching order to march on the earth. *Thy kingdom come. Thy will be done on earth as it is in heaven.*

265

May that which is already happening in heaven—God's glory filling the heavens, God's will being done—may that be done on earth as the armies go forward in the name of God, by the power of the Holy Spirit.

In addition to seeing the Holy Spirit's presence as a witness, we also see it as glory in the burning bush, where we see his presence as fire. Earth, wind, and fire. God's holy presence and judicial witness come together in the concept of his glory. That's what makes this a holy land. There is no Holy Land anywhere in the world today. There is no land that is holy. The Church of the Nativity in Bethlehem isn't holy. The temple isn't holy in Jerusalem. No building is holy in the new covenant. But we are holy; we are the temple of God. Yet in Exodus, God makes his dwelling in that burning bush. It is holy land. It is glory land. The pillar and the cloud that led Israel through the waters, through the wilderness, and finally into the Promised Land, that filled the tabernacle and then filled the temple when they got to the Promised Land—that glory was so essential that Moses said, "God, if your glory doesn't go with us, just kill us here on the other side of the Red Sea."

That pillar and cloud, radiant with winged creatures, pulled off an enormous feat, as we read in Exodus 14.

> Then the angel of God who was going before the host of Israel moved and went behind them, and the pillar of cloud moved from before them and stood behind them, coming between the host of Egypt and the host of Israel. And there was the cloud and the darkness. And it lit up the night without one coming near the other all night. (vv. 19–20)

"There was the cloud and the darkness." That's new-creation language again: darkness and void and the Holy Spirit creating light. At this point Moses stretches out his hand and the waters separate.

> And the people of Israel went into the midst of the sea on dry ground, the waters being a wall to them on their right hand and on their left. The Egyptians pursued and went in after them into the midst of the sea, all Pharaoh's horses, his chariots, and his horsemen. And in the morning watch the LORD in the pillar of fire and of cloud looked down on the Egyptian forces and threw the Egyptian forces into a panic, clogging their chariot wheels so that they drove heavily. And the Egyptians said, "Let us flee from before Israel, for the LORD fights for them against the Egyptians." (vv. 22–25)

In the Hebrew this is a bit more interesting, because while the Father, the Son, and the Holy Spirit are all present in the glory cloud, it's the Spirit who is actually reaching down—not just clogging the wheels with mud but unscrewing the wheels. That's what's happening here: the Holy Spirit makes his people cross on dry land. Here again, the foolishness of God is wiser than the wisdom of man. Here again, the pillar and the cloud lead God's people toward God's temple land.

The Spirit is present in the wilderness, and in the wilderness, even when the people grumble, the Holy Spirit maintains his presence in the tabernacle outside the camp. When Moses is frustrated that he has to carry the people all by himself, the Holy Spirit comes upon seventy of the elders. Joshua comes back to Moses and says, "I've got a report of something very urgent. News flash! A couple of people over here are prophesying without a license. They're not elders." I don't think what Moses does next is justify the undermining of office. This is an opportunity for him to say something that will help us look forward to what is to come.

So Moses says to Joshua, probably putting his hand on his shoulder to calm him down, "Are you jealous for my sake? Would that all the LORD's people were prophets, that the LORD would put his Spirit on them!" (Num. 11:29). Wouldn't that make his job easier? It would result in a kingdom of priests, a kingdom of witnesses to the glory of God, taking God's Word to the ends of the earth. Zeal for God's house consumes Moses. Moses pleads for that outpouring to be made in his day, so his people will be prophets and witnesses to God.

But we know what happens not only in the wilderness but also in the Promised Land. Even Moses is disobedient and so he doesn't lead the people into the Promised Land. Instead Joshua takes the people into Canaan, and yet it isn't, at the end of the day, the ultimate Canaan. It's not the ultimate Sabbath rest.

God's people eventually start imitating the world. The glory of God that filled the temple weighed lightly upon them. God warned them; he sent them prophets, and they stoned them and threw them into wells. Isaiah prophesied, in essence: "A day is coming. A day is coming when my presence will not be associated with that temple, and people will say, 'The temple of the Lord. The temple of the Lord. The temple of the Lord.' It won't mean anything at all to me, because the temple will return to *tohu wa-bohu,* to darkness and void, and I will take my Spirit back up into heaven." Isaiah 34 prophesies a day of confusion and emptiness—the world before the Holy Spirit made it a habitable place for us.

God's people will be carried off not only because they are unfaithful to the temple, but because they are unfaithful to their witness. Here's the language of the wind again. They will be carried off to exile. It's not just the exigencies of history involved here. The Holy Spirit will carry his people out of his land and evict them like a landlord evicts his tenants; he will send them into exile because there is no witness in the land of Israel, no one keeping in step with the Spirit below, no one listening to the marching of the armies in the treetops and keeping their armies moving below so that God's will is done on earth as it is done in heaven. No witness.

The accusation of a covenant prosecutor is seen again and again. The prophet is always proclaiming, "My people are deaf, dumb, and blind." That refers to witness. The people can't witness to anything because they haven't seen it. They haven't heard it. They don't speak up when God's name is profaned. They don't announce the good news that will come to the ends of the earth. They don't represent the Word of God. As Jeremiah says, in essence, "The prophets are filled with their own lies. 'The Lord told me this. The Lord told me that.' But nobody cares about the Word of the Lord." That judicial witness is noted in the legal language throughout the prophets. "Hear ye, hear ye, O Israel, the Lord has a case to bring against the people and all the inhabitants of the land. There is no truth. There is no justice. There is no mercy in the land." The result is that the Holy Spirit, the glory cloud, is taken back up into heaven and there is no dwelling of God on earth. *Ichabod*: the glory of God has departed.

The Anticipation of the Spirit's Outpouring

Even in the midst of that judgment, there is that prophecy of return—a return not just for Israel but for Israel coming back to the land with the nations in tow. We must remember that Israel was just a little country, one that couldn't defend itself during this period in its history. Israel had been carted off. Israel was weak and powerless. That's why Israel was looking for help from Assyria or Egypt, help from some empire rather than from God and his empire. Israel kept saying, "Some earthly empire will defend us." Yet the prophets declared, "A day is coming when you will come as conquering generals with all of the nations behind you led in a captives' train."[2] That is exactly the image we see again and again.

It is seen in Isaiah 61, when all the ships are coming to Israel. Think of it in light of today's news. Warships are coming into the harbor, and everybody's terrified. But wait! Don't worry. They're coming with gifts. They're coming to convert. They're coming to lay their treasures in Jerusalem and to worship with Israel.

There are many wonderful passages in Isaiah, too many for a short chapter.

> In that day there will be five cities in the land of Egypt that speak the language of Canaan and swear allegiance to the LORD of hosts. One of these will be called the City of Destruction.
>
> In that day there will be an altar to the LORD in the midst of the land of Egypt, and a pillar to the LORD at its border. (Isa. 19:18–19)

Remember, the person who is penning this is a Jew, and the people who are reading it are Jewish, and they remember what happened once upon a time when they cried out as slaves in Egypt and God heard them. The story isn't supposed to go like this.

> It will be a sign and a witness to the LORD of hosts in the land of Egypt. When [the Egyptians] cry to the LORD because of oppressors, he will send them a savior and defender, and deliver them. And the LORD will make himself known to the Egyptians, and the Egyptians will know the LORD in that day and

---

2. One such example is Psalm 68:18: "You ascended on high, leading a host of captives in your train and receiving gifts among men, even among the rebellious, that the LORD God may dwell there."

worship with sacrifice and offering, and they will make vows to the LORD and perform them. And the LORD will strike Egypt, striking and healing, and they will return to the LORD, and he will listen to their pleas for mercy and heal them.

In that day there will be a highway from Egypt to Assyria, and Assyria will come into Egypt, and Egypt into Assyria, and the Egyptians will worship with the Assyrians.

In that day Israel will be the third with Egypt and Assyria, a blessing in the midst of the earth, whom the LORD of hosts has blessed, saying, "Blessed be Egypt my people, and Assyria the work of my hands, and Israel my inheritance." (Isa. 19:20–25)

Doesn't that anticipate the outpouring of the Spirit in the last days?

Also in Isaiah, the preincarnate Christ says,

> "Draw near to me, hear this:
> from the beginning I have not spoken in secret,
> from the time it came to be I have been there."
> And now the LORD God has sent me, and his Spirit.
> (Isa. 48:16)

Not only the Father will send the Son but the Spirit as well, and then the Son will send the Spirit. In Isaiah 61:1–2, you have this famous prophecy: "The Spirit of the Lord GOD is upon Me, because the LORD has anointed me to bring good news to the poor . . . to proclaim the year of the LORD's favor."

The Spirit-filled Witness

So witness is absolutely central to the empowerment of the Holy Spirit. You see it in the temple, where the whole earth

271

will be full of the glory of God. But Scripture also notes that one day God will send his Mediator to earth, who will be an Advocate for his people. Isaiah 59:16 says, "He saw that there was no man." There was no man to speak up, to intercede for sinners, and so his own arm worked salvation for him, and his own right hand brought redemption. The glory came down again.

The glory came down by the Spirit when the Spirit came to the Virgin Mary and announced to her that her *tohu wa-bohu*, her darkness and the void of her womb, would become the birthplace of the new world, the birthplace of the new creation. Her womb would be the burning bush—only this time it wouldn't be a theophany. This time God would pitch his temple, not outside the camp where the tabernacle was, but among us, and would maintain his holy presence among us in righteousness and in truth.

He's the temple, the witness, and the glory. That which is happening in heaven will happen on the earth, the prophets say. God's glory will return to his temple, and the nations will stream into it.

That age does dawn, for Jesus is the glory-filled temple. He is the Spirit-filled temple. He pitches his tent among us. He tells his critics, "If you tear down this temple, I will rebuild it in three days," referring to his resurrection (see John 2:19).

At Jesus' baptism, the Spirit descends as he did at creation, as he did in leading his people through the Red Sea and through the wilderness. That same Spirit, that same glory cloud, lights above Jesus' head, this time in the form of a dove, and gives his benediction to the new world, to the new creation, as Jesus stands in the water—the water witnessing that he is the Lamb of God who takes away the sin of the world. Jesus is not only the Spirit-filled temple but also the Spirit-filled witness.

Jesus is the true Israel, the true Israelite who takes God's Word to the ends of the earth. "If it is by the Spirit of God that I cast out demons," he said, "then the kingdom of God has come upon you" (Matt. 12:28). Jesus also said, "I saw Satan fall like lightning from heaven" (Luke 10:18). The Spirit led him into the wilderness to be tempted just as Adam had been tempted, just as Israel had been tempted in the wilderness—only he, the true Adam, the true faithful Israel, fulfilled the probation on our behalf. "Father. . . . for their sake I consecrate myself, that they also may be sanctified in truth" (John 17: 11, 19). Jesus fulfilled the law by the power of the Spirit, not just because he was God. When he was in trouble in temptation, he did not draw on his deity. He came down in incarnate humility. He drew on the Spirit just as we do. He relied on the Holy Spirit to get him through trial instead of murmuring against God's will, and he fulfilled the law and witnessed this time, not to what was going to come, but to himself as the one who has come.

And Jesus promised the Spirit. John the Baptist said, "I baptize you with water, but he who is mightier than I is coming, the strap of whose sandals I am not worthy to untie. He will baptize you with the Holy Spirit [salvation] and with fire [judgment]" (Luke 3:16). Again we are harking back to the Red Sea.

Jesus is the temple. He is God's holy dwelling. He is God's Spirit-filled witness. Hebrews 1:3 says he is "the radiance of the glory of God." He will incorporate us into his Spirit-filled existence when the Spirit comes upon the rest of his Body. It won't just be an "inside thing" that he enjoys; those who are incorporated into him will be living stones, built into the temple that is Jesus Christ. Then the Spirit will descend from heaven, and there will be a temple on earth that will reach out to the ends of the earth.

273

The Age of the Spirit Inaugurated at Pentecost

The age of the Spirit came at Pentecost. At this point Jesus has promised, "I am with you always, to the end of the age" (Matt. 28:20), and he has given his disciples the Great Commission—to go from Jerusalem to Judea to Samaria to the uttermost parts of the earth.

Then it was Pentecost.

Pentecost was known as the Feast of Firstfruits. You can tell what the whole harvest will look like based on what comes in from the firstfruits. In this we see that Jesus' resurrection isn't a separate resurrection from ours. It's the beginning of our resurrection. It's the firstfruits of the whole harvest, and so we know how the whole harvest will turn out. We're not left wondering.

At Pentecost, Jews and proselytes were together in one place. Whereas you had in Eden a scattered Adam because of sin, at Babel scattered nations and scattered languages, and in the exile scattered Israel, at Pentecost you have the Spirit coming and gathering the nations to himself, uniting them in one gospel so that they can even hear and understand that gospel in their own tongue. They are the temple now. Those gathered in one place are the temple of God. They are living stones, being built up together in him. But they are also witnesses, and that's why you have the wind.

> And suddenly there came from heaven a sound like a mighty rushing wind, and it filled the entire house where they were sitting. And divided tongues as of fire appeared to them and rested on each one of them. And they were all filled with the Holy Spirit and began to speak in other tongues as the Spirit gave them utterance. (Acts 2:2–4)

The earth, wind, and fire are all in one place. The wind rushes into the room, and the tongues of fire, the burning bush, appear over everyone's head. Here the Spirit, who hovered over the waters, who created the world out of darkness and void, who issued that judicial benediction, is hovering over each believer and over the whole assembly gathered in that house. The dry bones prophesied in Ezekiel 37 come together. The army below hear the marching in the rooftops as the wind comes into the upper room and are now prepared to go out into the world. They're no longer deaf, dumb, and silent but are witnesses to what God has done in Jesus Christ outside the center city of Jerusalem.

> Now there were dwelling in Jerusalem Jews, devout men from every nation under heaven. And at this sound the multitude came together, and they were bewildered, because each one was hearing them speak in his own language. And they were amazed and astonished, saying, "Are not all these who are speaking Galileans? And how is it that we hear, each of us in his own native language?" (Acts 2:5–8)

This shows us that tongues—at least the tongues indicated by this passage—are known languages. They are not spiritual languages known only to the believer and the Holy Spirit. They are known linguistic structures, because the people were surprised not that they were chattering unintelligible words, but that they were preaching the gospel in their native language. Furthermore, the tongues weren't for the believers' private edification but for witness to the mighty works of God. The tongues of fire resting on each person corresponded to each of these spoken languages. As Paul says, "Thus tongues are a sign not for believers but for unbelievers" (1 Cor. 14:22). It's all to send the people of God out to be witnesses to God to the ends of the earth.

What's the effect of this Pentecost, the effect of the Spirit descending in power, this day everyone's been waiting for, this festival of harvest? What's the result? Something spectacular. A healing line. Many more resurrections. What's the spectacular, amazing, unbelievable saving event that happens on the heels of this? Peter preaches Christ.

If you don't think that's a miracle, go back and read Peter's story. This is the man who denied Jesus three times. This is the man who took Jesus aside every time he talked about the cross and said, "Stop talking about the cross." Jesus said, "Get thee behind me, Satan." But now Peter is a witness to Christ, no longer deaf and dumb in things pertaining to the gospel.

The good news is God has raised this Jesus from the dead. He has ascended to the right hand of the Father. The prophecy of Joel 2, Peter says, has been explicitly fulfilled. The Spirit has been poured out on all flesh. And you know what? He says you're included. "For the promise is for you and for your children and for all who are far off, everyone whom the Lord our God calls to himself" (Acts 2:39).

"Brothers, what shall we do?" they cry out (v. 37). He says, "Repent and be baptized every one of you in the name of Jesus Christ for the forgiveness of your sins" (v. 38). There's the water again, the water standing as the Holy Spirit's witness: the sign and seal that they belong to him. Everything else that follows is the record of the church growing by Word and sacrament in the power of the Holy Spirit as he witnesses through his people to the ends of the earth.

We have been enveloped into that glory cloud of witnesses, surrounded by the cloud of witnesses that Hebrews 12:1 talks about, a cloud teaming with the winged preachers of God's Word along with the myriad saints who have gone before us. We are ourselves, right at this very moment, enveloped in the glory cloud, which is the temple of God. Every believer is incorporated into Christ by the Holy Spirit. The Spirit has made every Christian a living stone in Christ, the only temple of God on earth. As he witnesses through those whom he blows wherever he will, we form a cloud of glory as we witness, going from glory to glory as we behold God's glory in the face of Christ.

So Paul says, "Let us also keep in step with the Spirit" (Gal. 5:25). *Thy kingdom come. Thy will be done on earth as it is in heaven.* May the whole earth be filled with the glory of God from Jerusalem to Judea to Samaria to the uttermost parts of the earth.

13

Born of the Spirit

PHILIP GRAHAM RYKEN

"ARE YOU A BORN-AGAIN Christian?" That's a question that a lot of people were asking particularly back in the 1970s, and then into the 1980s and I suppose still today. Are you born again? People were asking that question back then because being born again had unexpectedly become a matter of national politics. For many Americans, politics is the ultimate religion. They pay relatively little attention to Christianity until Christians start getting involved in politics, and then all of a sudden they're interested in religion again.

They were interested in 1976, when President Jimmy Carter told the world that he was a born-again Christian. This was in the same year that Charles Colson, who had been imprisoned for Watergate, came out with his famous spiritual autobiography, a book called *Born Again*.[1] Suddenly "born again," a phrase that had been used only in Sunday school or perhaps on a film night

1. Charles Colson, *Born Again* (Grand Rapids: Chosen Books, 1976).

at the local Christian church, started appearing in places such as *TIME* magazine.

My high-school debate partner went to summer school at Georgetown University. He came back to Wheaton, Illinois, talking about having had a coach who was a born-again Christian and how strange it was. I said, "John, *I'm* a born-again Christian." He looked at me with a puzzled expression and said, "Maybe this guy was born the first time. He was a lot stranger than you are." I didn't have the heart to tell him that Wheaton was full of born-again Christians in those days, as it still is.

What is a born-again Christian, anyway? Different people would answer in different ways. Some say a born-again Christian is a person who has made a decision for Christ, maybe by going forward at an evangelistic rally. Others would say it's a person who has prayed the sinner's prayer. Perhaps it's a person who has an evangelistic witness, the kind of person who passes out tracts and witnesses to people on an airplane. A fuller answer is given in a book called *Growing Up Born Again*, which is a humorous look back at what it was like to be a GUBA. In a chapter called "If You're Saved and You Know It," the authors wrote this:

> *Saved. Born again. Redeemed. Converted.* Those of us who grew up in BA families knew that we belonged to a very select body of people. We were special, set apart, chosen. We were real Christians. . . . How did we know? . . . Much like natural birth, being born again is an historical event. It takes place at a specific time and in a real location. For example, you may have been born again on June 5, 1958, at summer camp with your counselor after devotions. Or on October 11, 1953, at home with Mother. It's helpful to write this information on the flyleaf of your Bible. If you've

accepted Jesus as your personal Savior you know that, unlike your first birth experience (nobody asks to be born!), your second birth was a totally voluntary act of your own will. . . . Growing up born again doesn't just happen. It starts when you answer yes to the question, "Have you accepted Jesus as your personal Savior?"[2]

I'm not at all implying that there's anything wrong with making a decision to follow Christ or praying to receive him as Savior. In fact, repenting and believing in Christ are essential to your salvation. Nor is there anything wrong with sharing your faith. The Bible says we are always to be prepared to give an answer to everyone who asks us to give the reason for the hope that we have (1 Peter 3:15). But there is a danger in the way that people sometimes talk about born-again Christianity. The danger is in viewing conversion as something we have decided to do rather than something God does for us and in us by his grace, so that that grace is the foundation of any response that we make to God.

In an important book called *Against the Protestant Gnostics*, Philip Lee comments that

whereas classical Calvinism [Reformation theology] had held that the Christian's assurance of salvation was guaranteed only through Christ and his Church, with his means of grace, now assurance could be found only in the personal experience of having been born again. This was a radical shift, for Calvin had considered any attempt to put "conversion in the power of man himself" to be gross popery [works righteousness]. In fact, rebirth in God is the exact opposite of rebirth into

2. Patricia Klein, *Growing Up Born Again: Or a Whimsical Look at the Blessings and Tribulations of Growing Up Born Again* (Old Tappan, NJ: Fleming Revell, 1987), 52–53.

a new and more acceptable self, as the self-acclaimed born-again Christians would see the event.[3]

Do you see the difference? If being born again is based fundamentally on what we decide or what we do, then our faith and assurance always rest on the shaky foundation of our own spiritual experience. But if the new birth is a supernatural work of the Sovereign God, then our whole Christian life and experience flows from the life of God's Spirit. We have to be clear about what it means to be born again in the biblical sense. A born-again Christian is not something that we can choose to become but something the Spirit delivers. To understand what it really means to be born again, we need to go back to the Scriptures and particularly to John 3, for there we find that the new birth is not a cultural phenomenon unique to the American evangelical church. It's a biblical truth sometimes called the doctrine of regeneration. It's a spiritual reality that comes from the supernatural work of the Holy Spirit. We don't want to base our theology on our own experience. We want to understand our experience according to the Scriptures.

Nicodemus and the New Birth

Probably the first person who ever heard Jesus teach about the new birth was Nicodemus. His is one of the first Bible stories I can remember hearing. I can still picture my father sitting on the edge of my bed in the evening, reading about Nicodemus coming to Jesus by night. Nicodemus's encounter with Jesus seemed very similar to my own setting in the evening on the edge of the bed,

3. Philip J. Lee, *Against the Protestant Gnostics* (Oxford University Press, 1987), quoted in Michael Scott Horton, *In the Face of God* (Dallas: Word, 1996), 34.

and I can still remember the sense of joy in my soul as I heard what Jesus had said about being born again. It sounded like the most wonderful thing in the whole world, which in a way it is.

The story in John 3 begins matter-of-factly. "Now there was a man of the Pharisees named Nicodemus, a ruler of the Jews" (v. 1). In other words, he was a member of the Sanhedrin, a group of seventy religious leaders who governed God's people from Jerusalem. Nicodemus was a great man—a scholar, a teacher, a member of the ruling elite—and he was curious about Jesus of Nazareth. It was becoming more and more obvious that Jesus was a man from God. He taught such magnificent truths and performed such stupendous miracles that Nicodemus wondered who he was and what he had come to do.

So Nicodemus came to Jesus at night and said, "Rabbi, we know that you are a teacher come from God, for no one can do these signs that you do unless God is with him" (v. 2). This is phrased as a statement, but I think Nicodemus was probing into the question of Jesus' true identity. He knew that Jesus was a man from God, but exactly who was he? Nicodemus hinted that Jesus might be the Messiah whom God had promised to send. I think the question that he couldn't quite bring himself to ask but that he only implied was this: Jesus, are you the Savior?

If I'm right about that, this was the first of three questions that Nicodemus posed. In his answers, Jesus teaches three fundamental truths about regeneration: (1) the necessity, (2) the possibility, and (3) the sovereignty of the new birth.

The New Birth: Necessary for Salvation

First, Jesus teaches Nicodemus that the new birth is necessary for salvation. "Jesus answered him, 'Truly, truly, I say to you, unless one is born again he cannot see the kingdom of God" (v. 3). The kingdom of God was one of the central themes of Jesus' teaching. Here he is looking forward to his eternal kingdom, where he would rule in all his kingly glory. He is speaking to Nicodemus about eternal life, about the resurrection life of the age to come, which no one can enter without being spiritually reborn. It takes a new birth to see the new world. Jesus is warning Nicodemus that he has to be born again to be saved.

What do you think Nicodemus thought about that answer? That was hardly the answer he would have expected. He was there to examine Jesus, not to be examined *by* him. Certainly he treated Jesus with some respect. He recognized him as a teacher, praised his miracles, and even called him Rabbi. But Nicodemus still wanted to retain the right to judge Jesus for himself, to sit back and evaluate his ministry by his own criteria. You get the sense from the way he uses "We know" that he is appealing to all the other religious leaders and their opinion of Jesus.

But Jesus responds by entirely turning the tables on Nicodemus. Rather than submitting to Nicodemus's judgment, Jesus confronts him with God's requirements for salvation, and the real question is not whether Jesus is the Savior. He is. The real question is whether Nicodemus is saved. This is a reminder that there is a lot more to salvation than recognizing Jesus as a good teacher and a miracle worker; Jesus demands from you more than your respect. He demands your total spiritual transformation. You cannot see the kingdom of God unless you are born again.

What a remarkable thing that was to say to a man like Nicodemus, a man who thought he had every assurance of salvation. He was a Jew. He was a member of God's covenant people. More than that, he was a Pharisee, a man who kept God's law down to the very smallest detail. Notice that Jesus refers to him as Israel's teacher (v. 10)—perhaps *the* leading Bible scholar of his day. Yet

Nicodemus still hasn't gone far enough. With one short sentence, Jesus dismisses every one of his religious credentials and warns him that he still lacks the one thing that God requires for entrance into his kingdom: the new birth. Nicodemus must have been shocked. What Jesus said to him stands as a warning to every religious person, even to every churchgoer. It doesn't matter what family you're from or what church you attend or how smart you are or even what doctrinal position you hold intellectually or how much you know of the Bible. You must be born again.

What does it mean to be born again? The Greek word Jesus used for "born" is *gennao*, which is the origin of the English word *genesis*. It can refer either to the action of the father ("to beget") or to the action of the mother ("to give birth"). In either case, it refers in some way to the generation of a new life. Jesus used the term in its spiritual sense, telling Nicodemus that he needed new spiritual life. He needed that radical change of nature from spiritual death to spiritual life, wrought in us by Christ through the power of the Spirit.[4] That's the first word, the word *born*.

Like the word *born*, the word often translated *again* has two meanings. The Greek term *anothen* often refers to something repeated; it provides the basis for our English word *another*. To be "born again," therefore, would mean to be "reborn" or "born anew." Obviously this is the way Nicodemus understood Jesus, because you can see his objection in verse 4. "How can a man be born when he is old? Can he enter a second time into his mother's womb and be born?"

This idea of being born again is also where we get the theological term *regeneration*. If *gennao* means "generation" and *anothen* means "again," Jesus was telling Nicodemus that he needed a re-generation, another genesis.

---

4. Bruce Demarest, *The Cross and Salvation: The Doctrine of Salvation*, ed. John S. Feinberg (Wheaton, IL: Crossway, 1997), 285.

There is another way to translate *anothen*, however, and that is "from above." That gives what Jesus said a slightly different emphasis: no one can see the kingdom of God unless he is born from above. This is the way John uses the term elsewhere. In John 3:31, for instance, Jesus declares, "He who comes from above is above all," and in John 19:11, Jesus tells Pilate, "You would have no authority over me at all unless it had been given you from above." *Anothen* is used in both cases. So the idea of being born from above fits the context well, because Jesus goes on to explain that regeneration is the work of the Holy Spirit sent from heaven.

Which of these two meanings did Jesus have in mind? Was he telling Nicodemus to be born again or to be born from above? Probably both. When Nicodemus spoke of a second birth, Jesus didn't correct him. Regeneration really does require a new spiritual birth. Yet where does this birth come from? It comes from above. Thus, there is a double meaning here. No one can see the kingdom of God without being reborn from above.

Three times Jesus says the new birth is essential for salvation. He says it in verse 3: "Unless one is born again, he cannot see the kingdom of God." He says it again in verse 5: "Unless one is born of water and the Spirit, he cannot enter the kingdom of God." He says it very simply in verse 7: "You must be born again." Jesus could hardly have made it any plainer. There is no spiritual life without spiritual rebirth. Either you are a born-again Christian in the biblical sense or you're not a Christian at all.

The Problem: Human Depravity

To see why the new birth is so necessary, we need to step back for a moment and remember what the problem of humanity is. The problem is our depravity. We see in Nicodemus a man who epitomizes the lost and sinful condition of us all. There may be spiritual significance in the fact that he came to Jesus at night. Nicodemus wanted to keep their meeting secret. He was perhaps afraid of what the other religious leaders would think. But John loved that symbolism of light and darkness; you see it right from the beginning of his gospel. He may have mentioned the night here to give us a clue about Nicodemus's spiritual condition. He was the kind of man Jesus describes in verses 19–20. "The light has come into the world, and people loved the darkness rather than the light because their deeds were evil. For everyone who does wicked things hates the light and does not come to the light, lest his deeds should be exposed."

The night was blacker than Nicodemus knew. He was lost in the darkness. He had not yet seen the light, and the reason he could not perceive the kingdom of God was because he was still unregenerate. He was the kind of man Jesus describes in verse 6: "That which is born of the flesh is flesh." Jesus is talking about natural physical childbirth, *flesh* often referring to fallen humanity and its frailty. The only thing that one human being can give birth to is another human being, one sinner giving life and birth to another sinner. As long as we remain unregenerate, we cannot see, cannot enter, and cannot believe in the kingdom of God.

Theologians call this the doctrine of total inability. As far as anything spiritual is concerned, in our natural, sinful condition, we are unable to follow after God. Unregenerate we are, and unregenerate we will remain until we are born again by God's Spirit. Nicodemus is the perfect example. He knew all kinds of things about the Bible, but he couldn't understand a word Jesus was saying about eternal life. He had not yet been born again.

What Nicodemus needed—what we all need—is nothing less than a whole new spiritual life, a total transformation from our total depravity. The great Scottish theologian Thomas Boston compared this universal change to the work of a skilled doctor: "Man is . . . altogether disjoined by the fall; every faculty of the soul is . . . dislocated: [but] in regeneration, the Lord loosens every joint, and sets it right again."[5] This is the marvelous work of the Holy Spirit, making a new spiritual person who is able to think, to will, to act, to believe, to feel, and to live for the glory of God.

This is the Spirit promised in the Old Testament, the Spirit sent by the glorified Christ to give new life to the people of God. There is a point where we move from talking about the great work of the Holy Spirit in the history of redemption and move to the work of the Spirit as he enters our own personal history and our own life with that same life-changing power.

A beautiful example of this work of the Spirit comes from the life of Edward Studd, father of the famous English sportsman and missionary C. T. Studd. Edward Studd was worth a fortune. He loved to spend his wealth on sports and entertainments of all kinds. He went on an endless round of horse racing, gambling, dancing, and theatergoing. But then he became a born-again Christian in the biblical way, and he was a changed man. From that point, his only ambition was to bring other people to Christ. He cleared out the hall of his country estate, brought in pews and benches, and turned it into a venue for evangelistic services. This was such a sudden reversal of priorities that one acquaintance wondered what had happened to the man. Arriving at the estate, he remarked to the coachman that

5. Thomas Boston, *The Complete Works of the Late Rev. Thomas Boston of Ettrick*, ed. by Samuel M'Millan (London, 1853; repr. Wheaton, IL: Richard Owen Roberts, 1980), 8:141.

he had heard that Mr. Studd had become religious. "Sir," said the coachman, "we don't know much about that, but all I can say is that though there is the same skin, there's a new man inside!"[6] That amazing inward transformation is necessary for anyone to see the kingdom of God.

But Is the New Birth Possible?

The new birth may be necessary for salvation, but is it possible? This is the second question Nicodemus has for Jesus. "How can a man be born when he is old? Can he enter a second time into his mother's womb and be born?" (v. 4). Nicodemus didn't understand what Jesus was saying. Maybe he was thinking too literally. When he heard the term *born again*, he assumed it was about natural childbirth. But how could a man possibly be born a second time? To show how absurd the idea was, Nicodemus imagined an old codger climbing back into his mother's womb and starting life all over again. He should have known better than that. He should have realized that Jesus was speaking spiritually but using natural childbirth to illustrate a spiritual truth. Yet Nicodemus couldn't understand it. How can a man be born again? Of course, the answer is the answer that salvation always gives. "With man this is impossible, but with God all things are possible" (Matt. 19:26). What is impossible for us in our depravity is possible for God in all his grace.

Jesus emphasizes this by describing the new birth in the passive voice. We use the active voice to describe something we do or we did. An example of the active voice is the sentence "I went to church." It shows something I did. But we use the passive voice

---

6. Norman P. Grubb, *C. T. Studd: Cricketer and Pioneer* (Atlantic City, NJ: World-Wide Revival Prayer Movement, 1933), 19.

to describe something that was done to us, as in the sentence, "My life was changed at church." The action is not something I did or an action I took, but something that happened to me. When Jesus talks about the new birth, he's using not the active voice but the passive voice. He tells Nicodemus, "You must *be* born again." It's not something you can do for yourself; it's something that must be done for you or to you.

You can see the analogy with natural childbirth; this is the way birth operates. Children never bring themselves into the world. They are always delivered by their mothers. In the same way, unregenerate sinners cannot regenerate themselves. No, we are as dependent on the Holy Spirit for our spiritual rebirth as we were on our parents for our physical birth. No matter how much you go into labor, no matter how much you read self-improvement books of the spiritual kind, no matter how many religious rituals you follow, no matter what moral codes you observe, there is no way you can deliver yourself into new spiritual life.

In all the talk about being born again, this is often misunderstood. Remember *Growing Up Born Again*: "Unlike your first birth experience . . . your second birth was a totally voluntary act of your own will." In the United States, this misunderstanding goes back more than a century. One of the men who has had the greatest influence on the evangelical church is the nineteenth-century revivalist Charles Finney. He was always coming up with new methods for bringing people into the kingdom of God, and he criticized anyone who said that the new birth is the supernatural work of God's Spirit. He was opposed to that biblical viewpoint. He said, "Instead of telling sinners to use the means of grace and pray for a new heart, we call on them to make themselves a new heart and a new spirit."[7] When you

---

7. Charles Grandison Finney, *Memoirs of Rev. Charles G. Finney, Written by Himself*, ed. J. H. Fairchild (New York: Revell, 1903), 189.

tell people to do that, they end up thinking they can make themselves born again.

By way of contrast, consider the story of the conversion of one of Finney's contemporaries, Archibald Alexander, who was one of the great Princeton theologians. During the days of the Second Great Awakening, Alexander had not yet come to Christ. His biographer describes Alexander's conversion this way:

> One day a Baptist carpenter suddenly asked Alexander whether he believed in the second birth. Taken aback, Alexander answered that he did. Asked then if he had experienced it, Alexander answered frankly, "Not that I know of." The conversation ended with the disturbing words, "Oh, if you had experienced this change you would know something about it!" And Alexander began seriously to consider the subject: "It seemed to be in the Bible; but I thought there must be some method of explaining it away; for among the Presbyterians I had never heard of anyone who had experienced the new birth, nor could I recollect ever to have heard it mentioned."[8]

The more Alexander studied the Scriptures, the more convinced he became that the new birth couldn't be explained away. It's usually that way as you search things out in the Scriptures; that was the way it was for Alexander. He became convinced that this was true biblical doctrine, and so he tried to become his own obstetrician. He sought to find some way to deliver himself into the kingdom of God.

> I prayed, and then read in the Bible, prayed and read, prayed and read, until my strength was exhausted. . . . But the more

---

8. David B. Calhoun, *Princeton Seminary; Volume 1: Faith and Learning, 1812–1868* (Edinburgh: Banner of Truth, 1994), 1:45.

I strove the harder my heart became, and the more barren was my mind of every serious or tender feeling . . . I was about to desist from the endeavor, when the thought occurred to me, that though I was helpless, and my case was nearly desperate, yet it would be well to cry to God to help me in this extremity. I knelt upon the ground, and had poured out perhaps a single petition . . . when, in a moment, I had such a view of a crucified Savior, as is without parallel in my experience. The whole plan of grace appeared as clear as day. I was persuaded that God was willing to accept me, just as I was, and convinced that I had never before understood the freeness of salvation, but had always been striving to bring some price in my hand, or to prepare myself for receiving Christ. Now I discovered that I could receive him in all his offices at that very moment. . . . I felt truly a joy which was unspeakable and full of glory.[9]

Archibald Alexander was born again, not by his own labors, but by the gracious work of God's Spirit. Did he make a decision to follow Christ? Yes, he did. Did he personally receive Jesus Christ as his Savior? He did. But he could not do those things until he was regenerated by God's Spirit. That's what makes the new spiritual life possible: the life-giving work of the Holy Spirit.

When Nicodemus doubted the new birth, Jesus provided this answer: "Truly, truly I say to you, unless one is born of water and the Spirit, he cannot enter the kingdom of God. That which is born of the flesh is flesh, and that which is born of the Spirit is spirit" (vv. 5–6). Regeneration is possible because it is the work of God's Spirit, who brings us into the family of God by spiritual rebirth.

9. Archibald Alexander, quoted in J. W. Alexander, *The Life of Archibald Alexander* (New York: Charles Scribner, 1854), 4.

But what did Jesus mean when he said, "born of water and the Spirit"? It is admittedly a difficult phrase. Many interpretations have been offered.

Some say the water refers to natural birth. I think this is a wrong interpretation for several reasons, including grammatical ones. Water and the Spirit are tied together. Jesus did not say, "*born of water* and *born of the Spirit*," but "born of water and the Spirit." Rather than describing two different births, "water and the Spirit" seems to describe one and the same birth.

A different way to interpret the water in this verse is to take it as a reference to baptism. This explanation makes a lot of sense, but I'm not sure it would have made as much sense to Nicodemus. We should take seriously the fact that Jesus does not say "baptism." He says "water." It wasn't until after the resurrection that baptism marked the entrance into God's family. Although the Bible sometimes associates baptism with regeneration, it never makes baptism the cause of the new birth. Baptism is a *sign* of salvation, but it is not the *basis* for the salvation it signifies.

Another interpretation is that water refers to God's Word. This was the view of the late James Montgomery Boice. If Dr. Boice was right, as he almost always was, then Jesus meant that the new birth comes in response to God's Word in the gospel. Certainly that's a biblical truth. The apostle Peter wrote, "You have been born again . . . through the living and abiding word of God" (1 Peter 1:23). Or consider the words of James: "Of his own will he brought us forth by the word of truth" (James 1:18). Both apostles taught that spiritual life is conceived by the dissemination of God's Word, and although regeneration is an immediate work of God's Spirit, the first stirrings of that new spiritual life come through hearing God's Word. That interpretation is possible.

A fourth interpretation is most likely of all. D. A. Carson says that we should think of the water and the Spirit as a conceptual unity.[10] Water and the life-giving Spirit are not two separate things but two words that together describe the spiritual purification of a sinner. According to Sinclair Ferguson, the Spirit "simultaneously gives new life and cleanses the heart."[11] What Jesus said might be translated like this: "Unless one is born of water, even the Spirit, he cannot enter God's kingdom."[12] And together water and the Spirit describe the life-giving, heart-cleansing work of God's Spirit.

What an appropriate thing that would be to say to Nicodemus. As a Pharisee he had very carefully followed all the biblical regulations for purification. He had performed all the outward rituals for cleansing, but what he really needed was inward cleansing, without which no one can see the kingdom of God. Nicodemus thought he was clean because he was a Pharisee. He didn't recognize his need for purification. He needed to be born again by water, even the Spirit, who makes us clean within.

We find a similar connection between water and Spirit in Titus 3:4–6.

> But when the goodness and loving kindness of God our Savior appeared, he saved us, not because of works done by us in righteousness, but according to his own mercy, by the washing of regeneration and renewal of the Holy Spirit, whom he poured out on us richly through Jesus Christ our Savior.

10. D. A. Carson, *The Gospel According to John* (Leicester: Inter-Varsity, 1991), 194.

11. Sinclair B. Ferguson, *The Holy Spirit*, Contours of Christian Theology (Downers Grove, IL: InterVarsity, 1996), 122.

12. Kenneth S. Wuest, *Wuest's Word Studies from the Greek New Testament* (Grand Rapids: Eerdmans, 1966), 3, iii.55–57.

As one of Israel's teachers, the Rev. Dr. Nicodemus should have known that he was a polluted sinner who needed to be purified from the inside out, and particularly because in these words of Jesus he should have heard an echo of the prophet Ezekiel. I think this is the clincher that "water" refers to the spiritual cleansing of the Holy Spirit. For in Ezekiel 36:25–26, we read, "I will sprinkle clean water on you, and you shall be clean from all your uncleannesses, and from all your idols I will cleanse you. And I will give you a new heart, and a new spirit I will put within you." Ezekiel was the prophet of the Holy Spirit, and he promised that when the Spirit came he would wash God's people clean and give us new spiritual life. He would purge away all the defilement of our sin and create in us a whole new life, a new birth by water and the Spirit. Jesus was offering the fulfillment of Ezekiel's promise—the gift of a clean, new, spiritual heart created by the new birth.

Whatever Jesus meant by "born of water and the Spirit," he was saying this: only God can change a sinner's heart. If you hear the testimony of any Christian, you'll find that it's a story of being reborn from above. Let me give you a couple of examples.

The New Birth . . . For Every Believer

An example from Scripture comes from Paul's missionary journey to Philippi. One Sabbath Paul went to speak to a group of women who had gathered by the river to pray. One of those listening to Paul was a woman named Lydia, a dealer in purple cloth and a worshiper of God. In Acts 16:14 we read, "The Lord opened her heart to pay attention to what was said by Paul." In other words, the Lord opened her heart to respond to Paul's message of the gospel, and Lydia became a believer in the Lord

Jesus Christ. What enabled her to believe was the opening of her heart—the regenerating work of God's Spirit. As she heard the message of the gospel she was born again, transformed from within by the Holy Spirit.

Another example, one from church history, is the story of Martin Luther. Like Lydia, Luther received the new birth while studying the Scriptures. He had been trying to figure out what the Bible meant when it said, "The righteous will live by faith" (Rom. 1:17). This frightened him because he knew he was unrighteous. Then he was given the spiritual insight to realize that God offered God's own righteousness as a gift for sinners to receive by faith. Luther described his spiritual transformation this way: "Now I felt as though I had been immediately born anew and had entered paradise itself, and from that moment, the face of Scripture as a whole became clear to me and my mind ran through the Sacred Books seeking the strength and the salvation and the glory of God."[13]

The new birth is not for just the women of the New Testament and the men of church history. It is for every believer. I think of a friend who was raised in the liberal church but started to feel like something was missing. She started to go to a Bible-teaching church, and from time to time she would go in and meet with the pastor and ask all her questions. They talked about the inspiration of Scripture and about God's work in creation and about the necessity of the atonement and about the role of women in the church.

It took a couple of years of detox to clean out her theology, but finally she was ready to receive Christ in a biblical way, yet she hesitated because she was afraid it wouldn't work. "What if

13. Martin Luther, quoted in Bernard M. G. Reardon, *Religious Thought in the Reformation* (London: Longman, 1981), 52.

it doesn't take?" she asked. "I'm worried that if I ask Jesus into my heart, nothing will happen. What will I do then?"

Her pastor explained that being a Christian isn't a matter of feeling a particular way. What's important is not the experience. What's important is Jesus Christ and trusting him. The pastor knew that when someone is truly born again, the Holy Spirit is present in a life-changing way with life-changing power. He prayed that by God's grace, the Spirit would give her unmistakable assurance that she could know for certain she was born again. That afternoon she got down on her knees, she repented of her sin, and she asked Jesus Christ to be her Savior and her Lord.

When she got back up, she didn't feel any different, yet she believed that God had answered her prayer and that she was saved. Then God did something more for her. The next morning when she woke up, she had overwhelming peace and joy. It was unlike anything she had ever experienced before, and she knew with absolute certainty that God had made her a completely new person. She knew she had been born again.

This is not to say that you have to have a certain experience. Every Christian testimony is unique. The point is that the Holy Spirit has the power to change your life forever. Those who have been born again by the Spirit testify that it is the most wonderful thing that ever happened to them. The great Reformation theologians who wrote the Canons of the Synod of Dort described it like this.

> This is the regeneration so highly celebrated in Scripture and called a new creation, a resurrection from the dead, a making alive, which God works in us without our aid. It is evidently a supernatural work most powerful and at the same time most delightful, most astonishing, most mysterious and

indescribable, not inferior in efficacy to creation or to the resurrection from the dead.[14]

Of all the wonderful works of the Holy Spirit—his creation of the world, his raising Jesus from the dead, his outpouring on the church—none is more amazing than his regeneration of the sinner.

God's Sovereignty in Regeneration

The new birth is necessary. No one can receive eternal life without it. The new birth is possible because God is able to save sinners who seem beyond the hope of salvation. But Nicodemus still had a question: "How can these things be?" (v. 9). It's his third question, and it brings to mind the comparison that Jesus made between the Holy Spirit and the wind. Jesus used this analogy to show God's sovereignty in regeneration, which is the sovereignty of the new birth. He said, "The wind blows where it wishes, and you hear its sound, but you do not know where it comes from or where it goes. So it is with everyone who is born of the Spirit" (v. 8).

What makes this illustration especially effective is the fact that in the Greek language, *wind* and *breath* and *spirit* are all the same word, *pneuma*. The Spirit is the breath of God, whose influence is like the wind. No one can control the wind or even see it, yet its effects are obvious wherever it blows. So it is with the Holy Spirit. No one can control his gracious influences. No one can see when he first slips into a sinner's heart. But he always has his effect, and soon it becomes obvious that the sinner has

14. Canons of the Synod of Dort (III/IV, Art. 12), in *The Creeds of Christendom*, ed. Philip Schaff, rev. David S. Schaff, 6th ed. (1931; repr. Grand Rapids: Baker, 1983), 3:590.

been born again by the power of the Holy Spirit. The Spirit blows where he wills. The regenerating, life-giving work of the Spirit is up to the sovereignty of God. This is taught elsewhere in Scripture, as in John 1:13, which speaks of the children of God being born "not of blood nor of the will of the flesh nor of the will of man, but of God," or in the words of James the apostle: "Of his own will [God] brought us forth by the word of truth" (James 1:18).

If that's true, what are we supposed to do? It sounds like everything is up to God. If the Spirit blows wherever he pleases, how can we get him to breathe on us? As Nicodemus put it, "How can this be?" He was saying something like, "I must be born again. I hear what you're saying; I must be born again. But how can I? I cannot give birth to myself; that is something that only God can do." Nicodemus could see that the one thing he needed was outside his power, and he struggled with that. He struggled with God's sovereignty in salvation. From beginning to end, salvation is all a matter of divine grace, and regeneration is no different in this respect from election, in which God chooses whom he will save. Nor is regeneration different in this way from faith, which the Bible describes as a gift from God. Nor is it different from justification, which is accomplished by the finished work of Jesus Christ. God determines whom he will save, and God alone saves them.

For Jesus, this was such a basic, fundamental, obvious truth that he didn't go through a long philosophical defense of the sovereignty of God. He often referred to it in passing whenever he talked about salvation. Whenever he did happen to refer to God's sovereignty, it always aroused questions and sometimes objections, as it did in the mind of Nicodemus. As far as Jesus was concerned, a man such as Nicodemus should have known better than to question God's sovereignty. He should have understood from the Scriptures that salvation does not come by human effort but only by divine grace.

So Jesus says, "Are you the teacher of Israel and yet you do not understand these things?" (v. 10). The real question is not how you can get the new birth but how God grants it and the way God does that. He grants this gift of the new birth on the basis of the work of Jesus Christ.

What did Jesus do with Nicodemus? He talked about the Holy Spirit first of all, but he didn't leave it there. Jesus proceeded to talk to him about his own saving work on the cross. He told Nicodemus that new spiritual life comes by trusting in Jesus Christ and that the gift of the Spirit comes on the basis of Christ's saving work. At the end of this conversation, Jesus calls Nicodemus not to be his own obstetrician. He calls him to trust in Jesus for salvation.

> And as Moses lifted up the serpent in the wilderness, so must the Son of Man be lifted up, that whoever believes in him may have eternal life. (John 3:14–15)

Jesus was referring to the cross, where he would be lifted up to die for sinners. He was describing the crucifixion in terms that Nicodemus could understand, using an illustration from the Old Testament, the story in Numbers 21 where the children of Israel were complaining against God. While they were grumbling, God sent poisonous snakes among them, and many people died. Finally the people realized that they had sinned and that they were under God's judgment, so they asked how they could be saved. God said to Moses, "Make a fiery serpent and set it on a pole, and everyone who is bitten, when he sees it, shall live" (v. 8). Moses did as God commanded. "So Moses made a bronze serpent and set it on a pole. And if a serpent bit anyone, he would look at the bronze serpent and live" (v. 9). Jesus used the story of the serpent to explain to Nicodemus what God was calling him to do.

Like the children of Israel and like Nicodemus, we are dying for our sins, but Jesus has come to save us. First he had to be "lifted up," a phrase John uses later in his gospel, in chapter 8 and again in chapter 12. In both instances, he's referring to the cross where Christ was crucified. The point is that everyone who looks to Jesus in faith will live. This was the answer to the question Nicodemus asked. His question concerned the sovereignty of the new birth. "If regeneration is a work of God's grace, how can I be born again?" Rather than giving him some five-step plan for spiritual rebirth, Jesus told him very simply to trust in Jesus for his salvation, because everyone who believes in the crucified Christ will receive eternal life.

God is not calling sinners to believe the doctrine of regeneration, not in the first place. What he calls us to do first is to exercise faith in Jesus Christ. And what is our gospel? It's not an experience—a born-again experience or any other experience. The gospel is the death and resurrection of Jesus. That's the gospel we preach: Christ crucified and Christ risen. God tells us about the new birth, so that we will see our need for regeneration, will understand that we need to look to Christ, and will understand the transforming work of his Spirit that he is able to do. But what God calls us to do is to trust in Jesus Christ. The statement "You must be born again" is a statement of fact. It's not given in the Scriptures as a command to obey. Jesus is not telling us to convert ourselves. He is telling us to look to him for our salvation, which you are able to do only when you are born again by the Holy Spirit.

Looking to Jesus

What about Nicodemus? Was he ever born again? I think he was. We get a glimpse of him at the end of John 7, where he tried to stand up for Jesus before the Jewish leaders who were plotting to kill him. Nicodemus asked, "Does our law judge a man without first giving him a hearing and learning what he does?" (v. 51). The other Pharisees brushed him off: "Are you from Galilee too? Search and see that no prophet arises from Galilee" (v. 52).

But Nicodemus *did* look into it, and he came to believe that Jesus was a true prophet from God. He was at the cross when the Son of Man was lifted up to die, and at great risk to his career, he helped to take Jesus' body down from the cross and have it buried in the tomb. How can you explain that unless you understand that Nicodemus was born again by God's Spirit, that he looked to Jesus and lived? A born-again Christian, in the true sense of the word, is someone who, by the work of the Holy Spirit, looks to Christ for salvation, looks to Christ, the Christ of the cross and the Christ of the empty tomb. Nicodemus looked to Jesus and lived.

One snowy Sunday morning, a young man was on his way to church. He trudged down a side street and came to a little chapel. Going in, he saw a preacher mounting the pulpit. He turned out not to be a minister at all but only a common laborer. Nevertheless, "though his grammar and diction left much to be desired, he spoke earnestly and directly to his audience of twelve. Finally the preacher looked at the young man . . . and said, 'Young man, you look very miserable . . . and you will always be miserable if you don't obey my text. Look to Jesus Christ! You have nothin' to do but to look and live!' "[15]

15. Anthony A. Hoekema, *Saved by Grace* (Grand Rapids: Eerdmans, 1989), 113.

At those words, the young man—whose name was Charles Spurgeon—was born again in the biblical way. He came to spiritual life. By the sovereign work of God's Spirit, he was enabled to look to Jesus Christ in faith and to receive eternal life. What about you? Are you looking to Jesus? "For God so loved the world, that he gave his only Son, that whoever believes in him should not perish but have eternal life" (John 3:16).

14

Life in the Spirit

HYWEL JONES

SERMONS CAN HAVE titles, and, after you've heard them, you may wonder what the sermon and title had to do with each other and what each had to do with the text. But there is a substantial connection between the title of this chapter and Romans 8:1–27, a passage of Scripture written by the apostle Paul.

First of all, I wish to draw your attention to some expressions that are found in this passage. You have only to look at the second verse of Romans 8 to see life connected with the Spirit. "For the law of the Spirit of life has set you free in Christ Jesus." In addition, verse 11 speaks of life in connection with the work of the Spirit. So without going much farther into this great chapter, life in the Spirit is a fitting theme for it.

There are many references to the Spirit in Romans 8. There are eleven in the first fourteen verses. Not all of them are preceded by the definite article in the original text, and not all of them have the initial letter for the Greek word *spirit* capitalized. But arguably, there are eleven references to the Holy Spirit in the first fourteen verses, and there are more to follow, up to verse 27. There is no explicit reference to the Holy Spirit between verses 27 and 39, yet I'm going to suggest that we cannot do justice to those massive statements of abundant confidence and triumph in that passage without thinking of the work of the Holy Spirit in the heart of a believer.

Now we don't do our theology by numbers. Eleven uses in fourteen verses says neither this nor that. If we were to do our theology by numbers, arguably the word *and* would be the most important word in the whole Bible. But when we have the Spirit, that's a different matter. All that we see in Scripture serves to remind us of the dignity, the deity, and the importance of the work of the Holy Spirit in connection with the triumph of our Lord and Savior Jesus Christ. From the very first page of the Bible through to the last, you have references to the Holy Spirit by way of imagery and also by way of instruction. The fact that in Romans 8 we have so many references to the Holy Spirit should draw us up short and make us ponder the significance of such frequent usage.

But it is also striking that here you have more references to the Spirit than in all the rest of the epistle to the Romans. Careful reading of the letter will indicate that to you.

In the first seven chapters, there are only five references to the Holy Spirit, then eleven in the first fourteen verses of chapter 8. What's the significance of that concentration? It's because of the point that Paul has reached in his treatment of the righteousness of God, which is the theme of this great epistle. That's what we read in Romans 1:17: "For in it the righteousness of God is revealed from faith for faith, as it is written, 'The righteous shall live by faith.'" The righteousness of God, as Luther was given wonderfully to see, was not the righteousness that God demanded, which Luther couldn't bring to God; that was a thought that crippled and terrified him. It was rather the righteousness that God not only requires but also graciously bestows to all who believe in the Lord Jesus Christ, who kept the Law and bore its curse. In this epistle the apostle is unfolding the theme of the gospel, the saving righteousness of God, and he's doing so on three levels.

He does so in terms of an eternal plan or divine arrangement—in terms of the covenant headship of Adam on the one hand and the Lord Jesus Christ on the other. The latter part of Romans 5 sets that out, so that from God's standpoint, on the one hand the way in which he deals with people is in terms of their union with Adam in his sin and in his guilt; therefore they are liable to condemnation. All men everywhere "have sinned and fall short of the glory of God" (Rom. 3:23). But on the other hand, he deals with an infinite number of sinners from every kindred tribe and tongue and nation by virtue of their union with Jesus Christ, the second Adam. That's the first level, so to speak, in the unfolding of his argument.

Second, Paul looks at the saving righteousness of God from the historical and scriptural angle. He looks at it as it has been made known in the course of history through the prophets and in the writings of the New Testament. Not only does he look forward with the prophets to the inauguration of this righteousness through Jesus Christ and describe it in the last days as having begun, but arguably he looks forward to the massive ingathering of the Jewish people by faith in Jesus Christ into the one church, which is his body.

The third level is the experiential level, where this great purpose formed before the dawn of time, progressively revealed in the Old and New Testaments, takes root and bears fruit in the hearts and lives of sinners who trust in the Lord Jesus Christ.

This is the level the apostle has reached in Romans 8, and it's not possible to think in terms of the experience of salvation, the application of salvation, and the increase in all its blessings and to ignore the Holy Spirit. It's not possible to marginalize him. Just as the Holy Spirit is the executor of the purpose of God the Father, accomplished by the Son to save, so he is the one who brings all this to fruition in our hearts.

The Holy Spirit's Identity

This is where we are in chapter 8, hence the abundant references to the person and work of the Holy Spirit. First of all, in general, note some details that we're given in this chapter about the identity of the Spirit. In the title of this chapter we have just "the Spirit," and in Romans 8:4–5 that is what we have too: just "the Spirit." That, of course, is a shorthand way of referring to the Holy Spirit. By itself, however, it would be inadequate. It would raise some questions. Whose spirit? Which spirit? Those were vital questions in the first century, just as they are in the twenty-first century. When the apostle was writing to the church at Corinth, he referred to the fact that there were many so-called gods acknowledged, in heaven or on earth, many gods, many lords (1 Cor. 8:5). Later on he spoke about demonic influences associated with idolatrous worship and practices.

Even in a letter written to Christian believers, it was not just enough to say "the Spirit." If that was true in the first century, it's true in the twenty-first, when we have a return to first-century paganism. Much is included under the umbrella of "the Spirit." Whose spirit? Which spirit? So I draw your attention to some other descriptions or designations of the Spirit that we have in

Romans 8. The first is found in two places, where we have these words: "the Spirit himself" (vv. 16, 26).

The addition of that reflexive pronoun *himself* is important. It's significant. It says something. It doesn't just fill a space. What it does is differentiate "the Spirit" from other spirits. As you read through Romans 8—and I urge you to do so carefully with this perspective in mind—you'll see that there are references to other spirits besides the Holy Spirit. For instance, in verse 15 we see the "spirit of slavery" and the "Spirit of adoption." In verse 16, we see "the Spirit himself" contrasted. So the Spirit is not to be identified with either of those spirits as if he were one and the same with them. Those other two spirits are spirits, attitudes, dispositions within the human being.

Arguably, the first is a reference to an awakened sinner, someone who is aware of sin's corrupting power and its enslaving domination, as Paul has highlighted in chapter 7: "Who will deliver me from this body of death?" (v. 24). It's an awareness of guilt. Paul hadn't preached in Rome yet. How had the church come into being? There were people from Rome in Jerusalem on the day of Pentecost. What happened to them? They heard Peter preaching, and they were pricked in their hearts and said, "Brothers, what shall we do?" (Acts 2:37) They knew they were hopeless, helpless, guilty, foul, and condemned. That's the spirit of bondage.

The second is the "Spirit of adoption as sons, by whom we cry, 'Abba! Father!'" (v. 15). Here's the spirit of the regenerate human being, assured in measure, conscious of having been not only justified and pardoned but also adopted into the very family of God. What I want to underline for you now is this: the Spirit on whom we are focusing our attention is not to be identified with either of those. The unregenerate human spirit, aware of the supernatural, aware of shame and condemnation, might be the *result* of the work of the Holy Spirit, but he is not to be identified with the Holy Spirit, neither is your sense of being adopted into the family of God. The Holy Spirit bears a distinction that it is vital to maintain here.[1]

It is important to maintain that distinction today, because so easily and so widely the stirrings of one's spirit, particularly in a religious setting, are automatically identified with the Holy Spirit. You see it in the wilder excesses of the charismatic phenomenon. But you can also see it in the more reserved, quiet atmosphere of Roman Catholic worship or Eastern Orthodox worship. Instead of the happy-clappy atmosphere, you get the sense of the numinous. It's not noise; it's silence, with all the smells and bells as well. But however stirring, awe affecting, and humbling the experience is, it is not the same as the Holy Spirit, "the Spirit himself." He has an identity.

In Romans 8 we don't have the expression "the Holy Spirit," with which we are so familiar and rightly use so often, but the next designations of the Spirit in the chapter connect the Spirit with God and with Christ. Look at verse 9. "You, however, are not in the flesh but in the Spirit, if in fact the Spirit of God dwells in you." In verse 10 we see, "If Christ is in you." The Spirit is connected with God on the one hand and with Christ on the other, who is described as God's "own Son" in verse 3. Here then is the divine Spirit, the Spirit of God, not merely a spirit as opposed to a human disposition, but a Spirit who is totally and utterly divine, as divine as God the Father is, as divine as God the Son is, and connected with both in terms of their activity,

1. Editor's note: Dr. Jones's position on the "spirit of adoption" deviates from that of the translators of the English Standard Version and of many other translators. The ESV capitalizes *pneuma* in Romans 8:15, as do the King James Version, New King James Version, New International Version, and most other translations, understanding the "Spirit of adoption" in Romans 8:15 to refer to the Holy Spirit. Dr. Jones takes a different position.

in terms of the great covenant of redemption, the purpose of which is to save mankind.

When we think of the Spirit, we are not thinking of the spirit of any so-called imaginary deity, any god whom people like to make, or any god that people imagine themselves to be. We are talking about the third person of the blessed Trinity, the one who actuates within the dead sinner, making him or her a believer. Thereby is the saving purpose of God secured and accomplished by the obedient righteousness of his Son, the Lord Jesus Christ.

Divine, Deathless, and Dominant: Life in the Spirit

The next general thing I want to point out is the quality of life in the Spirit. As we think about life in the Spirit, it is vital to ask the question, "Who is the Spirit?" But it's equally important to ask, "What kind of life are we thinking of?" The first thing surely must be this—that here is a divine life. Here is the life of the third person of the Holy Trinity. It's the life of God in the soul of the believer. It's not that religious sense, that awareness that each and every human being has by virtue of having been made in the image and likeness of God.

In Romans 2 Paul wrote about the Gentiles who have not the law, yet out of their own constitution as human beings made in the image and likeness of God, are not amoral or without conscience, even though they don't know the Law, the Decalogue revealed at Sinai. They're not without a sense of right and wrong. Though corrupted and attenuated because of sin and the fall, still they have an awareness of the fact that they are accountable and that there is someone bigger and greater than they are, and that before him they will one day stand. It is an awareness that they are out to stifle and to destroy, but that they can't.

Life in the Spirit is not the same as being religious. It's a divine life. It's a life of knowing God, of being in relationship with him and in communion with him.

It isn't only a divine life; it's a deathless life. Romans 8:10 says, "But if Christ is in you, although the body is dead because of sin, the Spirit is life because of righteousness." This life is characterized by resurrection—Christ's resurrection. I think the best understanding of verse 10 is this: "If Christ is in you, the body is dead [on account] of sin." Whose sin? Adam's sin. The human spirit is alive because of righteousness. Whose righteousness? Christ's righteousness.

Verse 11 adds, "If the Spirit of him who raised Jesus from the dead dwells in you, he who raised Christ Jesus from the dead will also give life to your mortal bodies through his Spirit who dwells in you." The life you have within your soul by virtue of faith in Jesus Christ cannot die. It's resurrection life. It's a life that is immortal. Death will not conquer it. Christians live, even in dying, and the Spirit will quicken a corpse. We are sown in corruption; raised in incorruption. Why? Because the second Adam, the last Adam, is a quickening, life-giving Spirit. If the Spirit of him who raised up Jesus from the dead dwells in you, he will quicken your mortal bodies by his Spirit who dwells in you. We're going to be totally redeemed, my friends. Not a single thing, not even a hoof, is going to be left behind.

Life in the Spirit is divine, deathless, and one other thing: life in the Spirit is a dominant life. The Spirit is sovereign.

A good many folk look at Romans 8 like this: "Romans 5 is about justification, just as Romans 3 and 4 are, of course. Then Romans 8 is about sanctification, and it ends with glorification." I'm not saying Romans 8 has nothing to do with sanctification, but you don't read the word *sanctification* in Romans 8, not even at the end. Verse 30: "Those whom he justified he also"—sanctified? No: "glorified."

In Romans 8 you and I as Christian people are not commanded to do anything with reference to the Holy Spirit. There's not an imperative verb in the whole chapter. That doesn't mean there's nothing here for us to do. There is. There is a considerable amount for us to do, but the emphasis falls not on our doing but on the Spirit's doing. It's his activity. He's in charge. Life in the Spirit is not a life that we initiate; it's a life that the Spirit initiates and we respond to him. Verse 14 notes, "For all who are led by the Spirit of God are sons of God."

In Ephesians 5 believers are commanded, "Be filled with the Spirit" (v. 18). We read in Galatians: "Walk by the Spirit" (5:16). But here the emphasis is on the Spirit leading, and therefore we must realize that we are being put in the position in Romans 8 of following, keeping in step, responding. It's like what we see in Philippians 2:12–13: "Work out your own salvation with fear and trembling, for it is God who works in you, both to will and to work for his good pleasure." God works in us. He's begun a good work in us. He won't leave it undone. We are being called upon to keep in step, to respond, to walk, to bring to resolution those promptings, stirrings, warnings, rebukings, encouragings of the Spirit, and to act upon them by the Spirit's enabling. In that way we work out our own salvation with fear and trembling.

The life that is described here is a life according to the Spirit. You find that in the second part of verse 5: "Those who live according to the Spirit . . ." It's a life that is made up of a mind and a walk. A mind consists of thoughts. A mind consists of desires. A mind consists of decisions. Mind, heart, and will are all being directed in accord with the leading of the Spirit so that what results is a walk, a conduct.

313

Walking according to the Spirit, we are under obligation. Though it is the Spirit who has us in hand and who takes us onward and upward and homeward, we are debtors, because what he is out to produce in us is the righteousness of the law. We have duties because we are debtors, but now we are free, and so what was formerly impossible and unattainable is now gloriously possible.

Verse 3 says, "For God has done what the law, weakened by the flesh, could not do." The law couldn't save. We might think it held out blessing on condition of obedience. It couldn't give blessing. Why? Because obedience wasn't forthcoming. What the law could not do, in that it was weak through the flesh, God did. How? "By sending his own Son in the likeness of sinful flesh and for sin, he condemned sin in the flesh" (v. 4). He dealt with sin that enslaves and binds so that the righteousness of the law might be fulfilled in us. The Ten Commandments taken up by your Lord and Savior and mine, interpreted, unpacked in the Sermon on the Mount—this is the way in which the Spirit leads not into paths of unrighteousness but into righteousness, so that the righteousness of the law might be fulfilled in us as we walk not according to the flesh, but according to the Spirit. This is a dominant life. We are under obligation, and we are not our own.

Life in the Spirit: Liberty and Leading

Let us look at this life in more detail. There are two parts: liberty and leading. We must begin with liberty (vv. 2–3), for liberty precedes leading. We cannot follow without being freed.

Freed from what? "The law of sin and death" (v. 2). What is that? Here *law* does not mean precept or commandment. It means power: controlling, dominating, enslaving power. Romans

2 and 3 unpack the condition of all mankind. What the law says, it says to those who are under the law. Those who are under the law are under sin's enslaving, dominating power, so that they can't keep the law. This is the universal human predicament. No one in the flesh can please God. This is the bondage that has to be shattered before the Christian life is possible.

"For those who live according to the flesh set their minds on the things of the flesh" (v. 5). Those who are in the flesh cannot please God. They who are in the Spirit mind the things of the Spirit. This is the fundamental dichotomy. You get from the one to the other in exactly the same way you get from Adam to Christ—by the atonement of the Lord Jesus Christ provided by the Father being applied in its benefit and efficacy to your soul by the Holy Spirit. Verse 2 calls this "the law of the Spirit of life." There is a conflict of forces: "the law of sin and death" versus the strong man armed, who keeps his goods in peace. The one stronger than he comes by the word of the gospel, and the power of the Holy Spirit binds him and takes away the goods in which he trusted.

Wesley was dead right.

> Long my imprisoned spirit lay
> Fast bound in sin and nature's night;
> Thine eye diffused a quick'ning ray;
> I woke, the dungeon flamed with light;
> My chains fell off, my heart was free;
> I rose, went forth, and followed thee.[2]

I didn't look for a key to unlock my chains. They fell off! You can't follow without being freed. It's not possible to live the

2. Charles Wesley, "And Can It Be That I Should Gain," *The Trinity Hymnal*, (Philadelphia: Great Commissions Publications, 1990), 455.

Christian life without trusting in Christ. If you trust yourself, you can't live this life. You must trust in the righteousness of Jesus Christ, who procured the Holy Spirit. Only then can you live the Christian life.

Romans 8 doesn't describe a higher life that we have to get into by getting out of something else, even though we are Christians. If we're Christians, we're free. We are no longer dominated by sin. That doesn't mean that sin's power is not a reality. It is. But we are no longer dominated by sin, and we are no longer under the law as a condition of our being accepted by God. You don't need to do a thing, my friend, to make yourself acceptable to God. Jesus has done it all. You don't need to fear a thing either, because he has borne it all. We are freed. In "the law of the Spirit of life," *life* initially means liberation.

Where the Spirit Leads: Holiness, Assurance, and Prayer

But this is just the beginning. Leading comes next, as we see in verses 14–27. There are three parts to it. Into what does the Spirit lead? He goes before. The Good Shepherd in John 10 goes forth before his own sheep, and the sheep follow him. They hear his voice. On his return to his Father's side, he hands over his own to the Holy Spirit, who goes ahead of them and says, "This is the way to heaven, to glory." He leads. He goes before, so keep in step. Follow him.

Where does the Spirit lead? He leads into greater conformity to Christ (holiness), greater confidence in salvation (assurance), and greater consolation in prayer (prayer). Holiness, assurance, and prayer are the three features of a life characterized by the Spirit's leading. He won't lead you into sin. He won't lead you into presumption, self-trust, and vainglory. He won't lead you to think that you never need to bend your knees and ask for help and mercy. The way he leads you home is by a highway of holiness. As he leads you along the path, he will bring to you those reminders of God's love and mercy in and through Jesus Christ, assuring you that you are his. On those occasions when you know that the help of man is vain and you can only turn to God and say, "O God," he'll help you. We are in his hands. Trust him. Follow him.

Romans 8:13 says, "For if you live according to the flesh you will die." That is a great general truth. If you follow the flesh, death will be the end. But if you follow the Spirit, life will be at the end. This involves putting to death the deeds of the body so that you will live.

Pietism is to be reprobated. It imagines that the world and your body are entirely evil and that the way to godliness and to holiness is to enter into a monastery, proverbially speaking. No. This world is God's world, and your bodies, made by God for you, are going to be redeemed by him. They are not evil in themselves, but this world and these bodies in which we find ourselves are part of Satan's usurped kingdom, in which the effects of the fall are present and active. The world and the flesh are the means by which the adversary of God and man seeks to invade our lives.

We have to resist him. We have to use the world but not abuse it or become immersed in it. We may give God thanks for it, but the world is not to capture our hearts. In exactly the same way, we are not to "present [our] members to sin as instruments for unrighteousness" and for sin (Rom. 6:13). Why? Because sin approaches us through our physicality, through our senses. This includes not merely what our hands do, what our eyes see, what our ears hear, where our feet go, but what we give our thoughts to. In all these ways, sin infiltrates. In John Bunyan's *Holy War*,[3] there are ways through the gates of the city Mansoul. You've got to guard them. You've got to mortify the deeds of the body. Say no, so that you might live.

Prior to his conversion to Christ, St. Augustine lived an immoral life. After he had come to know the grace of God, he was walking one day through the market, and one of his former lady friends called to him. "Augustine, it is I." No answer. Again: "Augustine, it is I." Eventually he stopped, turned around, and said, "But it is no longer I."

Reformed people need godliness. Don't give it a bad name by the use of the term *Pietism*. There is genuine piety. The Spirit leads to holiness.

The Spirit also leads to assurance and leads in prayer. I'll bracket these two together. On the one hand, the Spirit bears witness (v. 16), and on the other hand, the Spirit expresses himself with unutterable groanings (v. 26). Within the tradition to which we belong, there is discussion here over whether the witness of the Spirit is additional to the witness of our spirits already.

When we believe the gospel, the gospel is life and peace to us. We know that we are alive to God. We know we have peace with God. We know we are loved by God. Is there anything more? In exactly the same way, in the context of prayer, we are called upon to pray, and we do. But the Spirit helps us in praying. How? By helping us in our praying or by adding his yearnings and groanings to our praying. In commentaries you will find different views taken. I take the view that the Spirit is doing, in each case, something more than our own spirits, and the ground on which I base that view is this: "the Spirit

3. John Bunyan, *The Holy War*, 1682.

himself." That unique expression draws a line of demarcation between what may be true of our spirits and what is true of his.

Our spirits may say to us, and hopefully they do, "Abba, Father," enabling us to address God as our heavenly Father through Jesus Christ. But then there are occasions when the Spirit witnesses to our spirits. I'm not talking about an audible voice, and I'm not talking about extra revelation in addition to what is written in Holy Scripture, which is closed and final and sufficient. The witness of the Spirit to our spirits comes by the preached Word, by the read Word, in the context of prayer, as we come to the Lord's Table—however, wherever, whenever the Spirit, who is sovereign, comes to us and gives to us assurance that we are indeed children of God, "and if children, then heirs—heirs of God and fellow heirs with Christ" (v. 16). Many of God's saints have known something like this down through the centuries.

And the same in prayer, which we see in verse 26: "for we do not know what to pray for as we ought." We know what it is to face adversity. We know what it is to be plagued with infirmity. We have these twin curs snapping at the heels of our souls all our way home to glory, and they drive us to pray and to express the yearning that is metaphorically attributed to inanimate, dumb creation as it waits for the glorious liberty of the children of God. We know how to speak to God, how to address him. We know general requests that we are to make of him. But how do we pray for ourselves or for others in this situation and that? We don't know, but the Spirit himself makes intercession for us. He adds his intercession alongside ours. On those occasions when all you and I can do is say, "O God," he can interpret that. He can translate it into whatever language is necessary, so that "he who searches hearts knows what is the mind of the Spirit, because the Spirit intercedes for the saints according to the will of God" (v. 27).

You and I have the help of the Holy Spirit in praying. We have the advocacy of the Son of God at the right hand of the Father. "If God is for us, who can be against us?" You begin to see how the end of this wonderful chapter can only be as it is, the accumulation of the work of the Spirit in the believer.

"And we know that for those who love God all things work together for good, for those who are called according to his purpose" (v. 28). Yes, I know.

> For I am sure that neither death nor life, nor angels nor rulers, nor things present nor things to come, nor powers, nor height nor depth, nor anything else in all creation, will be able to separate us from the love of God in Christ Jesus our Lord. (Rom. 8:38–39)

No condemnation at the beginning. "There is therefore now no condemnation" (v. 1). No separation at the end, and no opposition in the middle, for what is the opposition? "If God is for us, who can be against us?" (v. 31).

Let us live in the Spirit, through faith in Jesus Christ, to the glory of God our Father. Amen.

15

Holy Spirit, Counselor

R. C. SPROUL

THE CENTRAL THEME of what is historically called the Upper Room Discourse in John's gospel is Christ's promise of the sending of the Holy Spirit in his absence. In fact, in those chapters, beginning in chapter 14, we have the most extensive and comprehensive teaching in all Scripture about the person and the work of the Holy Spirit.

Throughout this portion of the New Testament, a name or title occurs again and again from the lips of Jesus. It is in the Greek the name or the title *Paraklētŏs*, which transliterated into English is the name or title *Paraclete*.

Allow me to give you a pop quiz to see how attentive you are to the teaching of Scripture. Who is the Paraclete? If your final answer is the Holy Spirit, thanks for playing, but you are incorrect. The Holy Spirit is not the Paraclete in the New Testament. To get this straight, we have to go to John 14 where Jesus says, "And I will ask the Father, and he will give you another

Helper, to be with you forever, even the Spirit of truth, whom the world cannot receive" (vv. 16–17).

If we're paying attention to what Jesus says here, he promises his disciples that he is going to send to them another helper, which in the Greek is "another Paraclete." For there to be another Paraclete, there must be at least one prior Paraclete. My question was not, "Who is the other Paraclete?" I asked, "Who was *the* Paraclete?" Christ is the Paraclete.

In the history of translating the Bible into English, one of the things that amazes me is the confusion about translating the term or title *Paraklētŏs*. In 1 John 2, John is encouraging us not to sin, yet at the same time, he writes, "But if anyone does sin, we have an advocate with the Father, Jesus Christ the righteous" (v. 1). I've always wondered why the King James Version, for example, translates the term *paraklētŏs* in the gospel of John as the word *comforter* but translates the same word in John's epistle as the English word *advocate*. I think it's a little strange, and I also think it's a little confusing. It is my intention to cut through some of the fog of that confusion, so we may get a clear picture of what Jesus is saying in the Upper Room Discourse.

Other translations also translate *paraklētŏs* as "counselor" or "helper," so we're left with four titles attached to one Greek word—Comforter, Counselor, Helper, Advocate. Will the real meaning of *paraklētŏs* please stand up?

What Kind of Paraclete?

This provides me an opportunity to vent my own theological frustration. I don't like the term *counselor* here as a translation of *paraklētŏs* because it smacks too much of a mentor who gives us guidance, such as the guidance counselor in school, or somebody we go to in order to seek his or her advice. When Jesus talks about sending another *Paraklētŏs*, he's talking about sending one who is going to have a much more significant job to perform in the life of the church than to offer advice or counsel. So strike *counselor* from the record. Put a line through that option.

What about *helper*? Does that mean "helper," such as a candy striper at the local hospital or a carpenter's assistant? *Helper* is just too vague. Of course the Holy Spirit comes to help us, but that is too general to satisfy me.

Next let us examine the King James Version's usage of *comforter*. Now we're getting somewhere, except this is one of those cases where we encounter the problem of the fluidity of language, where the nuances of terms tend to change over time. The idea of a comforter meant one thing in seventeenth-century England, when the King James Version was translated, and it means something significantly different in our usage today. Who or what is a comforter? A comforter is somebody who comes to us when we are stricken with grief, or when we are in affliction, or if we are suffering some kind of pain.

It's certainly true that one of the things the Holy Spirit does in the life of the people of God is bring comfort. Jesus, in fulfilling the role of the original Paraclete, was also given the title. In Luke's narrative of the dedication of Jesus in the temple, we read that the aged Simeon was there, waiting, having been promised that before he died, he would see the Lord's Anointed, described as "the consolation of Israel" (Luke 2:25). One of the titles of Jesus is that he will be the one who brings consolation to a hurting people. That is our final hope when we enter into the gates of heaven, into the New Jerusalem, the heavenly city—that Christ and God will wipe away our tears.

This is what we think of when we think of bringing comfort, but it is not what Jesus is talking about in John 14. Don't misunderstand me; the Holy Spirit does comfort us, but when Jesus said, "I'm going to send another Paraclete," he was not saying, "I'm going to send somebody whose primary purpose will be to comfort you."

The reason the term *comforter* was used in the seventeenth century was that at that time the English language was much more closely aligned with Latin than it is today, and the word *comforter* comes from the Latin prefix and root *cum forte*. *Cum* means "with." *Forte* means "strength."

In the seventeenth century, a comforter is not one who comes and dries your tears away after you've been brutally beaten in the battle. No, a comforter is one who comes to give you the strength you need to *fight* the battle. That makes all the difference in the world—to be empowered to enter into the conflict as opposed to being taken care of in the hospital after the conflict. Preparing to send his disciples into the world, Jesus says, "I'm going to send another *Paraklētŏs*, who will come to strengthen you, because the world is going to hate you just as it hated me."

If you want to use the title *comforter* as they did in the King James Version, that's fine as long as you remember the original seventeenth-century meaning of the word.

Our Advocate, Our Defense Attorney

My preference of the four is the word *advocate*, because it is almost a literal translation from Greek to Latin. The word *paraklētŏs* has a preface, *para*, that you see in English all the time. It simply means "alongside." For example, a paraministry is a ministry that works alongside the church, a paramedic is someone who works alongside doctors, and a paralegal works alongside attorneys. The root *klētŏs* comes from the verb *kaleō*, which means "to call." Literally, a paraclete or a *paraklētŏs* was somebody who was called alongside.

It's easy to see the similarity between *paraklētŏs* in Greek and *advocate* in Latin. *Vocatiō* means "to call." A vocation is a calling, and an advocate is somebody who is called to you. The words have the same meaning in Latin and in Greek.

In the Greek world, a paraclete was an attorney—but not just any attorney. A paraclete was the family attorney, who was on a permanent retaining fee and who always came alongside you when you were in trouble. When you had to go before the powers-that-be, before the magistrate, or before those who were accusing you, you called your paraclete to come alongside you. I think it's fascinating that when Jesus speaks of the Holy Spirit, he says, "I am now going to pray that the Father sends you another Advocate"—another defense attorney. Christ himself is our Advocate.

I don't think we give enough attention to that role of Jesus that we see him fulfilling in the New Testament. Shortly after this discourse, our Lord was killed, was buried, and rose from the dead, and not long after that, he ascended into heaven. We say in the Apostles' Creed that he is now seated at the right hand of the Father, which is the side of the Father by which power and authority and dominion and kingship are exercised over the entire world. When the New Testament talks about Jesus' posture after the ascension, when he's in heaven, it speaks of him as the church speaks of him, as being seated at the right hand of God.

Remember what happened with the first Christian martyr in the New Testament, St. Stephen, who gave a controversial message, speaking to his people and telling them that they had crucified the Lord of glory. Those who were standing by were so infuriated by the sermon that they were gnashing their teeth at him. They had a kangaroo court, accused him of blasphemy, and picked up stones to execute him. While the mob was about to kill Stephen, Luke tells us in Acts 7 that God in his mercy opened up the curtains of heaven and gave Stephen a vision into the heavenly sanctuary. While the earthly court of the church was sentencing Stephen to death for blasphemy, Stephen said, "Behold, I see . . . the Son of Man standing at the right hand of God" (v. 56). When the earthly court was about to execute Stephen, God showed Stephen his Advocate standing at the right hand of God. The one who stands in the heavenly courtroom is the attorney. Stephen saw Jesus standing to plead his case.

Do you understand that God has appointed Christ to judge the earth? On the day of judgment, he is going to be our Judge. But when we go to the last judgment, the Judge is going to stand up from behind the bench, come around to the front, and be our defense attorney, our advocate. Isn't it incredible that Christ is our defender?

Parting . . . Such Sweet Sorrow?

In John 14:16, the announcement Jesus gave to his disciples caused great distress and sorrow in their hearts. A bit later, the Lord continued:

> But now I am going to him who sent me, and none of you asks me, "Where are you going?" But because I have said these things to you, sorrow has filled your heart. (John 16:5–6)

What was it that caused the hearts of the disciples to be filled to capacity with grief and sorrow? They had just heard the worst announcement they could possibly hear from Jesus. Here in the Upper Room Discourse, Jesus announced to his disciples,

"In just a little while I'm leaving you, and where I'm going (at this point) you can't come. You're not going to see me anymore because I'm leaving. I'm not going to leave you without hope. I'm not going to leave you without comfort, because I'm going to pray that the Father will send another Paraclete to you. But you have to understand this: I'm leaving you."

We live at the beginning of the twenty-first century, and we have a spiritual nostalgia for that period in redemptive history when our Lord was walking on this planet. What would you give to have been an eyewitness of the wedding feast at Cana; or to have been on the Mount of Transfiguration, seeing the glory of God bursting through the human veil of Christ; or to have been there on Easter morning as an eyewitness of the resurrection? The most privileged people in all history were those who were able to walk with him and sit at his feet and behold with their eyes the ministry that Jesus performed while he was on the earth. And then he said, "I'm leaving."

When Vesta and I were engaged, we went to different colleges, so the only time we had to see each other was during vacations. How I looked forward to Thanksgiving vacation and Christmas vacation, when she would come home from college on the bus from Ohio! At the end of the vacation, I would drive her to the Greyhound bus station in downtown Pittsburgh. The whole waiting room would be filled with college students and their public displays of affection—guys and girls kissing, holding hands, weeping. Guys would be putting their girls on the buses and watching until they disappeared on the horizon.

The moment would come when Vesta would get on the bus and I would know I wouldn't see her for months. The bus would pull out of the terminal, and I would watch it until it disappeared, and I would be angry with Shakespeare for writing such nonsense as "Parting is such sweet sorrow." I remember getting in my car and saying, "What's wrong with the Bard of Avon? There's nothing sweet about this at all." When the time came for her to leave, it was a time for me to experience sorrow.

I remember when my dad got on that bus, with his duffel bag over his shoulder, to go off to war. Even though I was a little boy, his words to me before he stepped on the bus were, "Be a good soldier." I was three years old. Even then I knew I might never see him again. There was nothing happy about walking back home from the bus stop.

I remember 1945, when the war was over. Thousands of servicemen were returning home, and I was at the train station in Pittsburgh waiting for my father to come home. I watched on the platform, and I saw way down in the distance, maybe a hundred yards away, a man with that duffel bag over his shoulder. I saw him . . . and I *knew* it was my dad. I broke loose from my mother. I ran as fast as I could, and from about thirty feet away, I got airborne, long before Michael Jordan even knew what it was to get airborne. My dad saw me coming. He dropped the duffel bag, and he scooped me up and caught me and hugged me. It was one of the happiest moments of my entire life. But the day he had left had been a day of sorrow, and there had been no joy in it. When Jesus said, "I'm leaving," sorrow filled the disciples' hearts.

Luke records the actual departure of Jesus in Acts 1.

And when he had said these things, as they were looking on, he was lifted up, and a cloud took him out of their sight. And while they were gazing into heaven as he went, behold, two men stood by them in white robes, and said, "Men of Galilee, why do you stand looking into heaven? This Jesus, who was taken up from you into heaven, will come in the same way as you saw him go into heaven."

> Then they returned to Jerusalem from the mount called
> Olivet, which is near Jerusalem, a Sabbath day's journey away.
> (Acts 1:9–12)

When Jesus left and ascended into heaven, the disciples were spellbound. They stood gazing into heaven. They peered into the sky, trying to get the last possible glimpse of Christ before he went into his Father's kingdom, so that the angels came and said, "What are you guys doing here, standing paralyzed gazing into heaven? Go on back to Jerusalem."

All Luke tells us in the first chapter of Acts is that that's what they did: they went back to Jerusalem. But he omits a detail in the Acts account of the ascension that he includes in his gospel account.

> Then he led them out as far as Bethany, and lifting up his
> hands he blessed them. While he blessed them, he parted
> from them and was carried up into heaven. And they wor-
> shiped him and returned to Jerusalem with great joy. (Luke
> 24:50–52)

How about that? In the upper room, Jesus said, "I am leaving," and John tells us that their hearts were filled with sorrow. When we read that he left them, they went back to Jerusalem rejoicing. What could possibly make them rejoice? What could possibly change and transform their emotions from being gripped with the pangs of sorrow at the thought of Jesus leaving to seeing him actually leave and then come back to Jerusalem filled with joy?

The answer is found in Jesus' words in John 16. Jesus says, "But because I have said these things to you, sorrow has filled your heart. Nevertheless, I tell you the truth . . ." (vv. 6–7). Did he really have to say to his disciples, "I'm telling you the truth"?

Did he ever tell them anything but the truth? Jesus was incapable of anything but the truth, but he wanted to emphasize this for them. They needed assurance because of the sorrow that had gripped them.

"I tell you the truth," he continued, "it is to your advantage that I go away, for if I do not go away, the Helper [Paraclete] will not come to you. But if I go, I will send him to you" (v. 7). The word that Jesus used that is translated "to your advantage" is the word *sumphĕrō*, which can be also translated "profitable" or "expedient." It involves an improved situation. Jesus is saying—and he prefaces it by saying, "I'm telling you the truth"— "It's better for you if I go than if I stay."

A Teaching the Church Has Never Believed

This is one teaching of our Lord Jesus Christ that the church has never believed. We just can't get it into our heads that the life we enjoy on this planet today is better than the situations that the disciples enjoyed during Christ's venue here on earth. Yet when he made a comparative analysis between his staying and his leaving, Jesus said, "It's better for you, it's advantageous, it's expedient, it's profitable for you if I leave."

Somewhere between having their hearts filled with sorrow and their returning to Jerusalem in great joy, a new understanding dawned on the disciples. Somewhere along the line, they came to believe what Jesus had said when he had said, "It's better that I leave," and they began to understand *why* it was better that he had left.

First, it was better because of where Jesus was going. He was going to his investiture as the King of Kings. Do you want him to stay on earth in his humiliation, or would you like him to go to the right hand of his Father? Would you like him to ascend into heaven as your Great High Priest, where he will intercede for you in the immediate presence of God in the heavenly sanctuary every single day? Do you want him to pray for you in the upper room, or do you want him to go into the real upper room as your Priest and as your King? Not only will that improve your present situation, because Jesus will be going to the seat of cosmic authority, where he will reign as the King of Kings and the Lord of Lords, but when he goes he will be authorized to send the other Paraclete, the Spirit of truth.

Please note what Jesus said he would do:

> And when he comes, he will convict the world concerning sin and righteousness and judgment: concerning sin, because they do not believe in me; concerning righteousness, because I go to the Father, and you will see me no longer; concerning judgment, because the ruler of this world is judged. (John 16:8–11)

D. A. Carson has written what I feel is one of the best and most definitive commentaries on the gospel of John that is available.[1] Not only does he deal with this passage in his commentary with great depth of understanding and insight, but he has also submitted several scholarly articles in journals on this very passage, pointing out the difficulty of discerning precisely what is in view here when Jesus says that the Spirit will convince or convict the world of sin, of righteousness, and of judgment.

There is a certain ambiguity in the term that is used here, coming from the verb *elegchō*, which is translated here as "to convict" but which can also mean "to refute, to persuade, to convince." It is a verb that suggests, particularly in the legal environment, the

---

1. D. A. Carson, *The Gospel According to John* (Grand Rapids: Eerdmans, 1991).

bringing forth of evidences in a law court in order to demonstrate truth of guilt or of innocence. Jesus is saying, "I'm going to send you another Advocate, another attorney, if you will, and his job is to *elegchō*, to convince or to persuade or to refute or to convince people of sin, of righteousness, and of judgment."

Here is where the ambiguity lies: perhaps Jesus is saying that the role of the Holy Spirit will be to come into this world and persuade the world of the truth of the claims of Jesus and to show the world what real guilt is, or to convince the world of the true standard of righteousness. One of the things Jesus did was expose false theories of righteousness. Those who were regarded as the paragons of virtue in Jerusalem—the scribes and the Pharisees—were the ones most highly exalted and esteemed as the righteous ones of Israel, but when the true righteousness appeared, the true exposed the counterfeit.

Now the true embodiment of righteousness is about to leave. Who is going to continue to demonstrate to the world what authentic righteousness is? Who is going to continue to display to the world what real sin is? Jesus said, "I'm sending another Advocate to carry out that role."

Perhaps what Jesus was saying is, "What I did in my earthly ministry, now the Spirit will do as my replacement—he will continue to manifest what true sin is, what true righteousness is, and what true judgment is." Maybe that's what Jesus meant. In that sense, Jesus would be saying that the ministry of the Spirit is objective: to demonstrate the objective reality of what sin is, of what righteousness is, of what judgment is. Or he could be speaking of the subjective work of the Holy Spirit, in which the Holy Spirit is the one who applies the objective work of Christ subjectively to our hearts. We speak of the conviction of the Holy Spirit, in which the Holy Spirit comes to us and convicts us inwardly of sin. I don't know which of those two things Jesus is talking about.

In one sense—and I don't mean to be glib—I don't care, because either one of those understandings of this text is consistent with what the Bible teaches all along about the ministry of the Holy Spirit. He does both of these things. The Holy Spirit does, in fact, manifest what true sin is, and the Holy Spirit objectively proves what righteousness is, and the Holy Spirit comes to judge as well, providing true judgment. But he doesn't just do it objectively; he does it subjectively.

Why are you a Christian? What brought you to repentance? It wasn't just the objective evidence of your sin. In addition to the objective evidence of your sin, the Holy Spirit cut through all your deceitful barriers that kept you from coming to the cross of Christ, throwing yourself at his mercy, and saying, "God, be merciful to me, a sinner." God had to melt your heart and turn that heart of stone into a heart of flesh before you were ever converted, and it was God the Holy Spirit who brought that inner conviction.

Calvin saw in this the conviction of the Holy Ghost, that the only righteousness by which we can be saved is an alien righteousness, a righteousness that is not our own, but a righteousness that is a heavenly righteousness—that is, the righteousness won for us by Jesus Christ. It is the righteousness that is imputed to the believer, so that God now counts us righteous in his sight, not because we are righteous in ourselves, but because Christ is our righteousness.

He Will Convict the World
concerning Righteousness

Jesus said, "He will convict the world concerning sin and righteousness" (16:8), because Christ would be taken out of the way. He would be in heaven. Does that mean that simply in his absence, the Spirit will teach righteousness? Calvin says no. He's going back to the testament that Paul tells us: that Christ is raised for our justification—that the resurrection shows God's acceptance of the atonement of Christ and the perfect work of Christ on our behalf, that he doesn't just die for our sins but is also raised for our justification. The word that is used in the text is the word *dikaiosunē*, the very word for *justification* that we find at the heart of Paul's teaching in Romans with respect to our justification by faith alone in Jesus Christ—the only grounds of our justification.

How are we convinced or persuaded of the gospel? It's the Spirit who reveals to me my helplessness in sin. It's the Spirit who reveals to me the utter sufficiency of the righteousness of Jesus Christ for my justification. Jesus is saying, "The world hates me, and the world is going to hate you, but I'm going to send the Paraclete to come alongside you to convince you and to convince the world of the righteousness that is the righteousness of God by which we are justified." Again and again, the ministry of the Holy Spirit is to apply the redemptive work of Christ to the lives of believers.

And so, beloved, our Lord said that it was to our advantage that he leave, because he was going to send the Spirit of truth, who will truly convict us and the whole world of sin and of righteousness and of judgment. Keep that in mind when you examine the culture in which you live, a culture that pretends there is no such thing as sin, no such thing as righteousness, no such thing as judgment, because moral relativity is at the heart of postmodernism. There is no sin, just bad choices.

One of the few benefits of 9/11 was that, for the first time in a long time, the secular world started talking about objective evil. Nobody talked about bad decisions or bad choices. They said, "This is evil." We live in a world that calls evil *good* and good *evil*, and the Christian who tries to be faithful to God in a pagan, barbarian land feels isolated and alone, feeling that nobody will ever be convinced of real righteousness, of real sin, of real judgment. But the only way that could ever happen would be if Jesus had lied instead of telling the truth. The Holy Spirit will not allow the world's view of sin, righteousness, and judgment to prevail, because he's the Spirit of truth, sent to the world by the Father and by the Son.

A L L I A N C E®
OF CONFESSING EVANGELICALS

What is the Alliance?

The Alliance of Confessing Evangelicals is a coalition of pastors, scholars, and churchmen who hold to the historic creeds and confessions of the Reformed faith and who proclaim biblical doctrine in order to foster a Reformed awakening in today's church. Our members join for gospel proclamation, biblically sound doctrine, fostering of reformation, and the glory of God. We work and serve the church through media, events, and publishing.

The work started in media: *The Bible Study Hour* with James Boice, *Every Last Word* featuring Philip Ryken, *Mortification of Spin* with Carl Trueman and Todd Pruitt, *No Falling Word* with Liam Goligher, and *Dr. Barnhouse & the Bible* with Donald Barnhouse. These broadcasts air throughout North America as well as online at AllianceNet.org.

PlaceforTruth.org is our online magazine—a free, "go-to" theological resource. ChristwardCollective.org is a theological conversation equipping believers for growth. And reformation21.org provides cultural and church criticism. Our online daily devotionals include *Think and Act Biblically* and *Making God's Word Plain*, as well as MatthewHenry.org, a resource fostering biblical prayer.

Our events include the Philadelphia Conference on Reformed Theology, the oldest continuing national Reformed conference

in North America, and regional events including theology and Bible conferences. Pastors' events, such as reformation societies, continue to encourage, embolden, and equip church leaders in pursuit of reformation in the church.

Alliance publishing includes books from trustworthy authors, with titles such as *Zeal for Godliness*, *Our Creed*, and more. We offer a vast list of affordable booklets, as well as e-books such as *Learning to Think Biblically* and *How to Live a Holy Life*. And we encourage sound biblical doctrine by offering a wide variety of CD and MP3 resources.